BATMAN

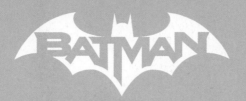

ZEROPOINT

FORTNITE®

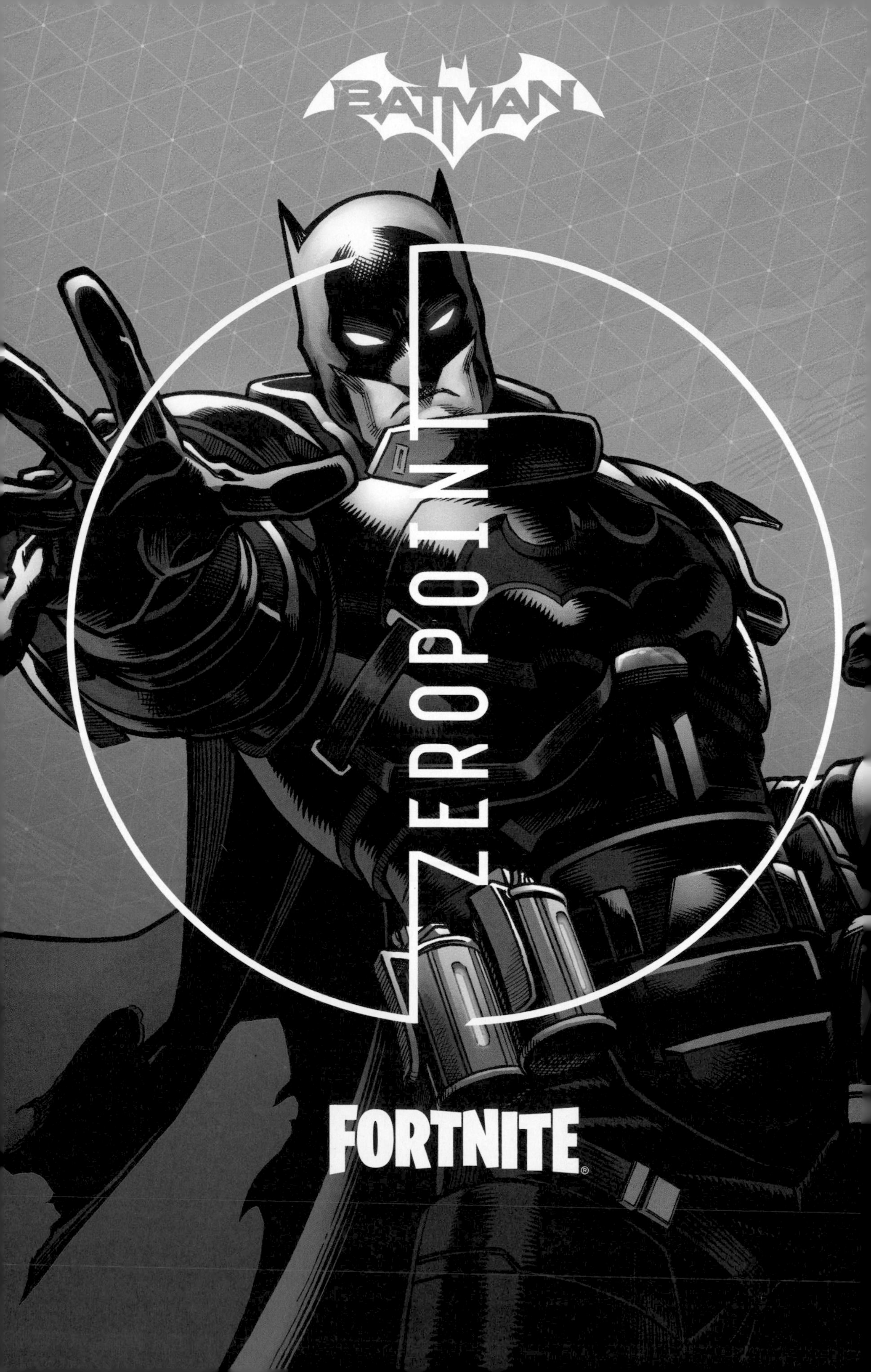
BATMAN
ZERO POINT
FORTNITE

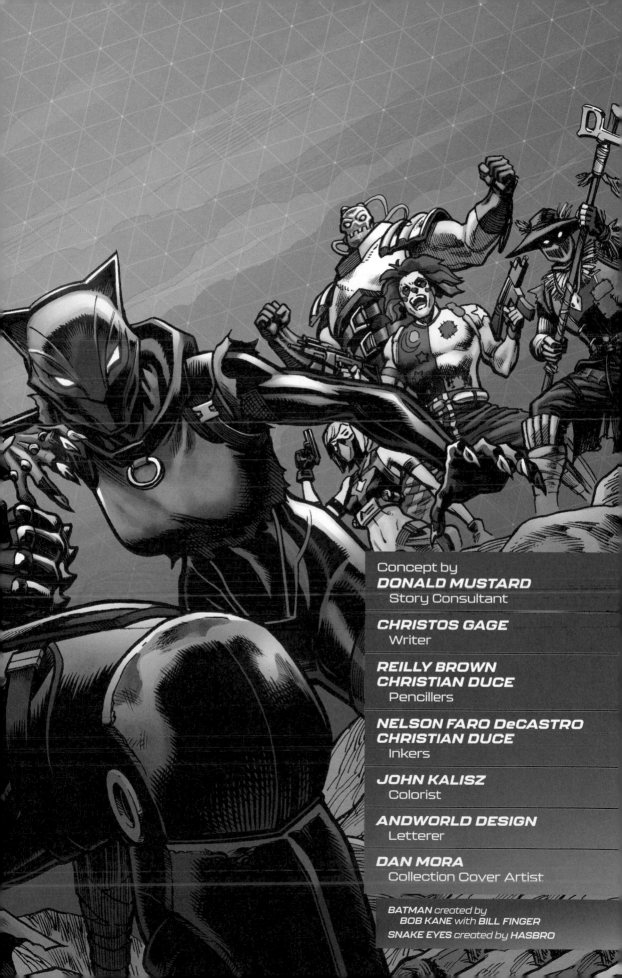

Concept by
DONALD MUSTARD
Story Consultant

CHRISTOS GAGE
Writer

REILLY BROWN
CHRISTIAN DUCE
Pencillers

NELSON FARO DeCASTRO
CHRISTIAN DUCE
Inkers

JOHN KALISZ
Colorist

ANDWORLD DESIGN
Letterer

DAN MORA
Collection Cover Artist

BATMAN *created by*
BOB KANE *with* BILL FINGER
SNAKE EYES *created by* HASBRO

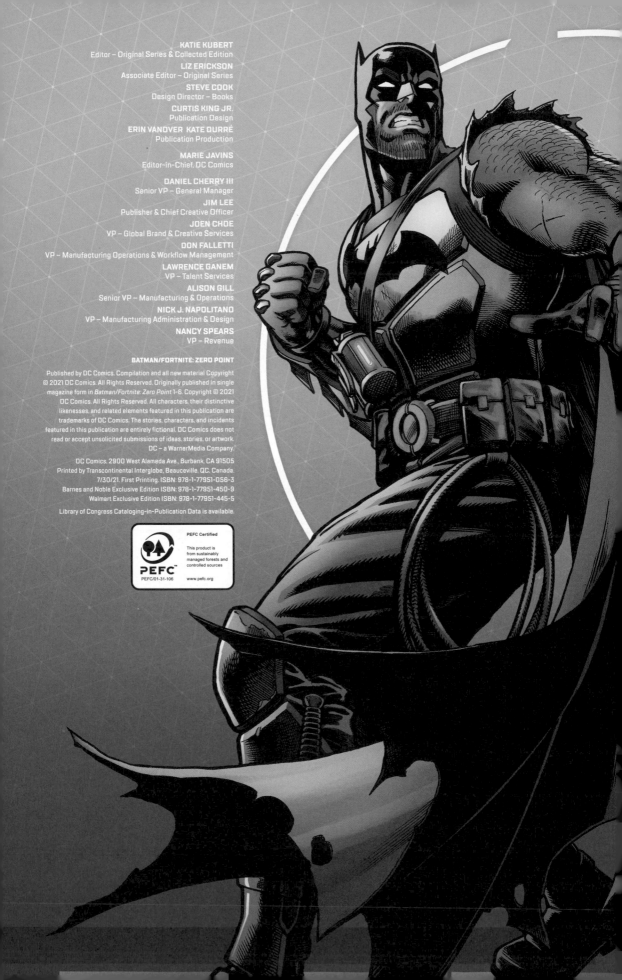

KATIE KUBERT
Editor – Original Series & Collected Edition

LIZ ERICKSON
Associate Editor – Original Series

STEVE COOK
Design Director – Books

CURTIS KING JR.
Publication Design

ERIN VANOVER KATE DURRÉ
Publication Production

MARIE JAVINS
Editor-in-Chief, DC Comics

DANIEL CHERRY III
Senior VP – General Manager

JIM LEE
Publisher & Chief Creative Officer

JOEN CHOE
VP – Global Brand & Creative Services

DON FALLETTI
VP – Manufacturing Operations & Workflow Management

LAWRENCE GANEM
VP – Talent Services

ALISON GILL
Senior VP – Manufacturing & Operations

NICK J. NAPOLITANO
VP – Manufacturing Administration & Design

NANCY SPEARS
VP – Revenue

BATMAN/FORTNITE: ZERO POINT

Published by DC Comics. Compilation and all new material Copyright © 2021 DC Comics. All Rights Reserved. Originally published in single magazine form in *Batman/Fortnite: Zero Point* 1-6. Copyright © 2021 DC Comics. All Rights Reserved. All characters, their distinctive likenesses, and related elements featured in this publication are trademarks of DC Comics. The stories, characters, and incidents featured in this publication are entirely fictional. DC Comics does not read or accept unsolicited submissions of ideas, stories, or artwork. DC – a WarnerMedia Company.

DC Comics, 2900 West Alameda Ave., Burbank, CA 91505
Printed by Transcontinental Interglobe, Beauceville, QC, Canada.
7/30/21. First Printing. ISBN: 978-1-77951-056-3
Barnes and Noble Exclusive Edition ISBN: 978-1-77951-450-9
Walmart Exclusive Edition ISBN: 978-1-77951-445-5

Library of Congress Cataloging-in-Publication Data is available.

PEFC Certified

This product is from sustainably managed forests and controlled sources

PEFC/01-31-106   www.pefc.org

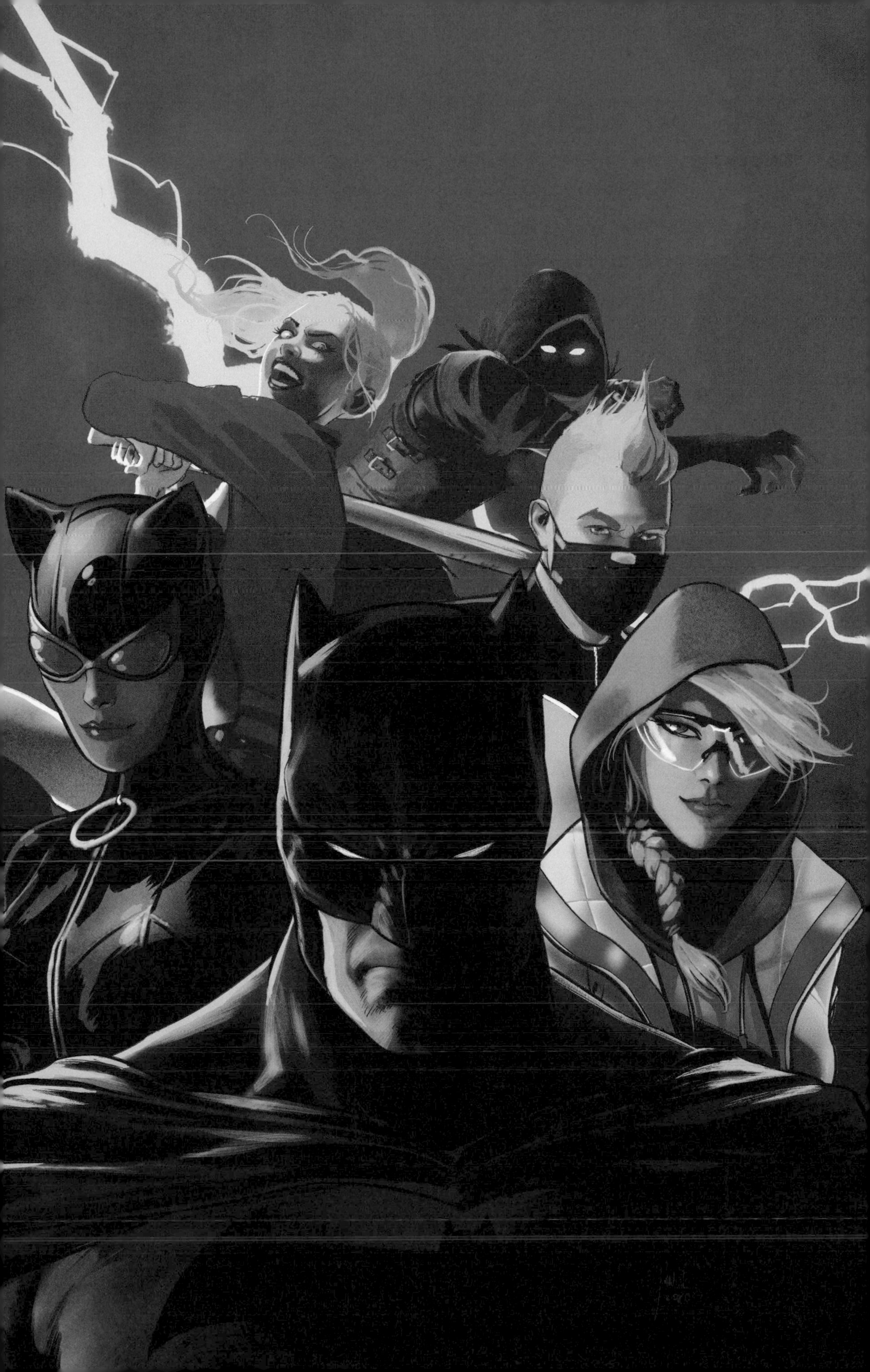

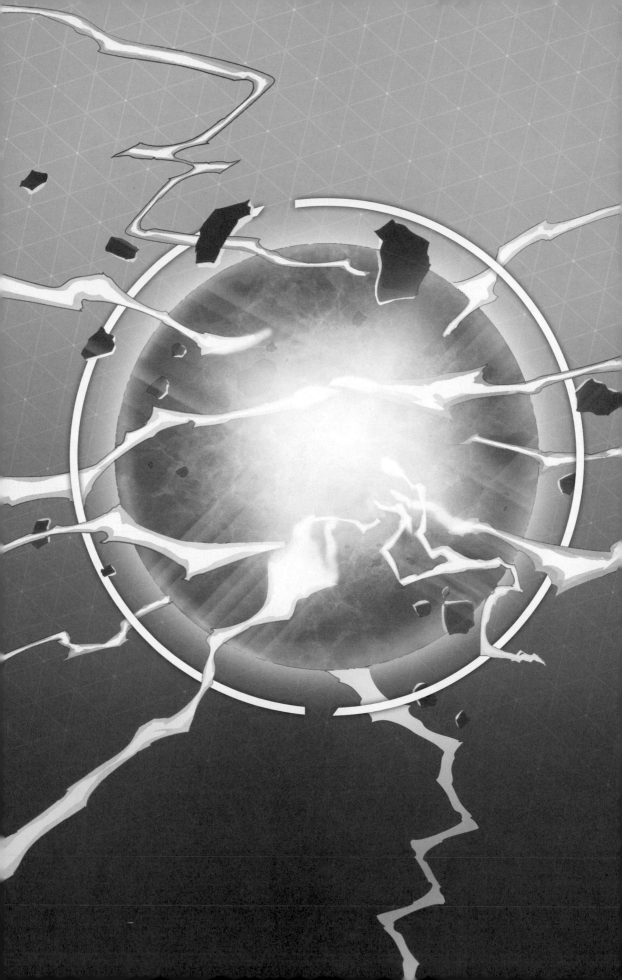

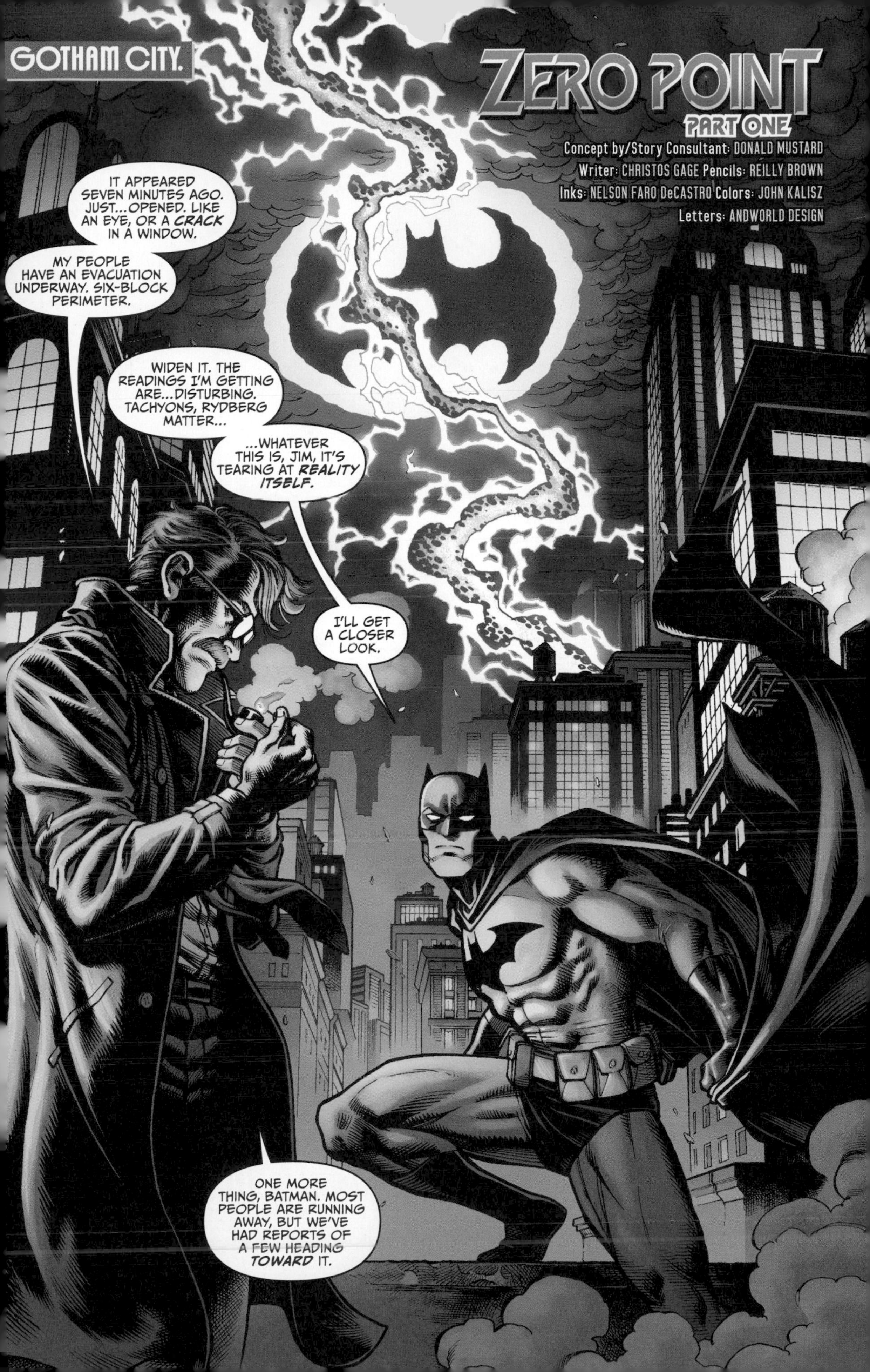

GOTHAM CITY.
ZERO POINT
PART ONE
Concept by/Story Consultant: DONALD MUSTARD
Writer: CHRISTOS GAGE Pencils: REILLY BROWN
Inks: NELSON FARO DeCASTRO Colors: JOHN KALISZ
Letters: ANDWORLD DESIGN
IT APPEARED SEVEN MINUTES AGO. JUST...OPENED. LIKE AN EYE, OR A *CRACK* IN A WINDOW.
MY PEOPLE HAVE AN EVACUATION UNDERWAY. SIX-BLOCK PERIMETER.
WIDEN IT. THE READINGS I'M GETTING ARE...DISTURBING. TACHYONS, RYDBERG MATTER...
...WHATEVER THIS IS, JIM, IT'S TEARING AT *REALITY ITSELF*.
I'LL GET A CLOSER LOOK.
ONE MORE THING, BATMAN. MOST PEOPLE ARE RUNNING AWAY, BUT WE'VE HAD REPORTS OF A FEW HEADING *TOWARD* IT.

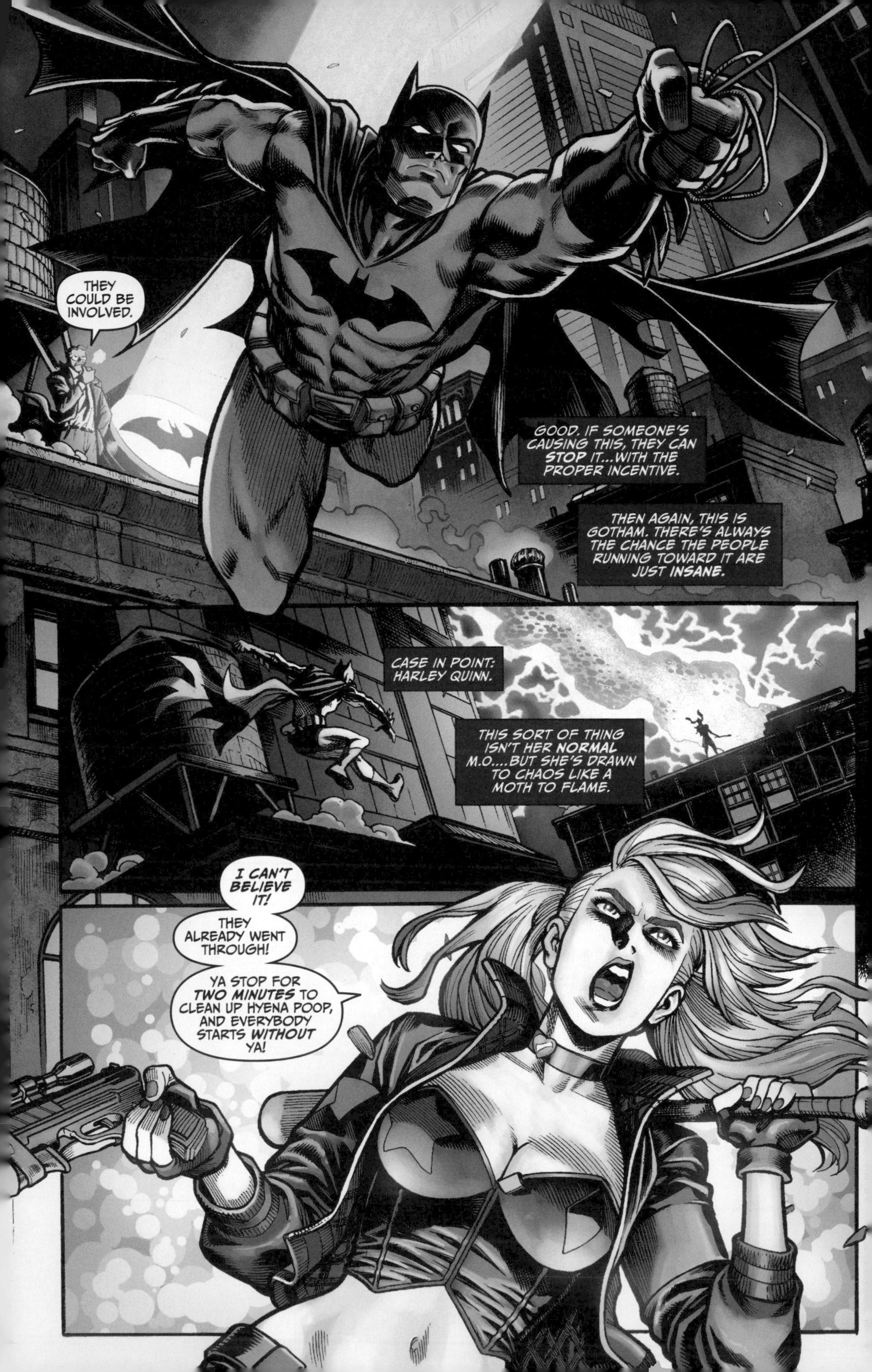
THEY COULD BE INVOLVED.
GOOD. IF SOMEONE'S CAUSING THIS, THEY CAN STOP IT...WITH THE PROPER INCENTIVE.
THEN AGAIN, THIS IS GOTHAM. THERE'S ALWAYS THE CHANCE THE PEOPLE RUNNING TOWARD IT ARE JUST INSANE.
CASE IN POINT: HARLEY QUINN.
THIS SORT OF THING ISN'T HER NORMAL M.O....BUT SHE'S DRAWN TO CHAOS LIKE A MOTH TO FLAME.
I CAN'T BELIEVE IT!
THEY ALREADY WENT THROUGH!
YA STOP FOR TWO MINUTES TO CLEAN UP HYENA POOP, AND EVERYBODY STARTS WITHOUT YA!

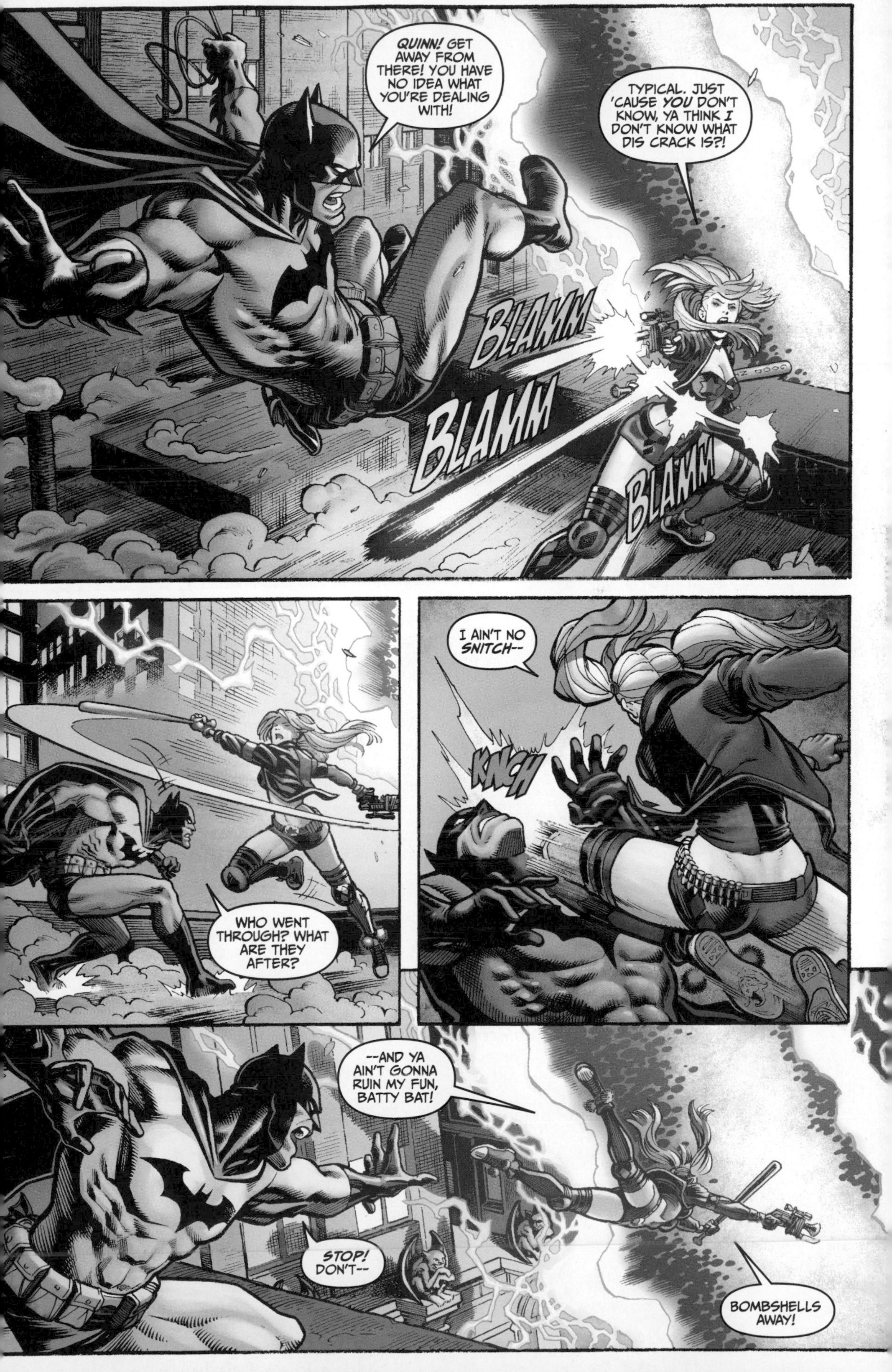
QUINN! GET AWAY FROM THERE! YOU HAVE NO IDEA WHAT YOU'RE DEALING WITH!
TYPICAL. JUST 'CAUSE YOU DON'T KNOW, YA THINK I DON'T KNOW WHAT DIS CRACK IS?!
BLAMM
BLAMM
BLAMM
WHO WENT THROUGH? WHAT ARE THEY AFTER?
I AIN'T NO SNITCH--
KNCH
--AND YA AIN'T GONNA RUIN MY FUN, BATTY BAT!
STOP! DON'T--
BOMBSHELLS AWAY!

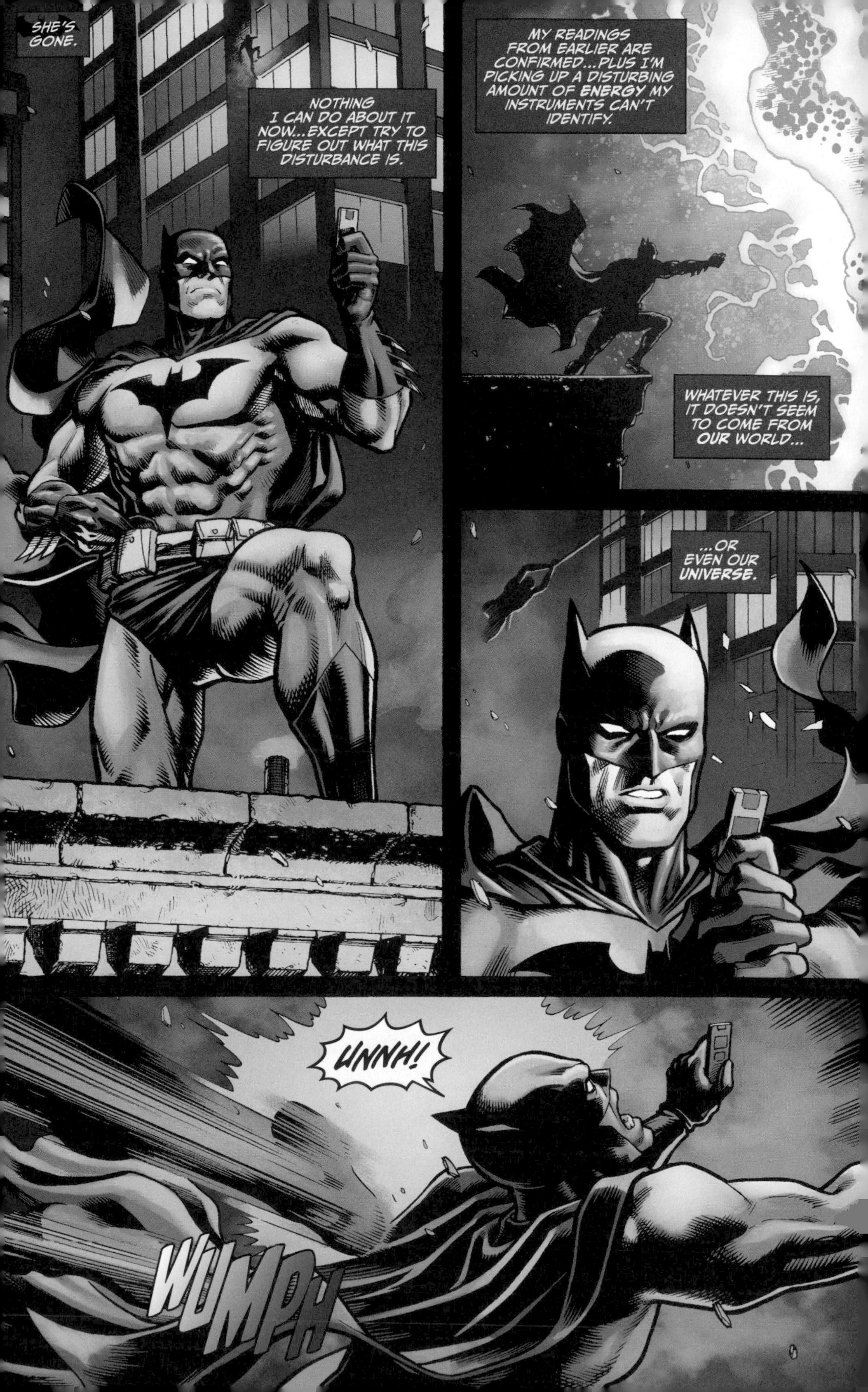
SHE'S GONE.
NOTHING I CAN DO ABOUT IT NOW...EXCEPT TRY TO FIGURE OUT WHAT THIS DISTURBANCE IS.
MY READINGS FROM EARLIER ARE CONFIRMED...PLUS I'M PICKING UP A DISTURBING AMOUNT OF ENERGY MY INSTRUMENTS CAN'T IDENTIFY.
WHATEVER THIS IS, IT DOESN'T SEEM TO COME FROM OUR WORLD...
...OR EVEN OUR UNIVERSE.
UNNH!
WUMPH

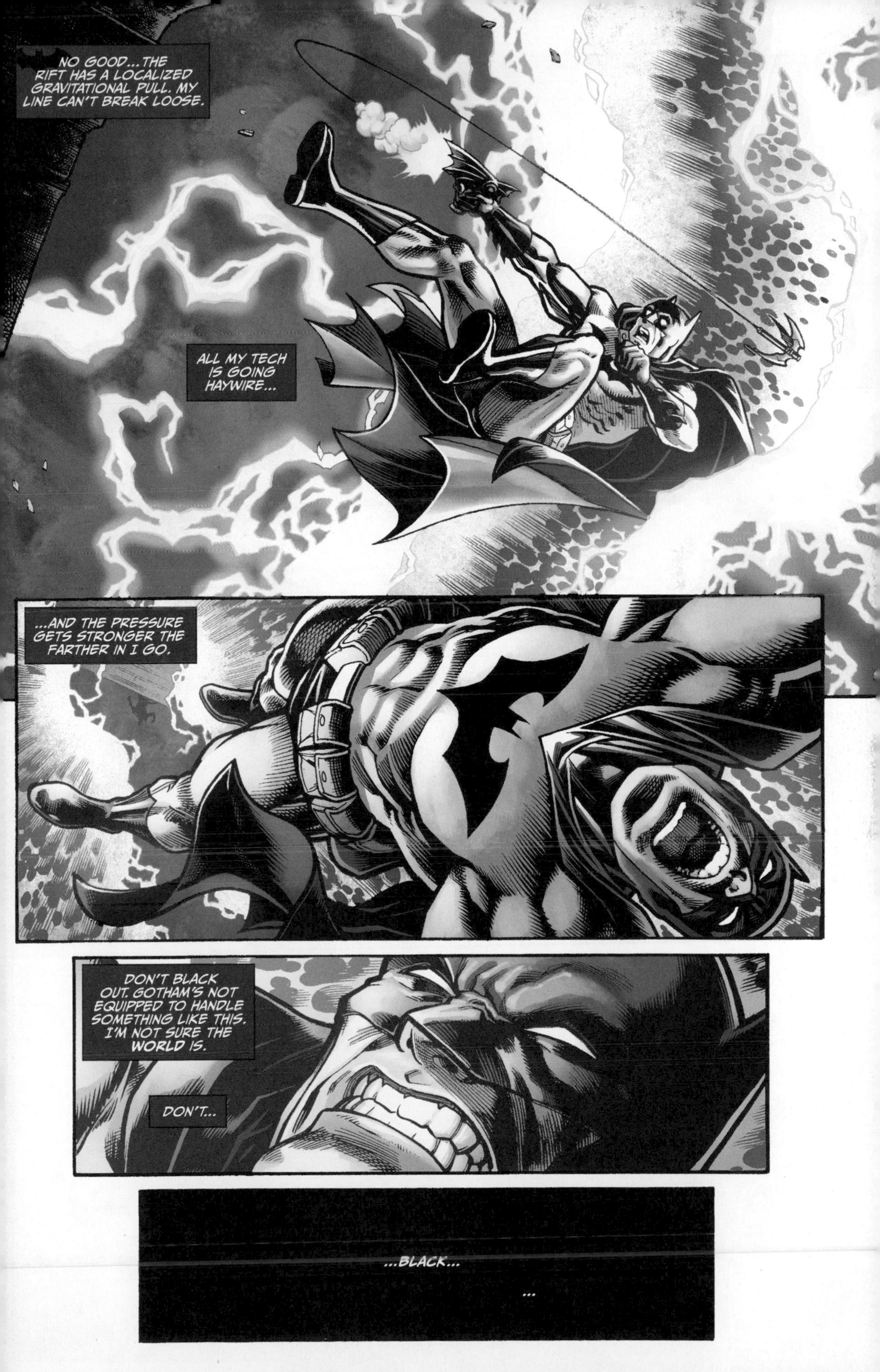
NO GOOD...THE RIFT HAS A LOCALIZED GRAVITATIONAL PULL. MY LINE CAN'T BREAK LOOSE.
ALL MY TECH IS GOING HAYWIRE...
...AND THE PRESSURE GETS STRONGER THE FARTHER IN I GO.
DON'T BLACK OUT. GOTHAM'S NOT EQUIPPED TO HANDLE SOMETHING LIKE THIS. I'M NOT SURE THE WORLD IS.
DON'T...
...BLACK...
...

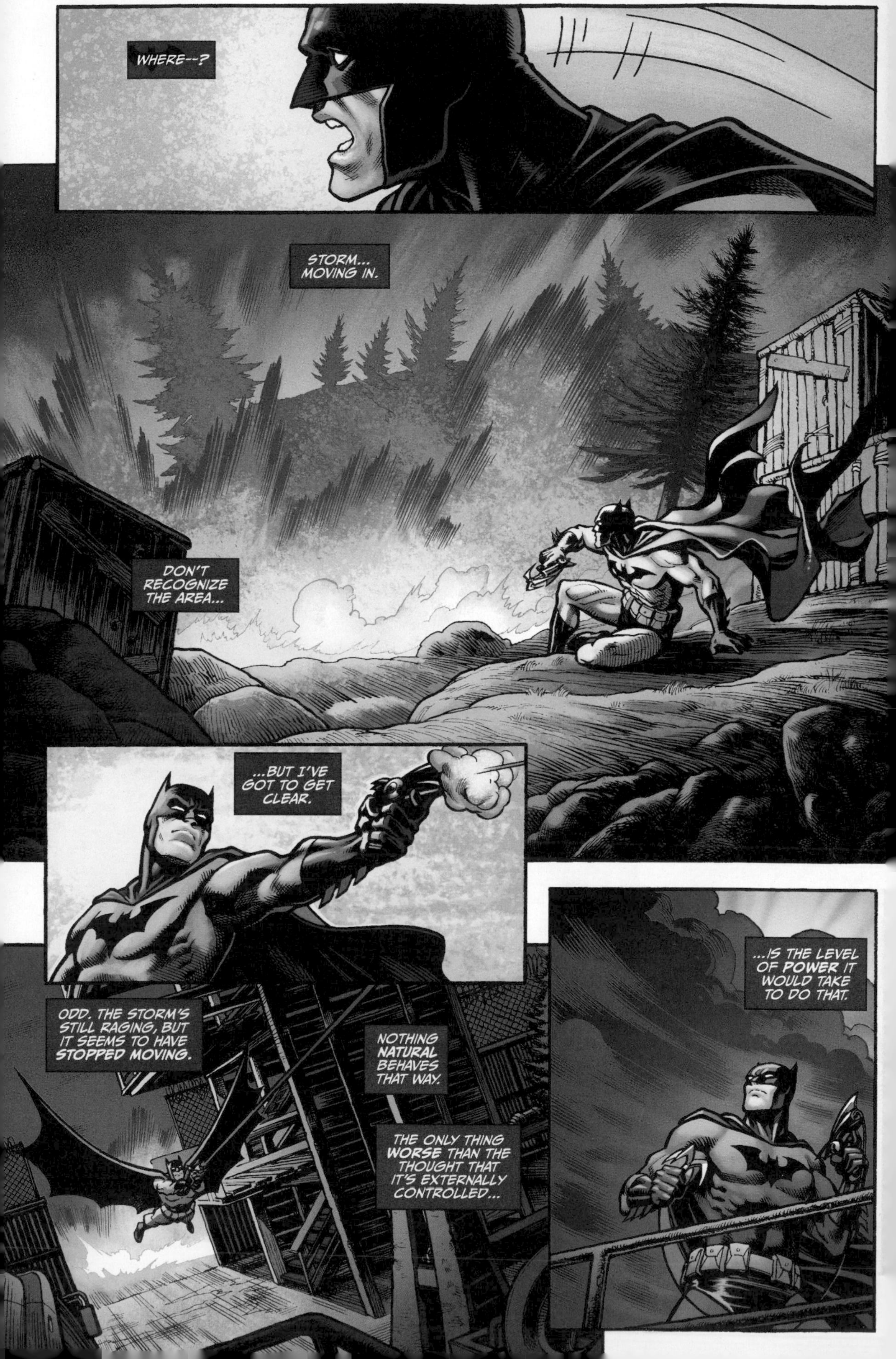
WHERE--?
STORM... MOVING IN.
DON'T RECOGNIZE THE AREA...
...BUT I'VE GOT TO GET CLEAR.
ODD. THE STORM'S STILL RAGING, BUT IT SEEMS TO HAVE STOPPED MOVING.
NOTHING NATURAL BEHAVES THAT WAY.
THE ONLY THING WORSE THAN THE THOUGHT THAT IT'S EXTERNALLY CONTROLLED...
...IS THE LEVEL OF POWER IT WOULD TAKE TO DO THAT.

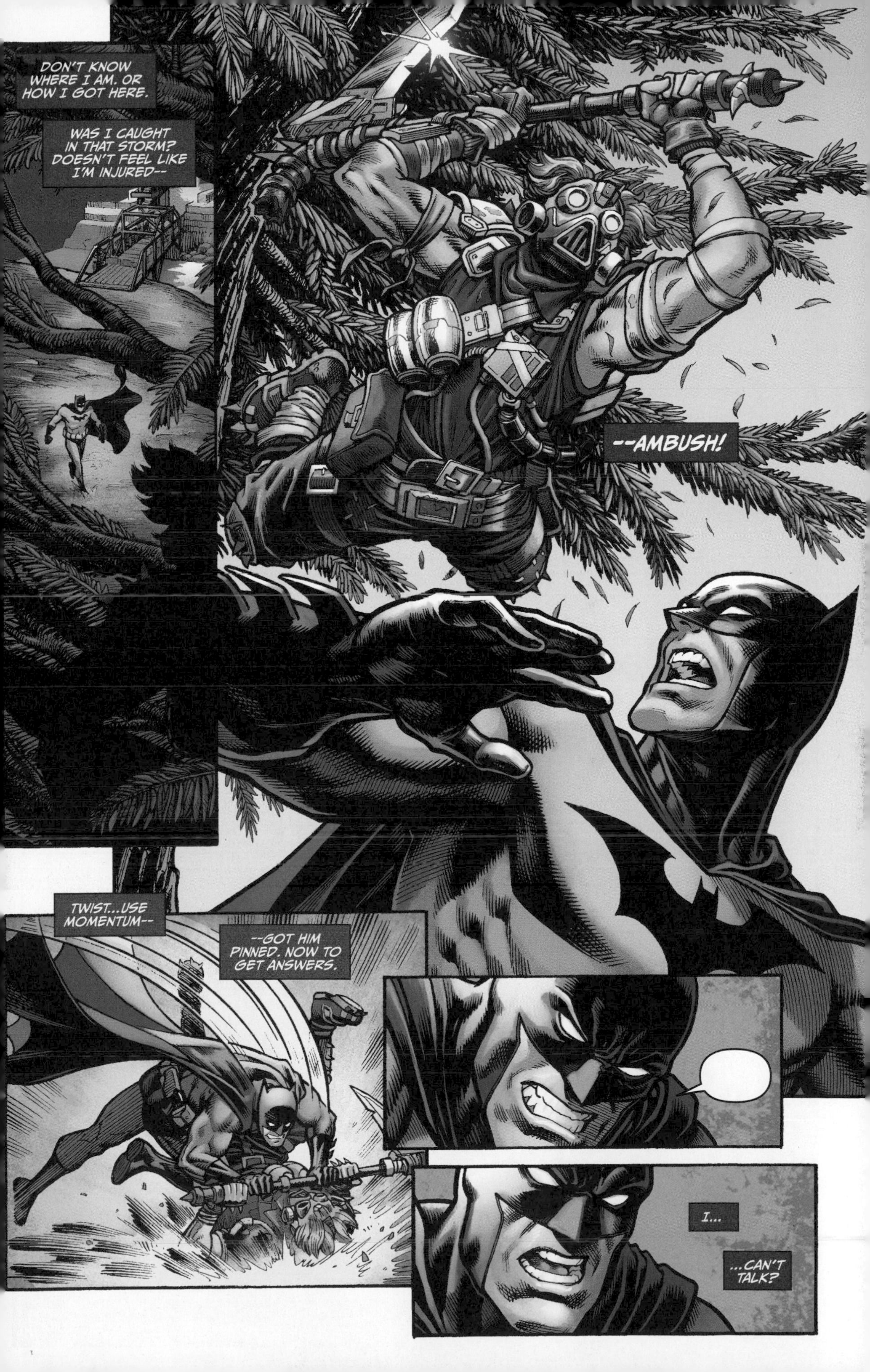
DON'T KNOW WHERE I AM. OR HOW I GOT HERE.
WAS I CAUGHT IN THAT STORM? DOESN'T FEEL LIKE I'M INJURED--
--AMBUSH!
TWIST...USE MOMENTUM--
--GOT HIM PINNED. NOW TO GET ANSWERS.
I...
...CAN'T TALK?

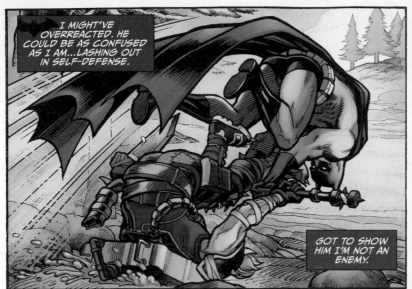

I MIGHT'VE OVERREACTED. HE COULD BE AS CONFUSED AS I AM...LASHING OUT IN SELF-DEFENSE.

GOT TO SHOW HIM I'M NOT AN ENEMY.

MAYBE I CAN COMMUNICATE THROUGH SIGN LANGUAGE.

"I AM..."

...I...

...I DON'T KNOW WHO I AM.

WHHSSTT!

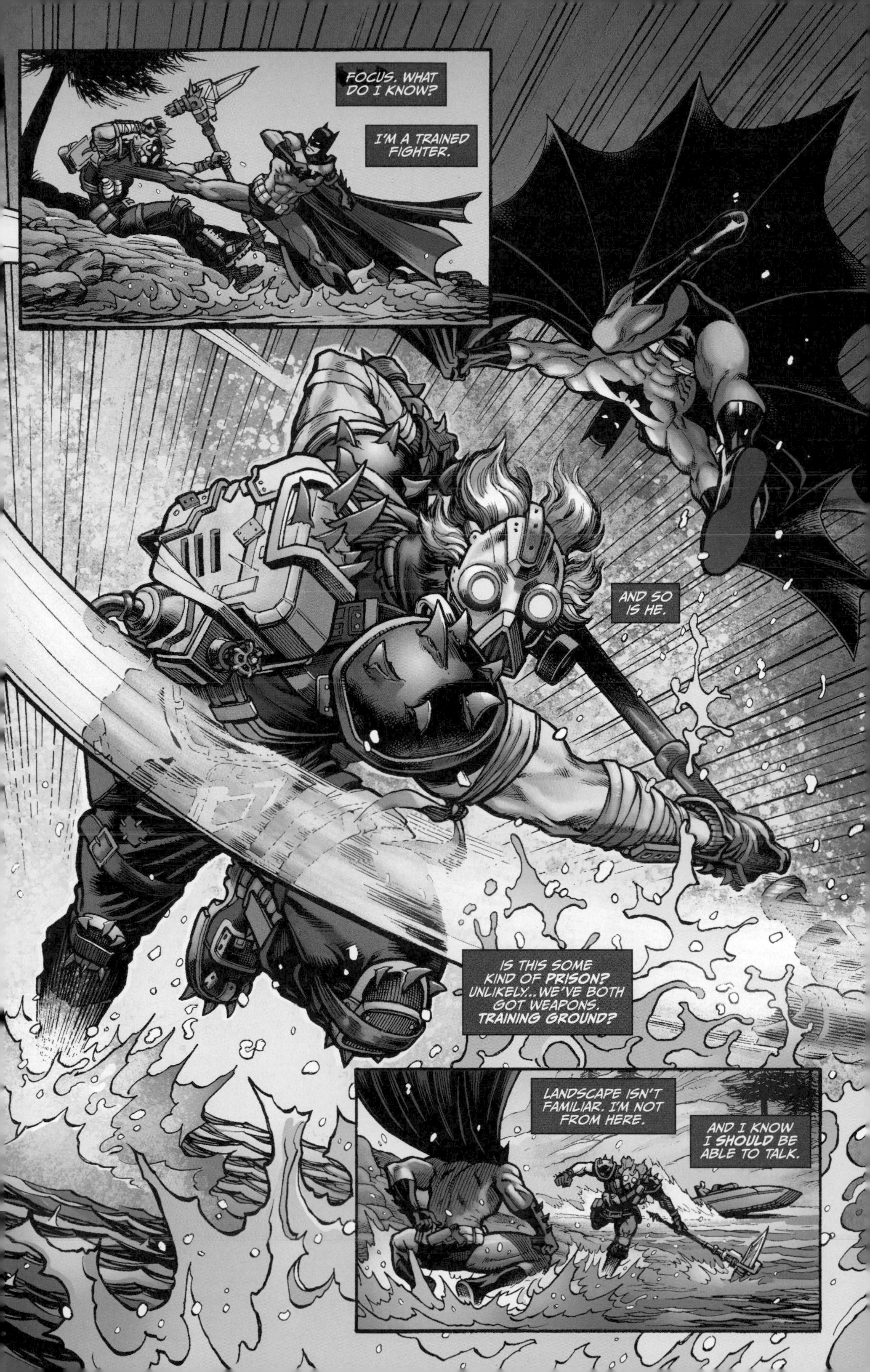
FOCUS. WHAT DO I KNOW?
I'M A TRAINED FIGHTER.
AND SO IS HE.
IS THIS SOME KIND OF PRISON? UNLIKELY...WE'VE BOTH GOT WEAPONS. TRAINING GROUND?
LANDSCAPE ISN'T FAMILIAR. I'M NOT FROM HERE.
AND I KNOW I SHOULD BE ABLE TO TALK.

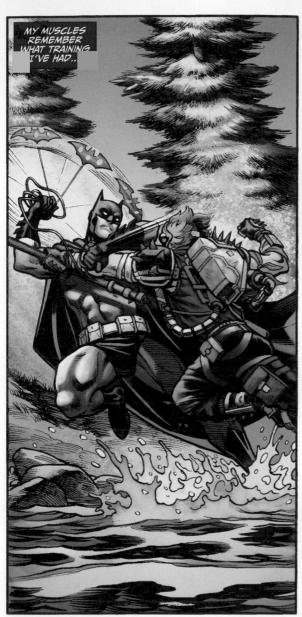

MY MUSCLES REMEMBER WHAT TRAINING I'VE HAD...

...AND HOW TO USE THESE WEAPONS.

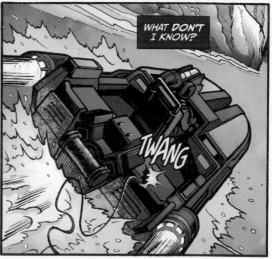

WHAT *DON'T* I KNOW?

TWANG

PRETTY MUCH EVERYTHING ELSE.

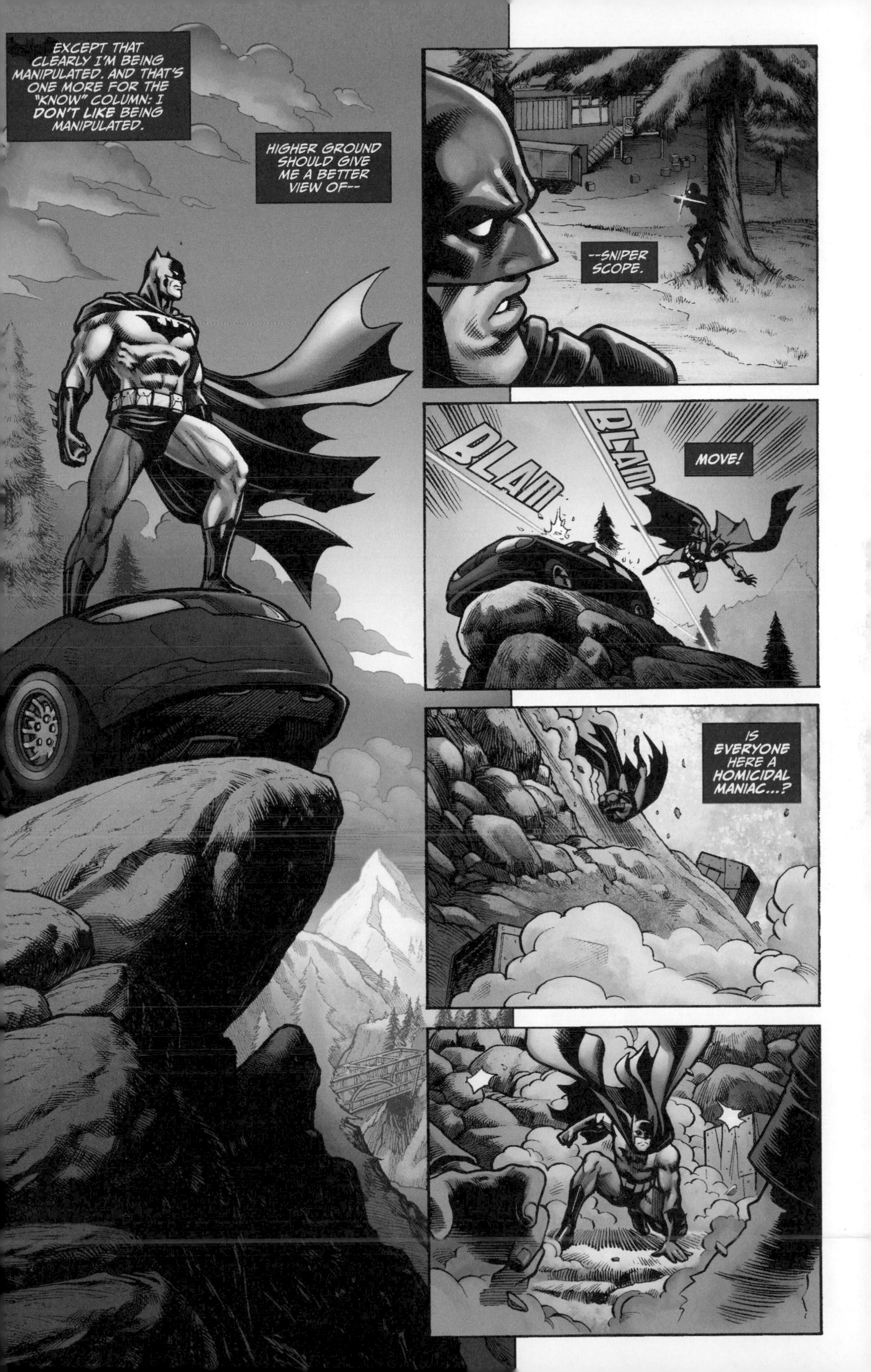
EXCEPT THAT CLEARLY I'M BEING MANIPULATED. AND THAT'S ONE MORE FOR THE "KNOW" COLUMN: I DON'T LIKE BEING MANIPULATED.
HIGHER GROUND SHOULD GIVE ME A BETTER VIEW OF--
--SNIPER SCOPE.
BLAM
BLAM
MOVE!
IS EVERYONE HERE A HOMICIDAL MANIAC...?

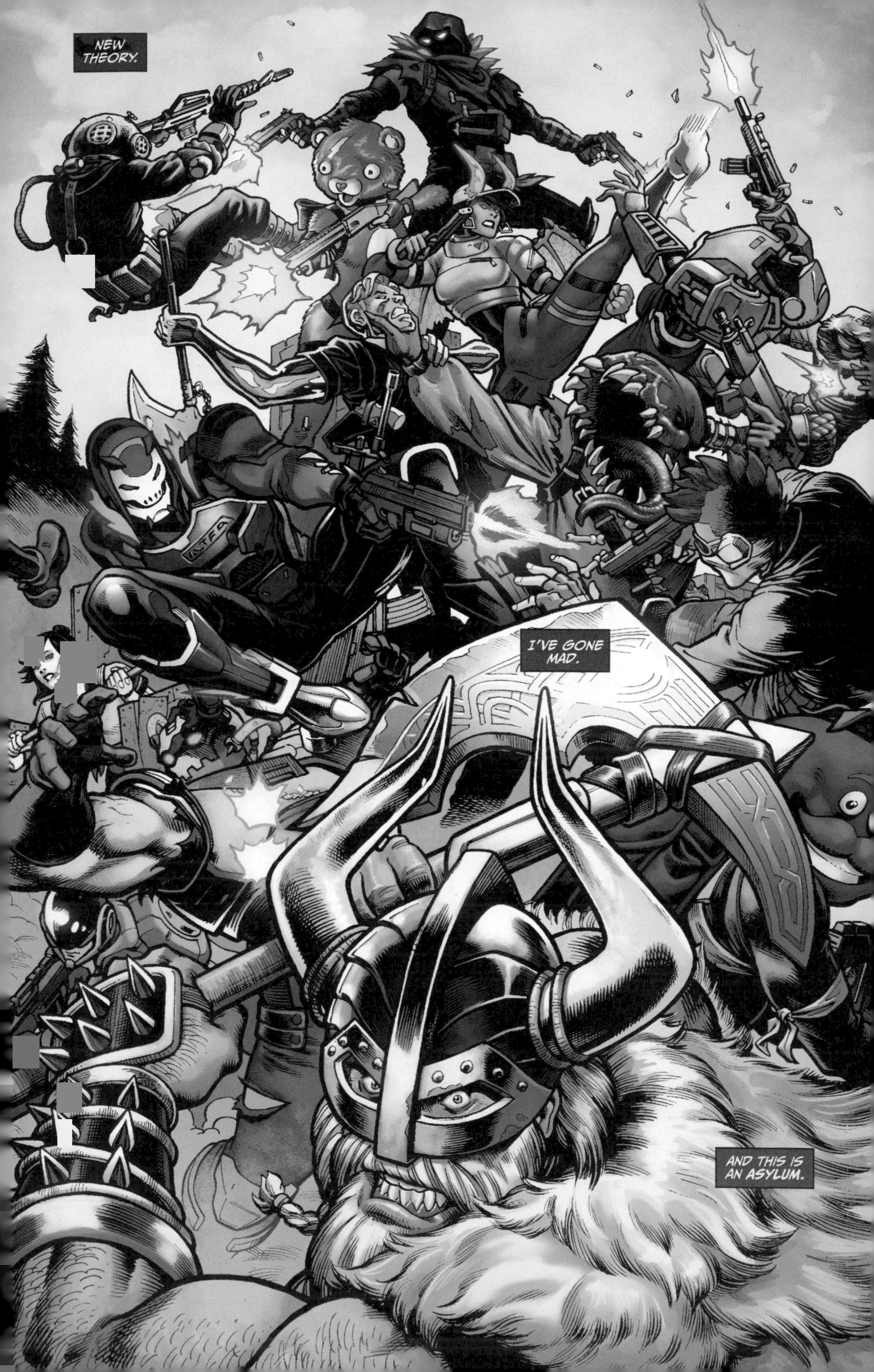
NEW THEORY.
I'VE GONE MAD.
AND THIS IS AN ASYLUM.

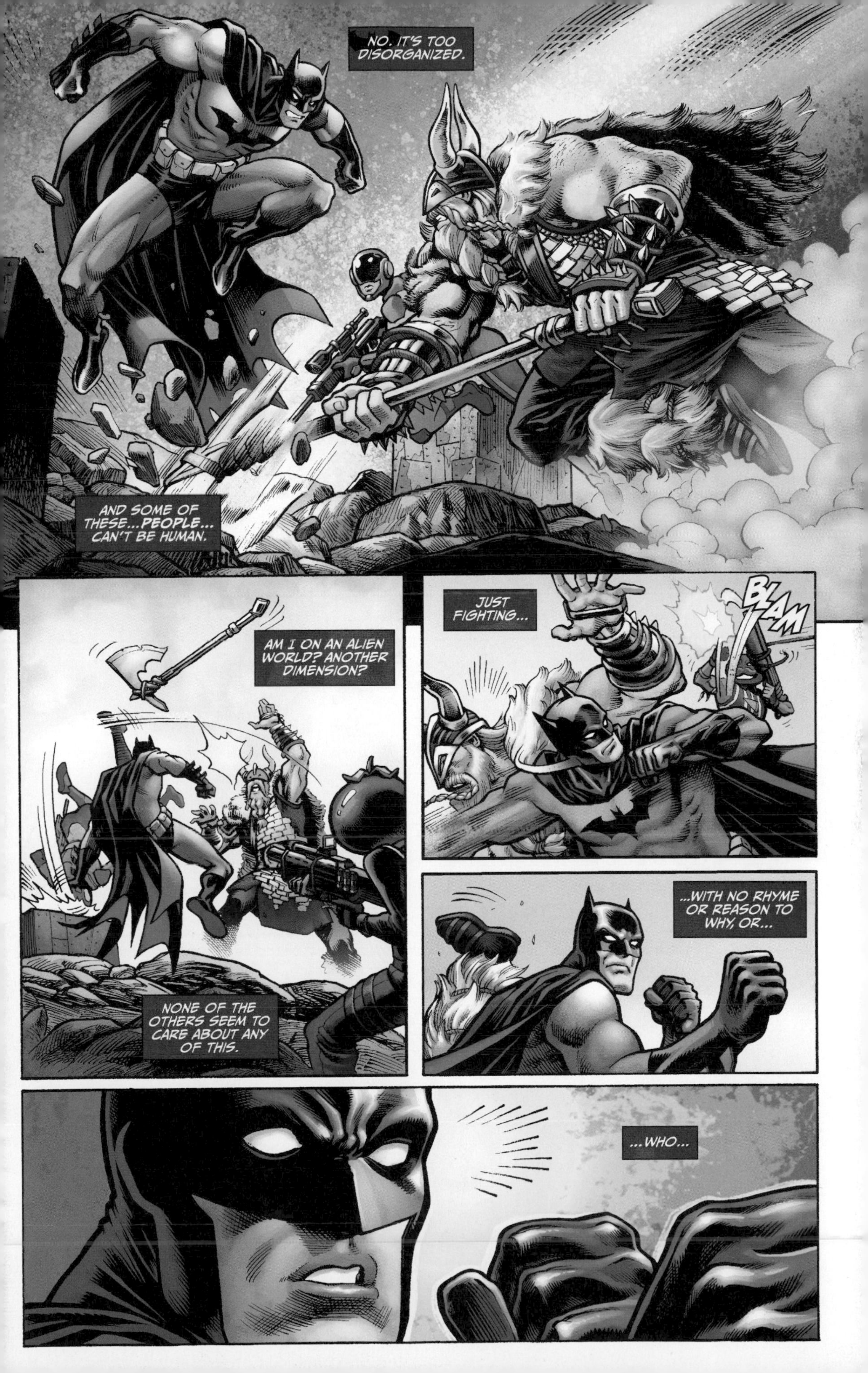
NO. IT'S TOO DISORGANIZED.
AND SOME OF THESE...PEOPLE... CAN'T BE HUMAN.
AM I ON AN ALIEN WORLD? ANOTHER DIMENSION?
NONE OF THE OTHERS SEEM TO CARE ABOUT ANY OF THIS.
JUST FIGHTING...
BLAM
...WITH NO RHYME OR REASON TO WHY, OR...
...WHO...

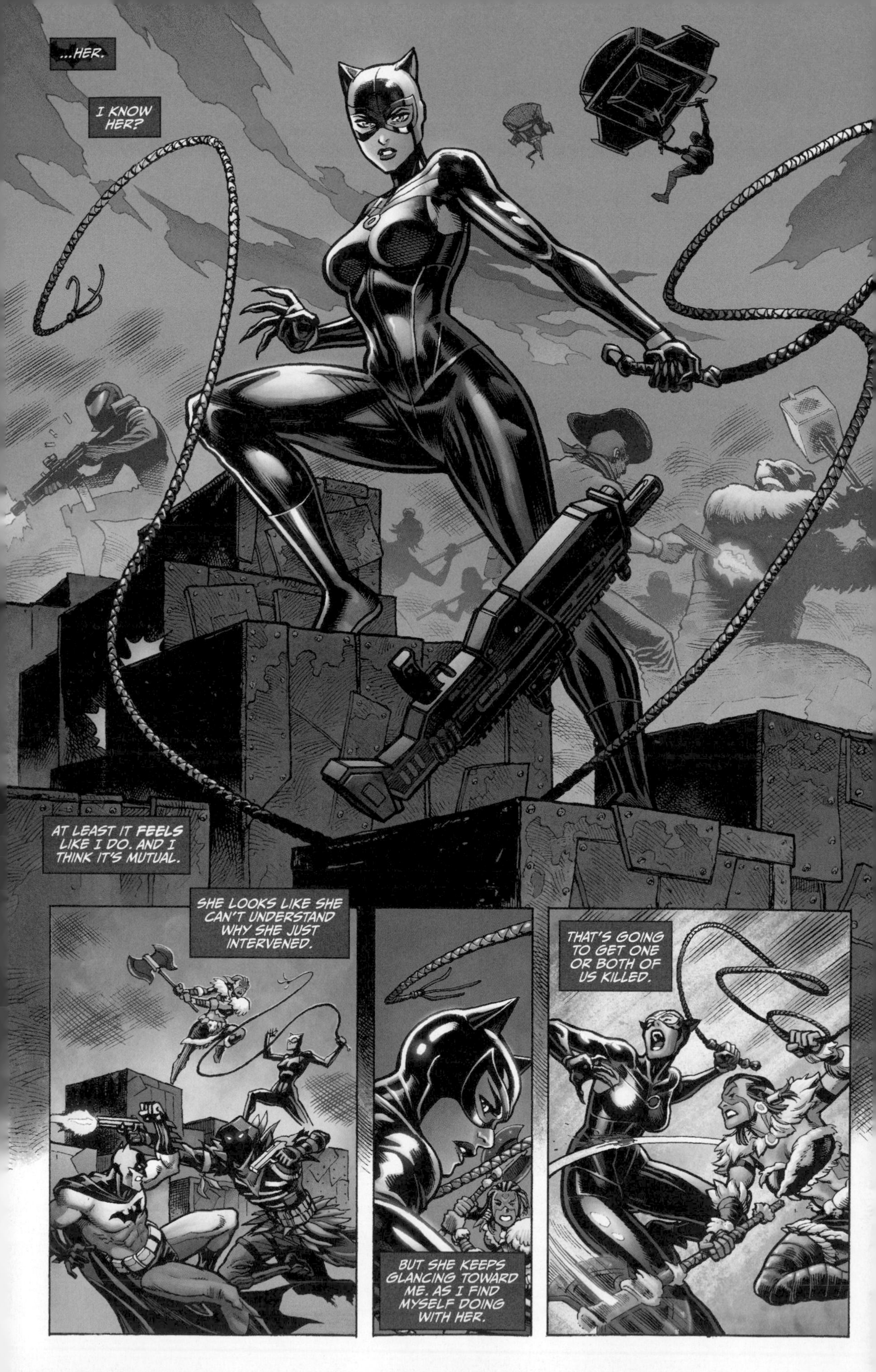

...HER.
I KNOW HER?
AT LEAST IT FEELS LIKE I DO. AND I THINK IT'S MUTUAL.
SHE LOOKS LIKE SHE CAN'T UNDERSTAND WHY SHE JUST INTERVENED.
BUT SHE KEEPS GLANCING TOWARD ME. AS I FIND MYSELF DOING WITH HER.
THAT'S GOING TO GET ONE OR BOTH OF US KILLED.

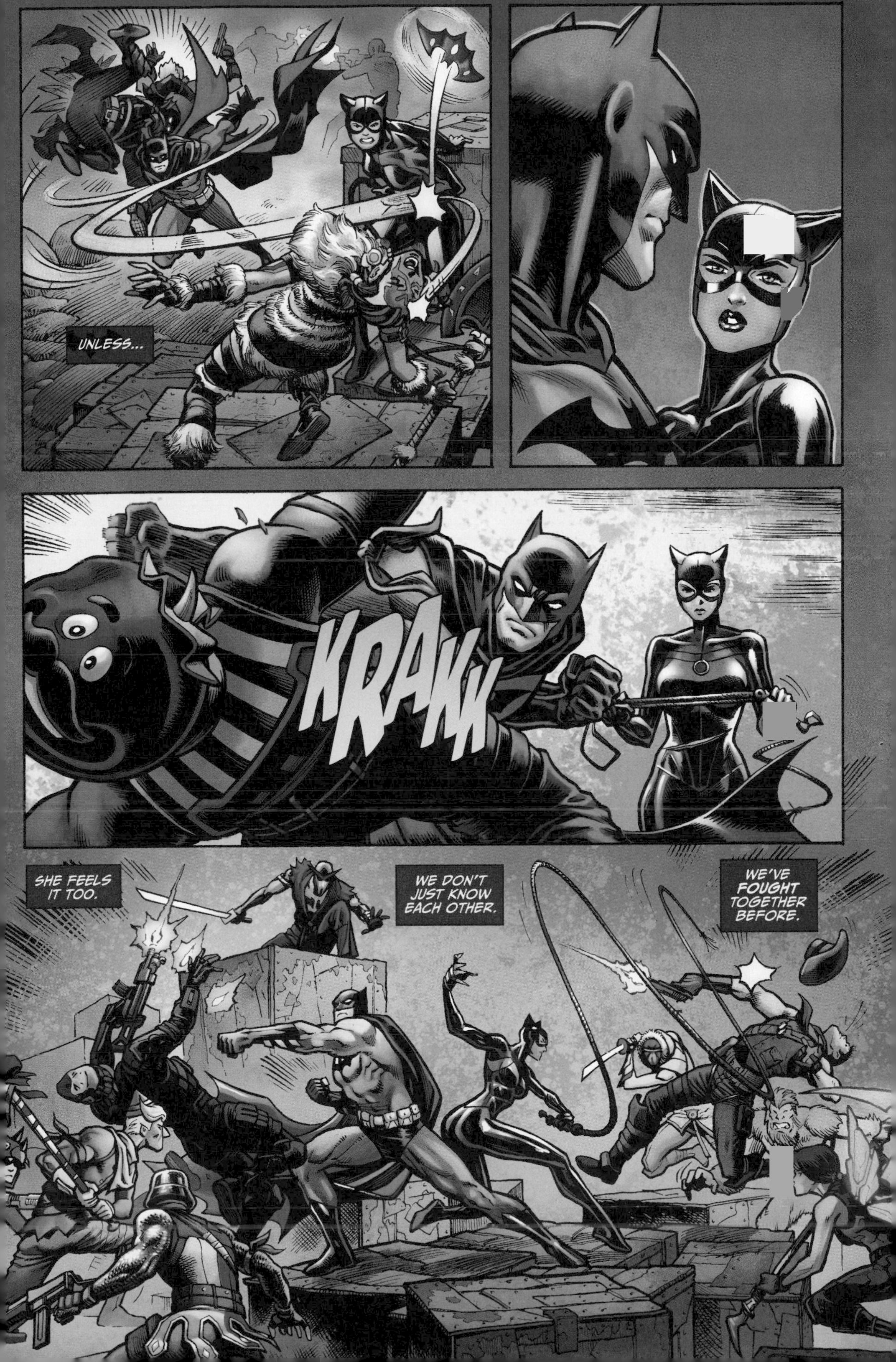
UNLESS...
KRAKK
SHE FEELS IT TOO.
WE DON'T JUST KNOW EACH OTHER.
WE'VE FOUGHT TOGETHER BEFORE.

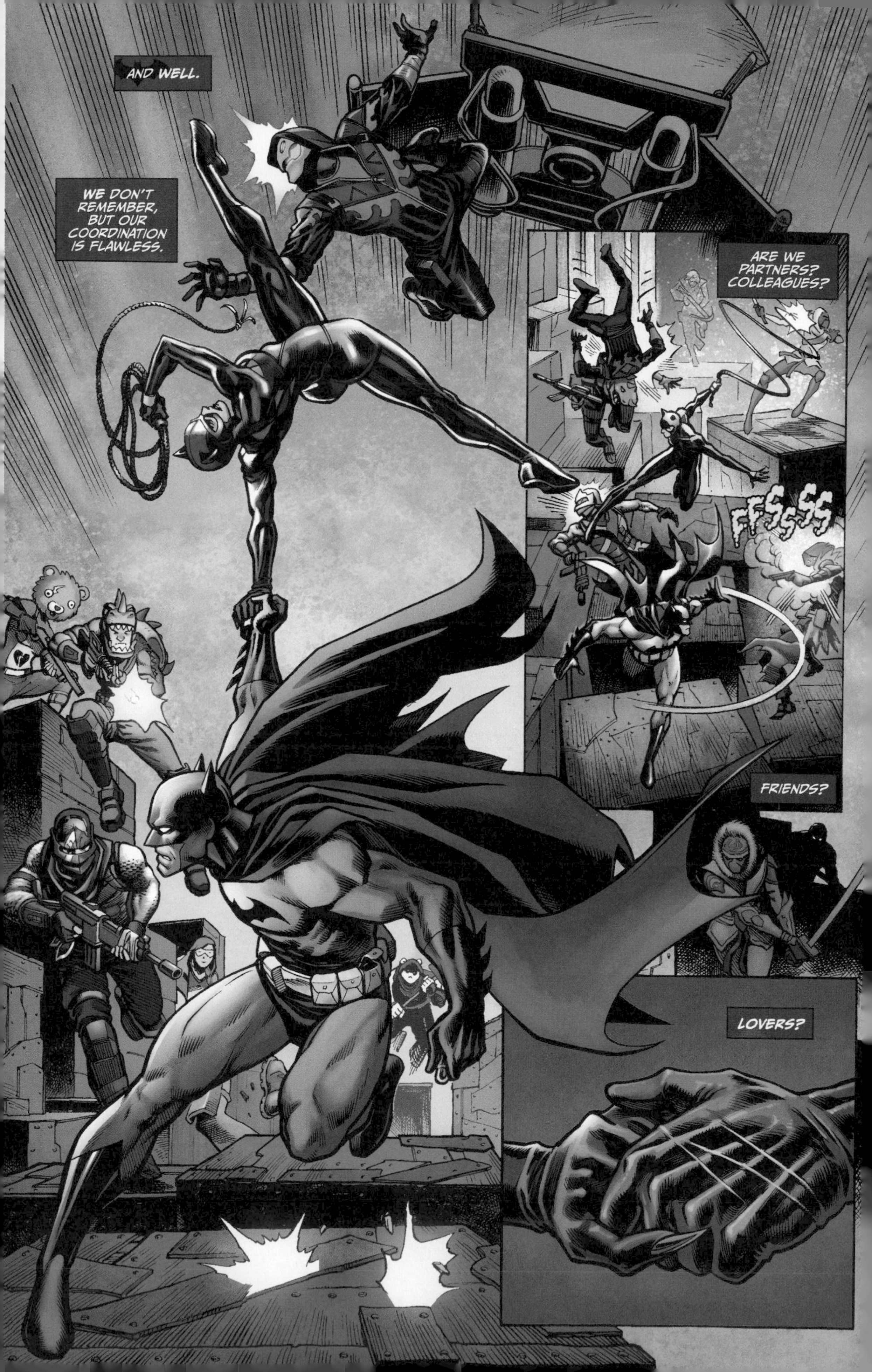
AND WELL.
WE DON'T REMEMBER, BUT OUR COORDINATION IS FLAWLESS.
ARE WE PARTNERS? COLLEAGUES?
FFSSSSS
FRIENDS?
LOVERS?

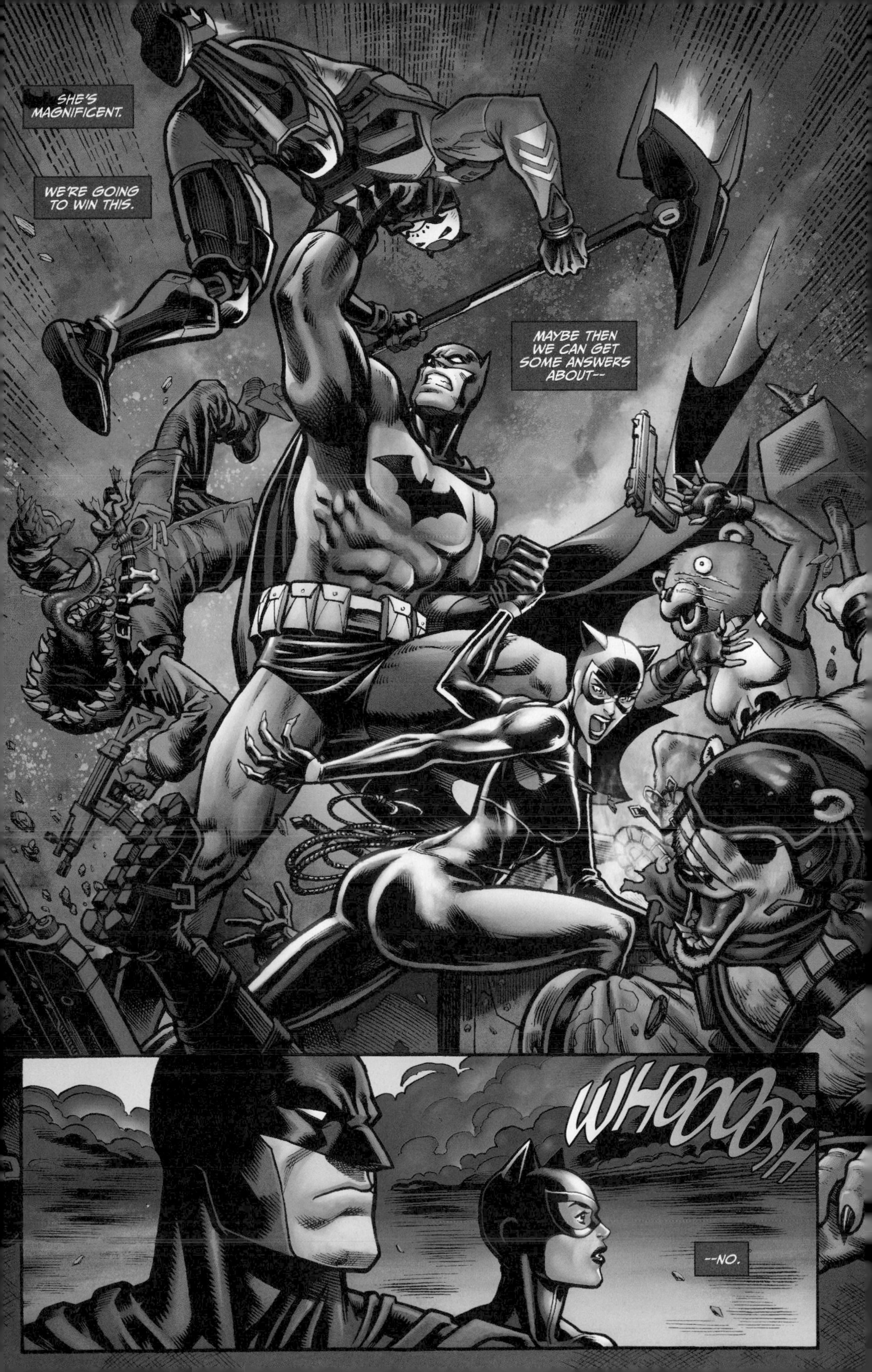
SHE'S MAGNIFICENT.
WE'RE GOING TO WIN THIS.
MAYBE THEN WE CAN GET SOME ANSWERS ABOUT--
WHOOOSH
--NO.

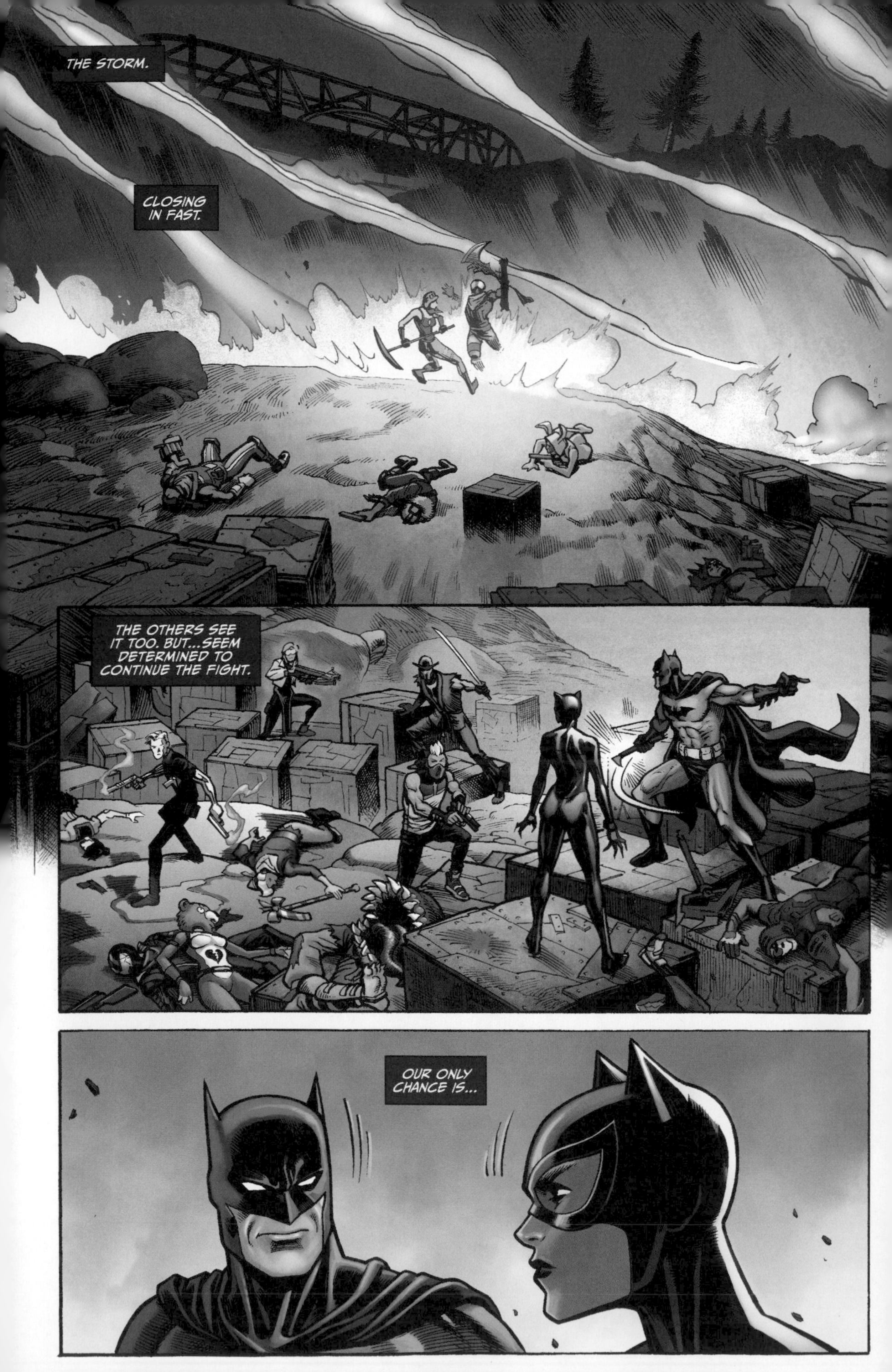
THE STORM.
CLOSING IN FAST.
THE OTHERS SEE IT TOO. BUT...SEEM DETERMINED TO CONTINUE THE FIGHT.
OUR ONLY CHANCE IS...

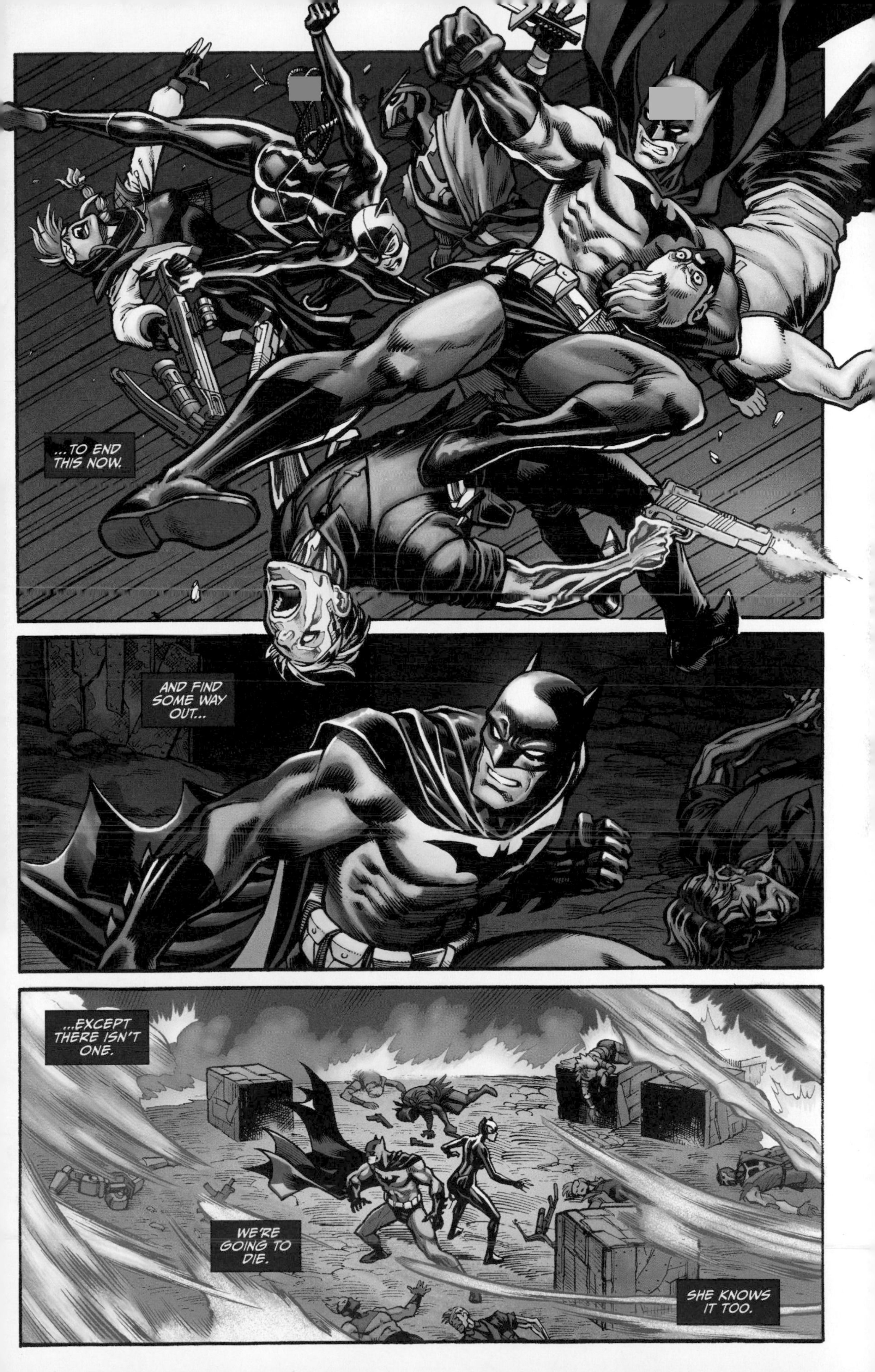
...TO END THIS NOW.
AND FIND SOME WAY OUT...
...EXCEPT THERE ISN'T ONE.
WE'RE GOING TO DIE.
SHE KNOWS IT TOO.

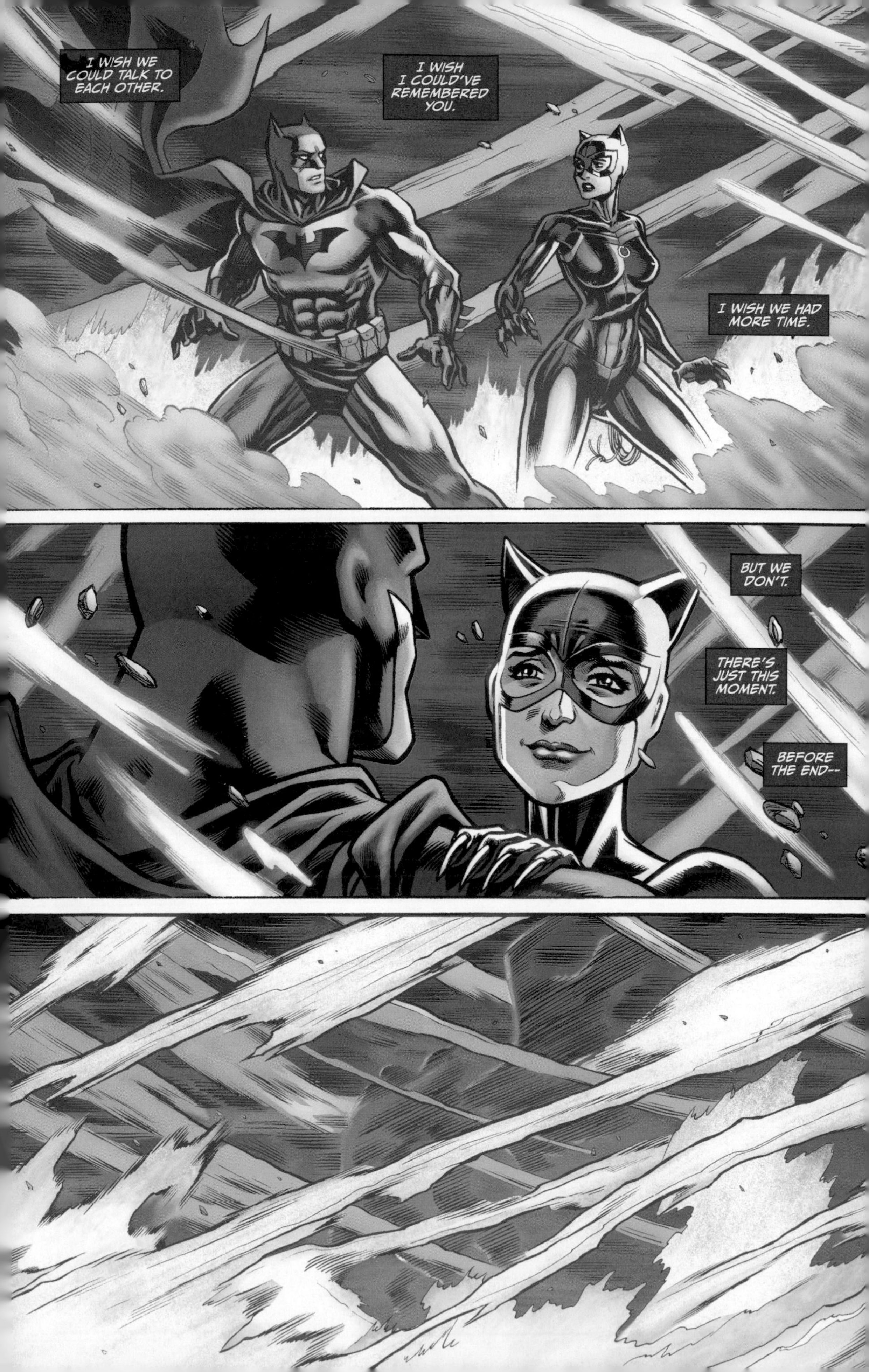
I WISH WE COULD TALK TO EACH OTHER.
I WISH I COULD'VE REMEMBERED YOU.
I WISH WE HAD MORE TIME.
BUT WE DON'T.
THERE'S JUST THIS MOMENT.
BEFORE THE END--

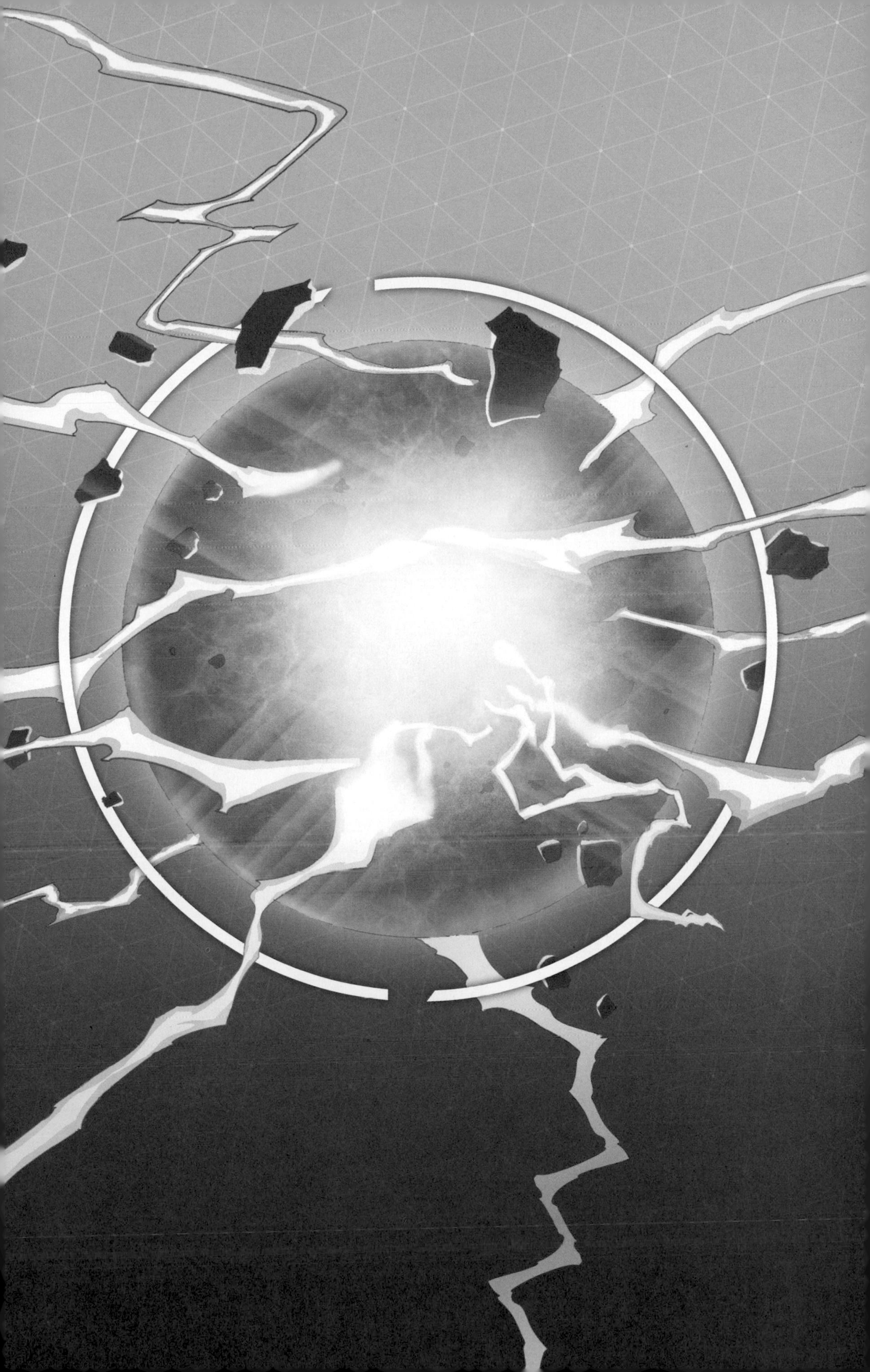

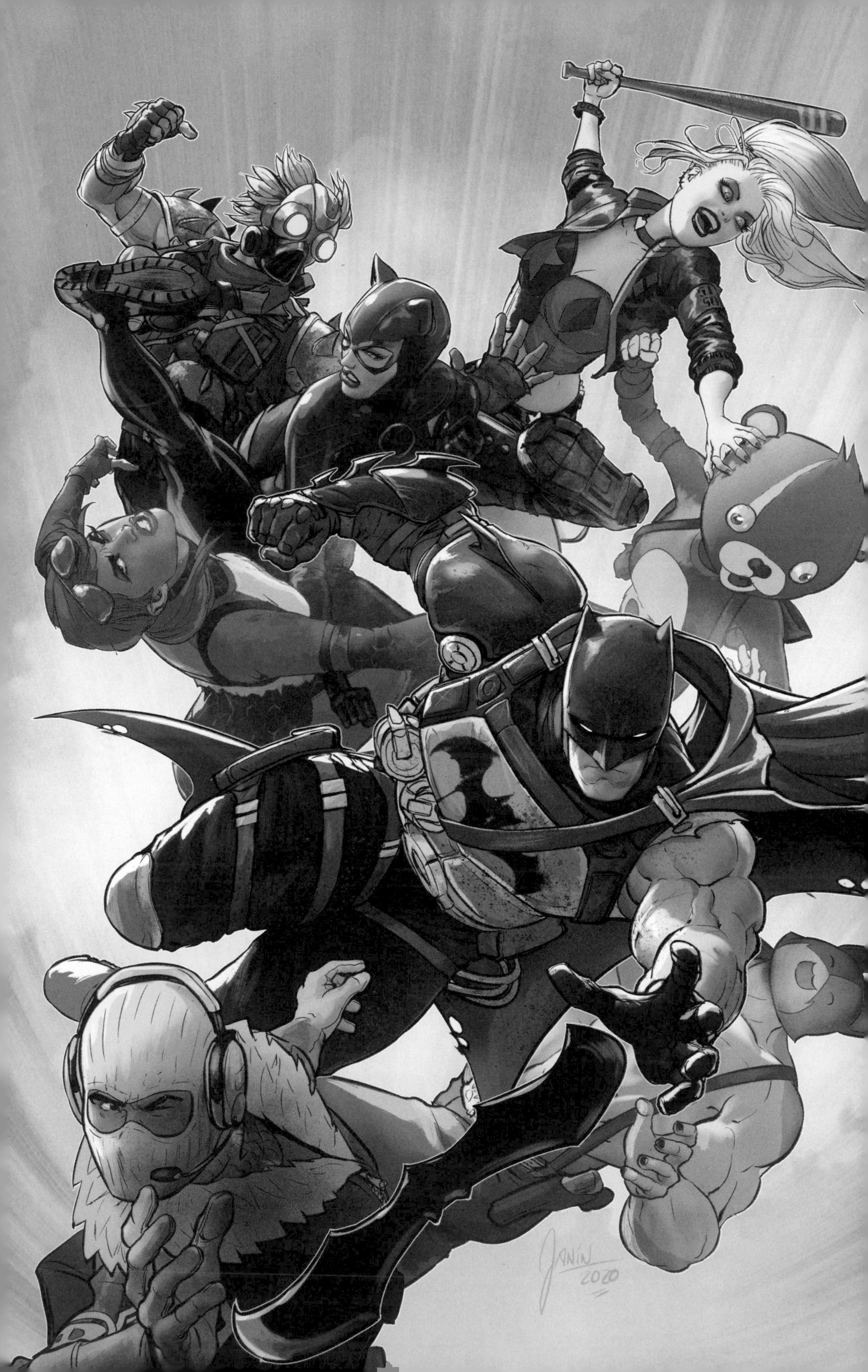
Janín
2020

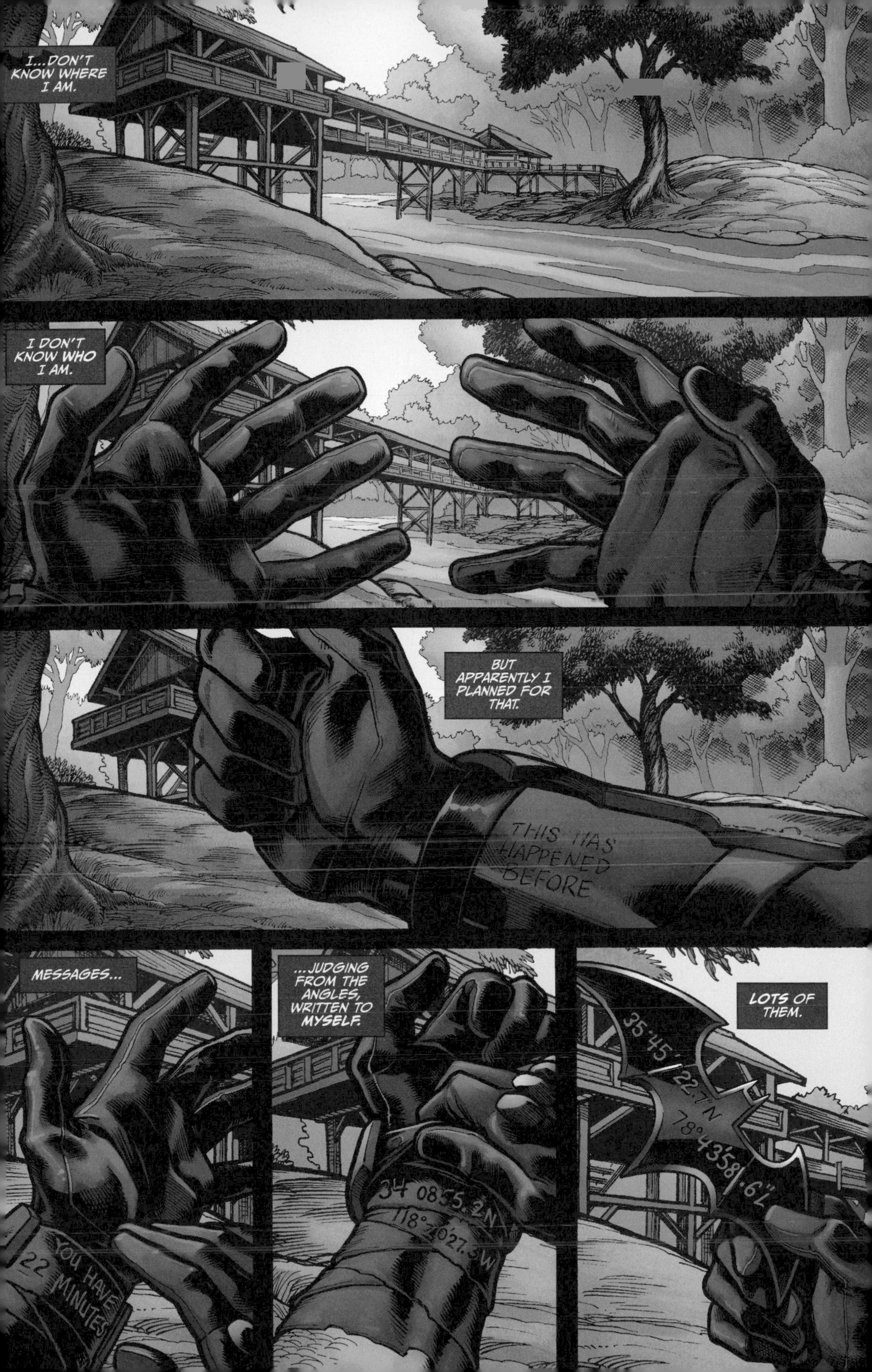
I...DON'T KNOW WHERE I AM.
I DON'T KNOW WHO I AM.
BUT APPARENTLY I PLANNED FOR THAT.
THIS HAS HAPPENED BEFORE
MESSAGES...
YOU HAVE 22 MINUTES
...JUDGING FROM THE ANGLES, WRITTEN TO MYSELF.
34 0855.2N 118°2027.3W
LOTS OF THEM.
35°45'22.7"N 78°43'58.6"

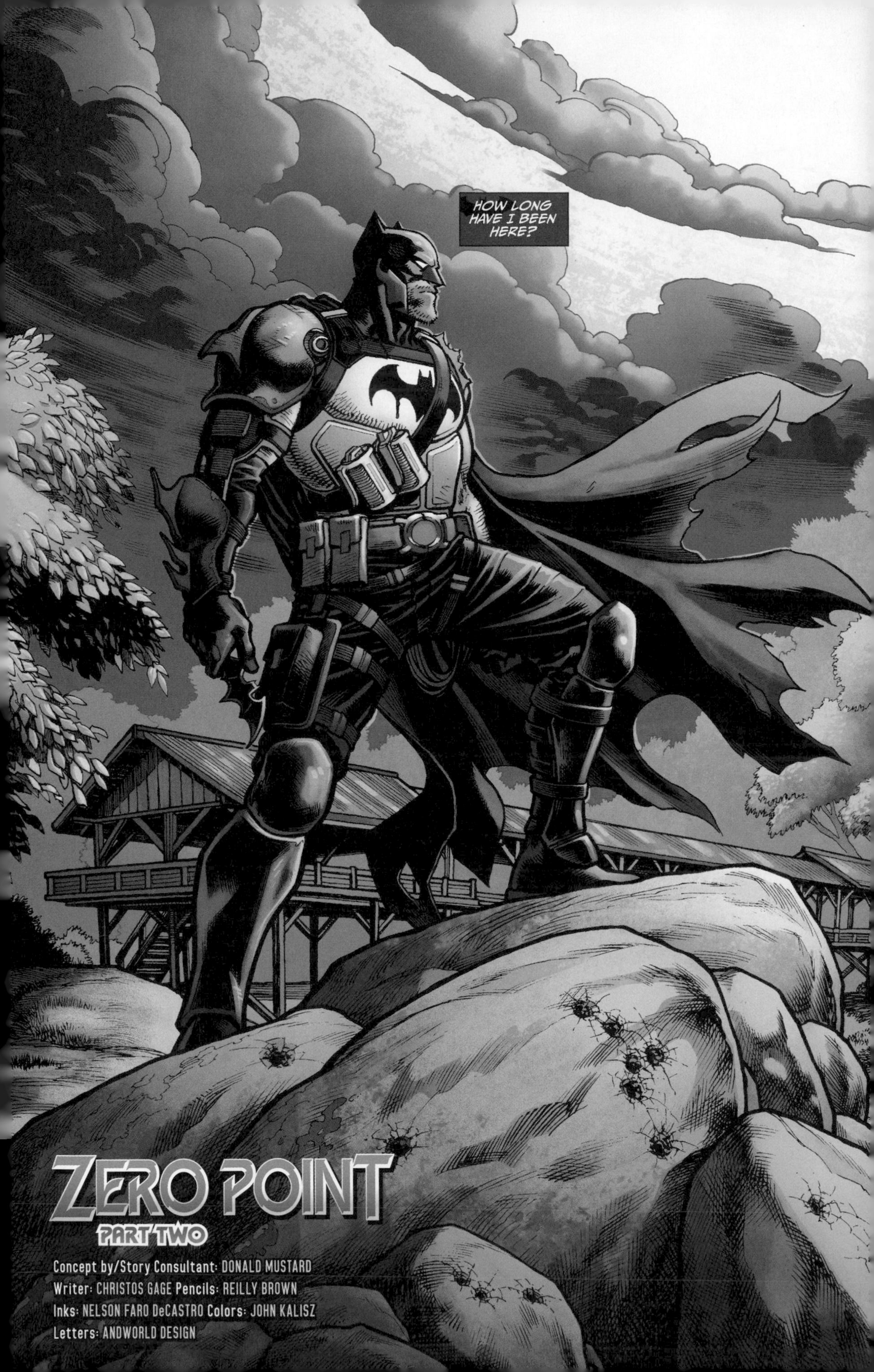
HOW LONG HAVE I BEEN HERE?
ZERO POINT
PART TWO
Concept by/Story Consultant: DONALD MUSTARD
Writer: CHRISTOS GAGE Pencils: REILLY BROWN
Inks: NELSON FARO DeCASTRO Colors: JOHN KALISZ
Letters: ANDWORLD DESIGN

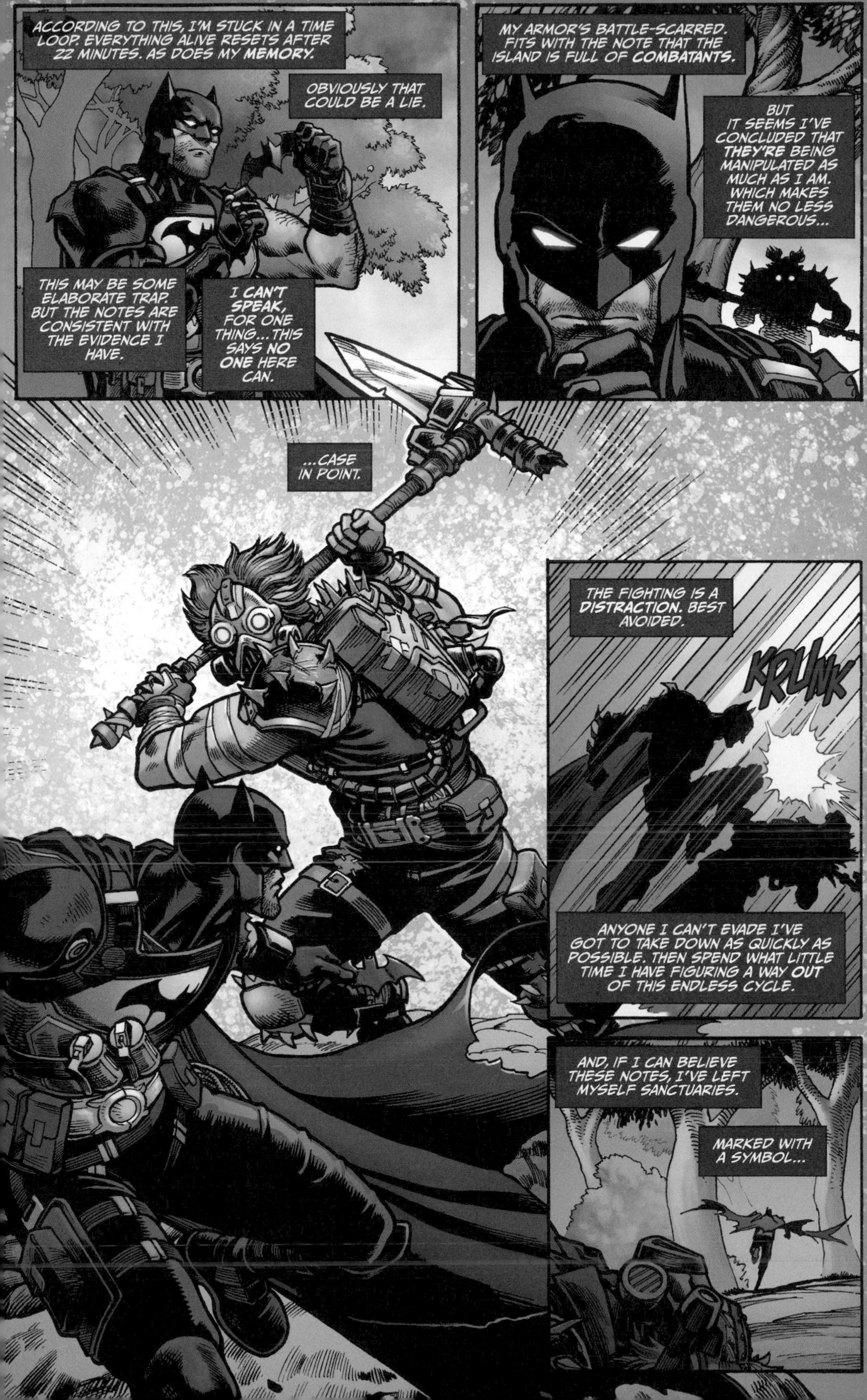
ACCORDING TO THIS, I'M STUCK IN A TIME LOOP. EVERYTHING ALIVE RESETS AFTER 22 MINUTES. AS DOES MY **MEMORY**.
OBVIOUSLY THAT COULD BE A LIE.
THIS MAY BE SOME ELABORATE TRAP. BUT THE NOTES ARE CONSISTENT WITH THE EVIDENCE I HAVE.
I **CAN'T SPEAK**, FOR ONE THING... THIS SAYS **NO ONE** HERE CAN.
MY ARMOR'S BATTLE-SCARRED. FITS WITH THE NOTE THAT THE ISLAND IS FULL OF **COMBATANTS**.
BUT IT SEEMS I'VE CONCLUDED THAT **THEY'RE** BEING MANIPULATED AS MUCH AS I AM. WHICH MAKES THEM NO LESS DANGEROUS...
...CASE IN POINT.
THE FIGHTING IS A **DISTRACTION**. BEST AVOIDED.
KRUNK
ANYONE I CAN'T EVADE I'VE GOT TO TAKE DOWN AS QUICKLY AS POSSIBLE. THEN SPEND WHAT LITTLE TIME I HAVE FIGURING A WAY **OUT** OF THIS ENDLESS CYCLE.
AND, IF I CAN BELIEVE THESE NOTES, I'VE LEFT MYSELF SANCTUARIES.
MARKED WITH A SYMBOL...

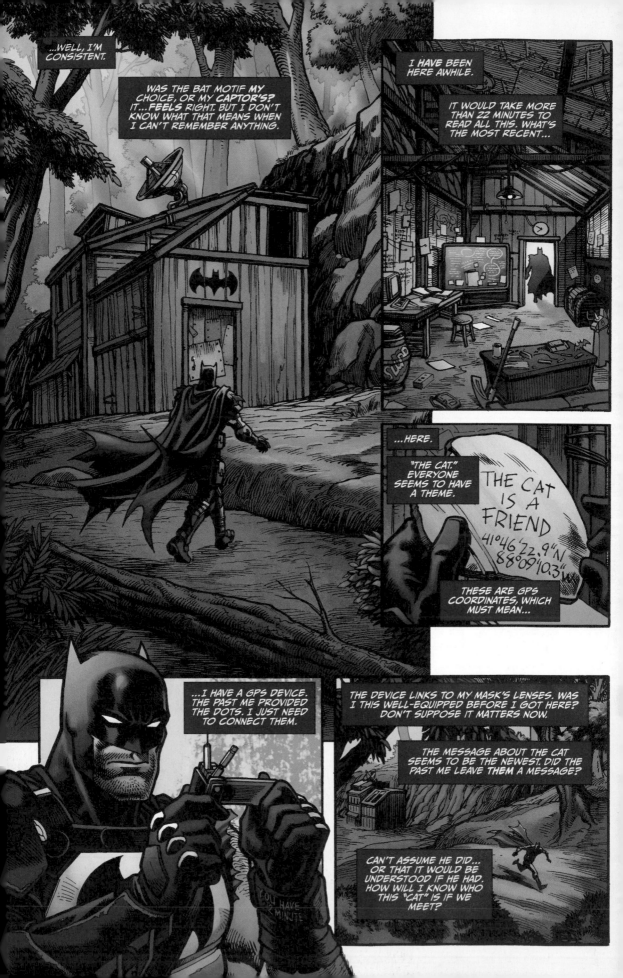

...WELL, I'M CONSISTENT.

WAS THE BAT MOTIF **MY** CHOICE, OR MY **CAPTOR'S?** IT...**FEELS** RIGHT. BUT I DON'T KNOW WHAT THAT MEANS WHEN I CAN'T REMEMBER ANYTHING.

I **HAVE BEEN** HERE AWHILE.

IT WOULD TAKE MORE THAN 22 MINUTES TO READ ALL THIS. WHAT'S THE MOST RECENT...

...HERE.

"THE CAT." EVERYONE SEEMS TO HAVE A THEME.

THE CAT IS A FRIEND
41°46'22.9"N
88°09'103"

THESE ARE GPS COORDINATES, WHICH MUST MEAN...

...I HAVE A GPS DEVICE. THE PAST ME PROVIDED THE DOTS. I JUST NEED TO CONNECT THEM.

THE DEVICE LINKS TO MY MASK'S LENSES. WAS I THIS WELL-EQUIPPED BEFORE I GOT HERE? DON'T SUPPOSE IT MATTERS NOW.

THE MESSAGE ABOUT THE CAT SEEMS TO BE THE NEWEST. DID THE PAST ME LEAVE THEM A MESSAGE?

CAN'T ASSUME HE DID... OR THAT IT WOULD BE UNDERSTOOD IF HE HAD. HOW WILL I KNOW WHO THIS "CAT" IS IF WE MEET?

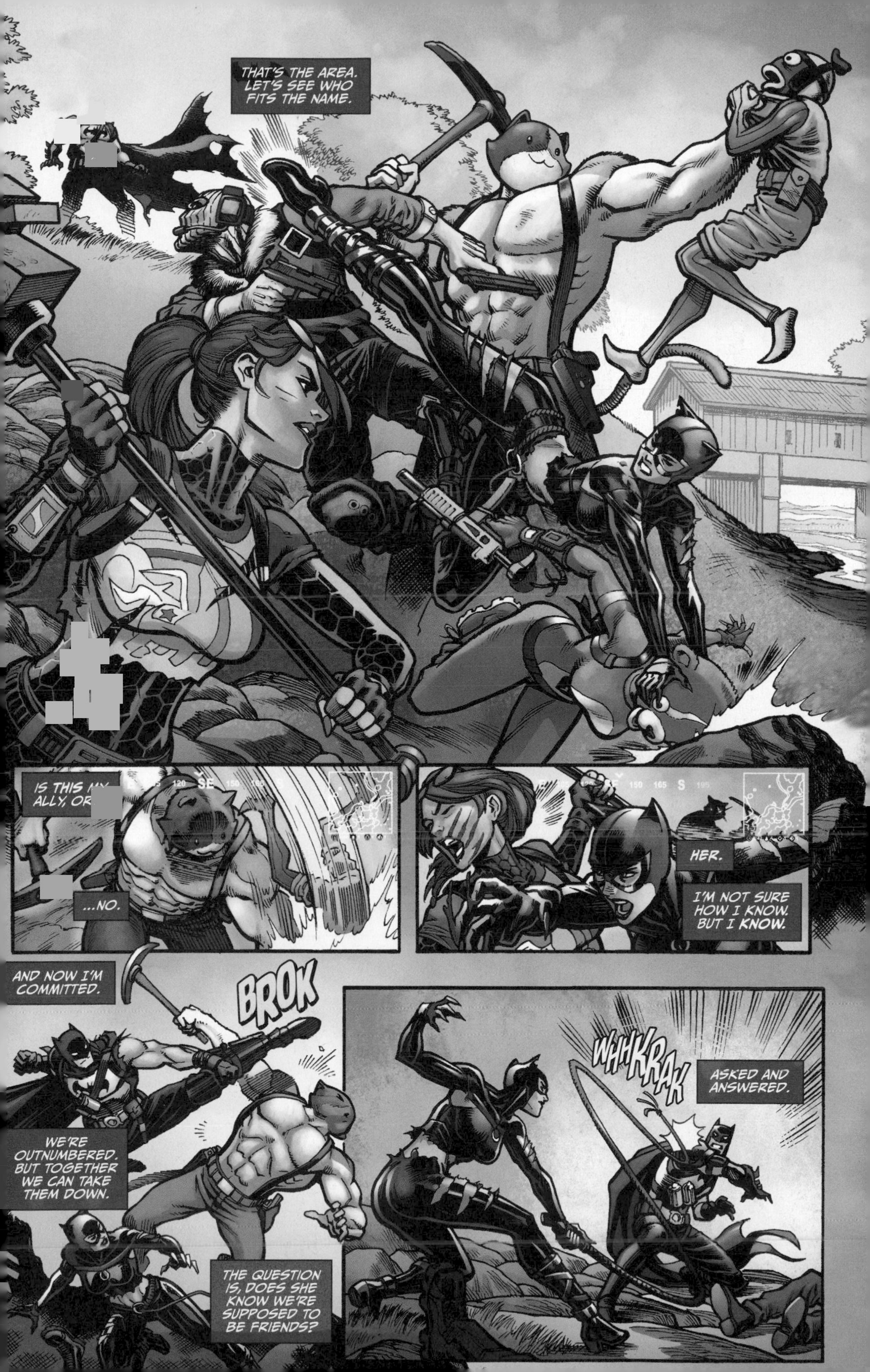

THAT'S THE AREA. LET'S SEE WHO FITS THE NAME.
IS THIS M ALLY, OR
...NO.
HER.
I'M NOT SURE HOW I KNOW. BUT I KNOW.
AND NOW I'M COMMITTED.
BROK
WE'RE OUTNUMBERED. BUT TOGETHER WE CAN TAKE THEM DOWN.
THE QUESTION IS, DOES SHE KNOW WE'RE SUPPOSED TO BE FRIENDS?
WHHKRAK
ASKED AND ANSWERED.

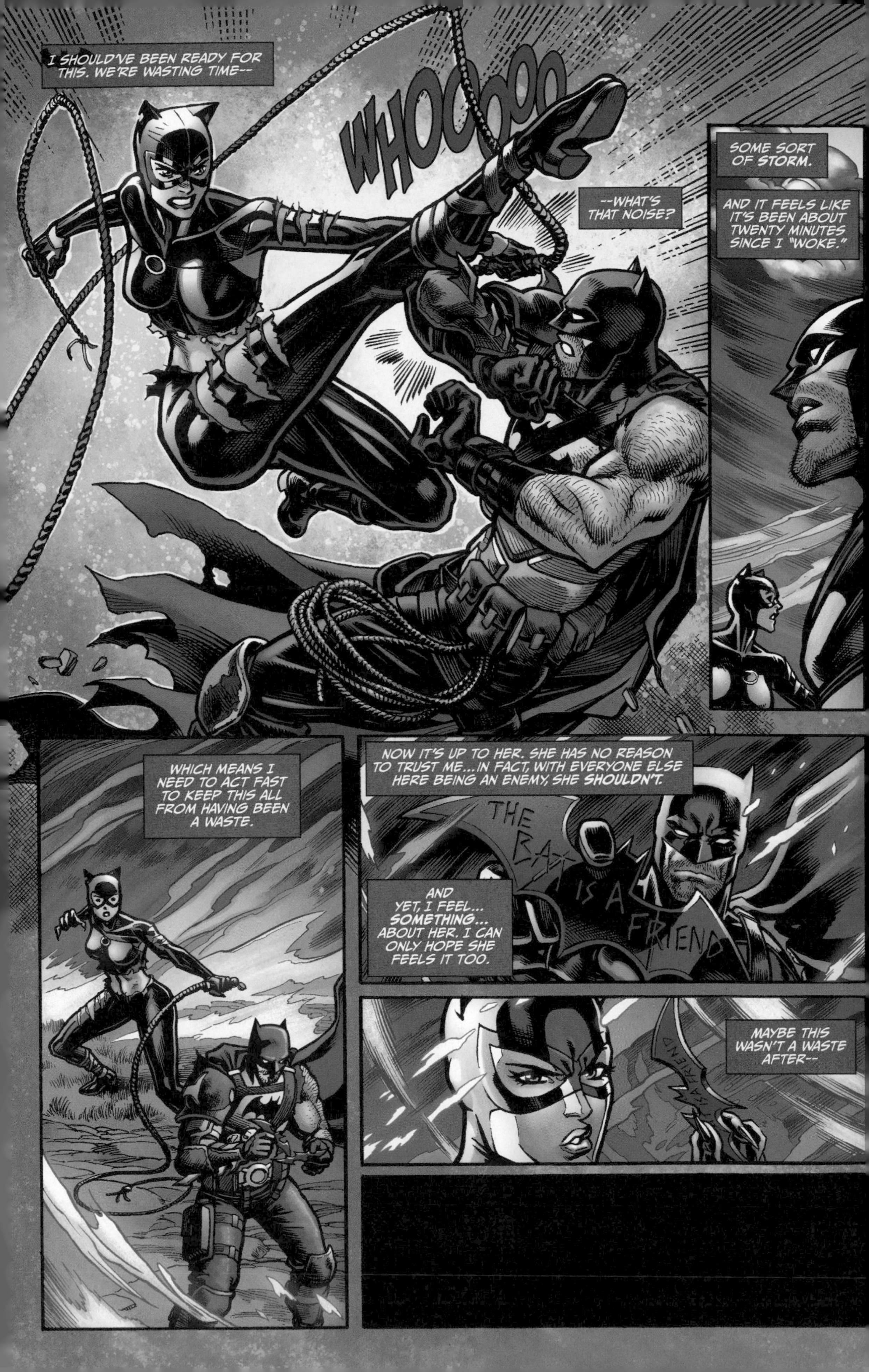
I SHOULD'VE BEEN READY FOR THIS. WE'RE WASTING TIME--
WHOOOOO
--WHAT'S THAT NOISE?
SOME SORT OF STORM.
AND IT FEELS LIKE IT'S BEEN ABOUT TWENTY MINUTES SINCE I "WOKE."
WHICH MEANS I NEED TO ACT FAST TO KEEP THIS ALL FROM HAVING BEEN A WASTE.
NOW IT'S UP TO HER. SHE HAS NO REASON TO TRUST ME...IN FACT, WITH EVERYONE ELSE HERE BEING AN ENEMY, SHE SHOULDN'T.
THE BAT IS A FRIEND
AND YET, I FEEL... SOMETHING... ABOUT HER. I CAN ONLY HOPE SHE FEELS IT TOO.
MAYBE THIS WASN'T A WASTE AFTER--

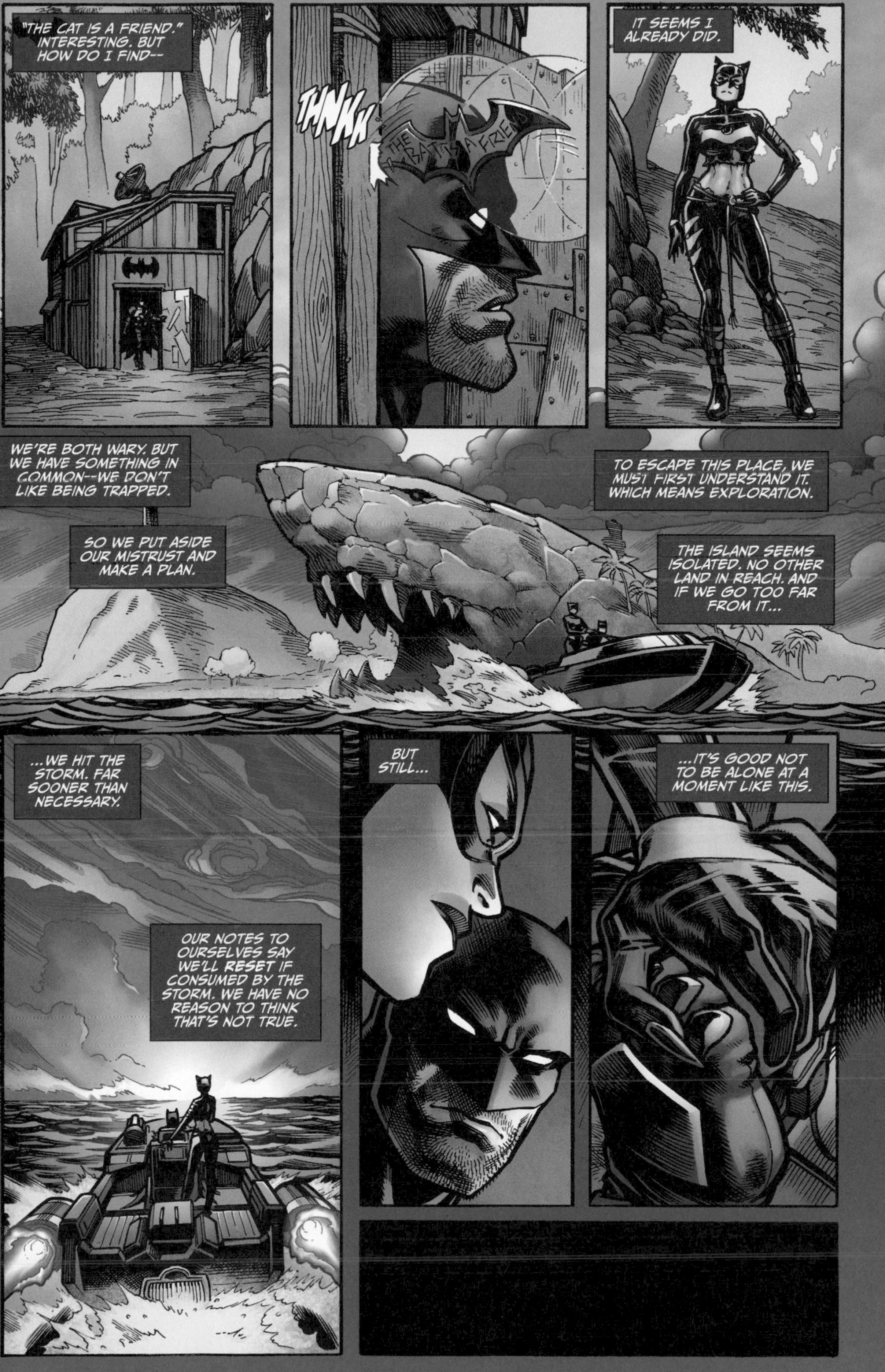

"THE CAT IS A FRIEND." INTERESTING. BUT HOW DO I FIND--
THNKK
THE BAT IS A FRIEND
IT SEEMS I ALREADY DID.
WE'RE BOTH WARY. BUT WE HAVE SOMETHING IN COMMON--WE DON'T LIKE BEING TRAPPED.
SO WE PUT ASIDE OUR MISTRUST AND MAKE A PLAN.
TO ESCAPE THIS PLACE, WE MUST FIRST UNDERSTAND IT. WHICH MEANS EXPLORATION.
THE ISLAND SEEMS ISOLATED. NO OTHER LAND IN REACH. AND IF WE GO TOO FAR FROM IT...
...WE HIT THE STORM. FAR SOONER THAN NECESSARY.
OUR NOTES TO OURSELVES SAY WE'LL RESET IF CONSUMED BY THE STORM. WE HAVE NO REASON TO THINK THAT'S NOT TRUE.
BUT STILL...
...IT'S GOOD NOT TO BE ALONE AT A MOMENT LIKE THIS.

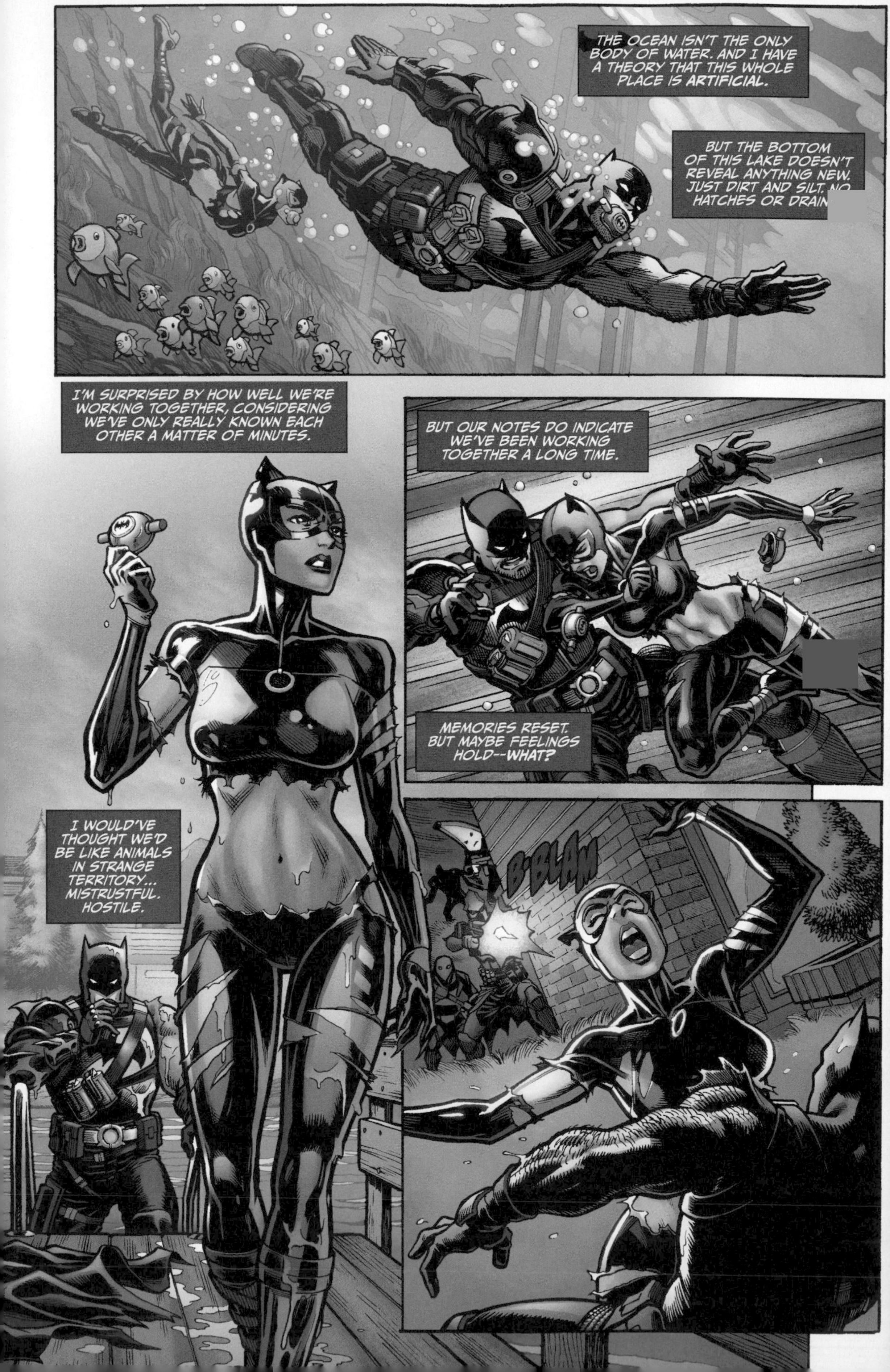
THE OCEAN ISN'T THE ONLY BODY OF WATER. AND I HAVE A THEORY THAT THIS WHOLE PLACE IS ARTIFICIAL.
BUT THE BOTTOM OF THIS LAKE DOESN'T REVEAL ANYTHING NEW. JUST DIRT AND SILT. NO HATCHES OR DRAIN
I'M SURPRISED BY HOW WELL WE'RE WORKING TOGETHER, CONSIDERING WE'VE ONLY REALLY KNOWN EACH OTHER A MATTER OF MINUTES.
I WOULD'VE THOUGHT WE'D BE LIKE ANIMALS IN STRANGE TERRITORY... MISTRUSTFUL. HOSTILE.
BUT OUR NOTES DO INDICATE WE'VE BEEN WORKING TOGETHER A LONG TIME.
MEMORIES RESET. BUT MAYBE FEELINGS HOLD--WHAT?
B'BLAM

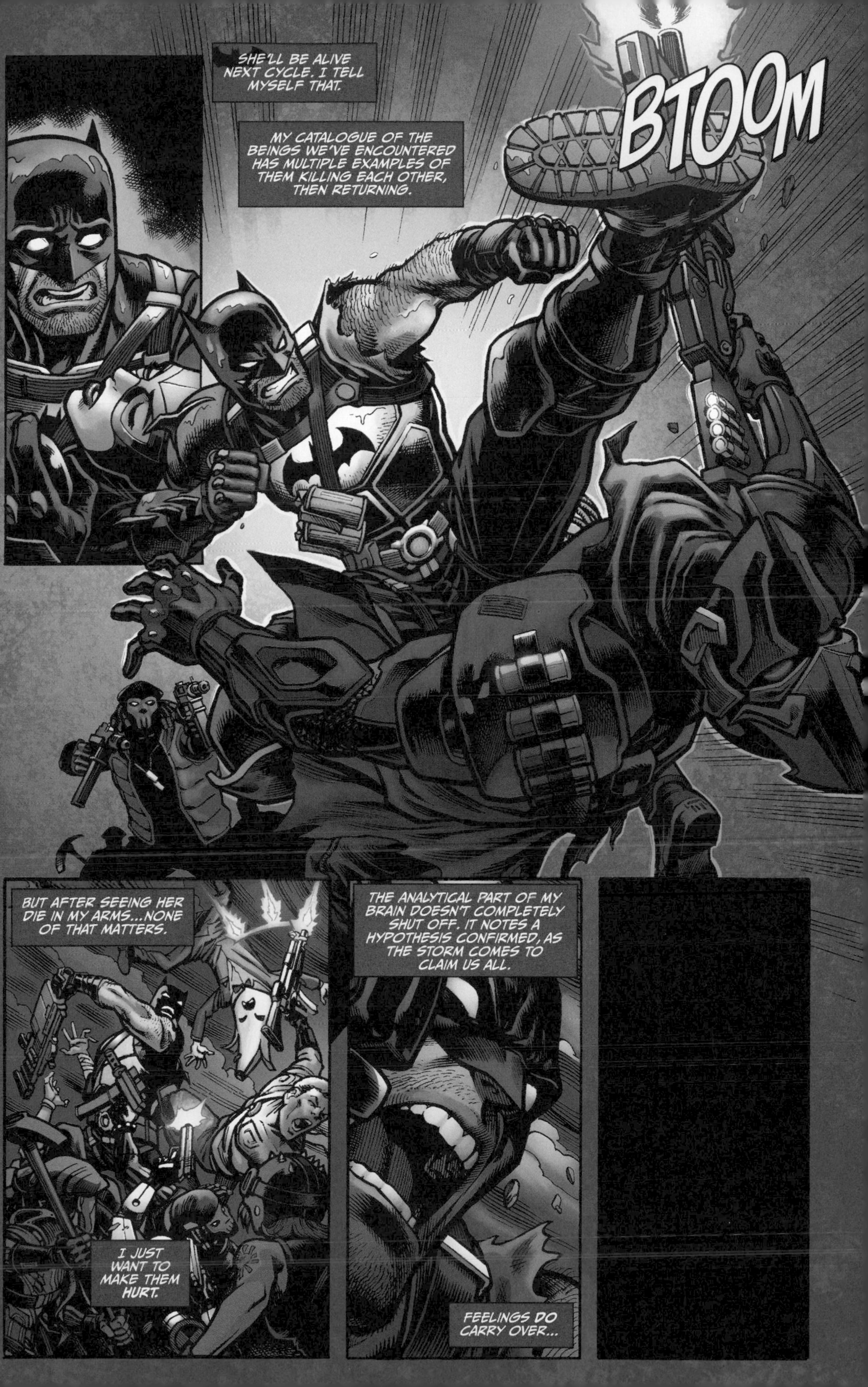

SHE'LL BE ALIVE NEXT CYCLE. I TELL MYSELF THAT.
MY CATALOGUE OF THE BEINGS WE'VE ENCOUNTERED HAS MULTIPLE EXAMPLES OF THEM KILLING EACH OTHER, THEN RETURNING.
BTOOM
BUT AFTER SEEING HER DIE IN MY ARMS... NONE OF THAT MATTERS.
I JUST WANT TO MAKE THEM HURT.
THE ANALYTICAL PART OF MY BRAIN DOESN'T COMPLETELY SHUT OFF. IT NOTES A HYPOTHESIS CONFIRMED, AS THE STORM COMES TO CLAIM US ALL.
FEELINGS DO CARRY OVER...

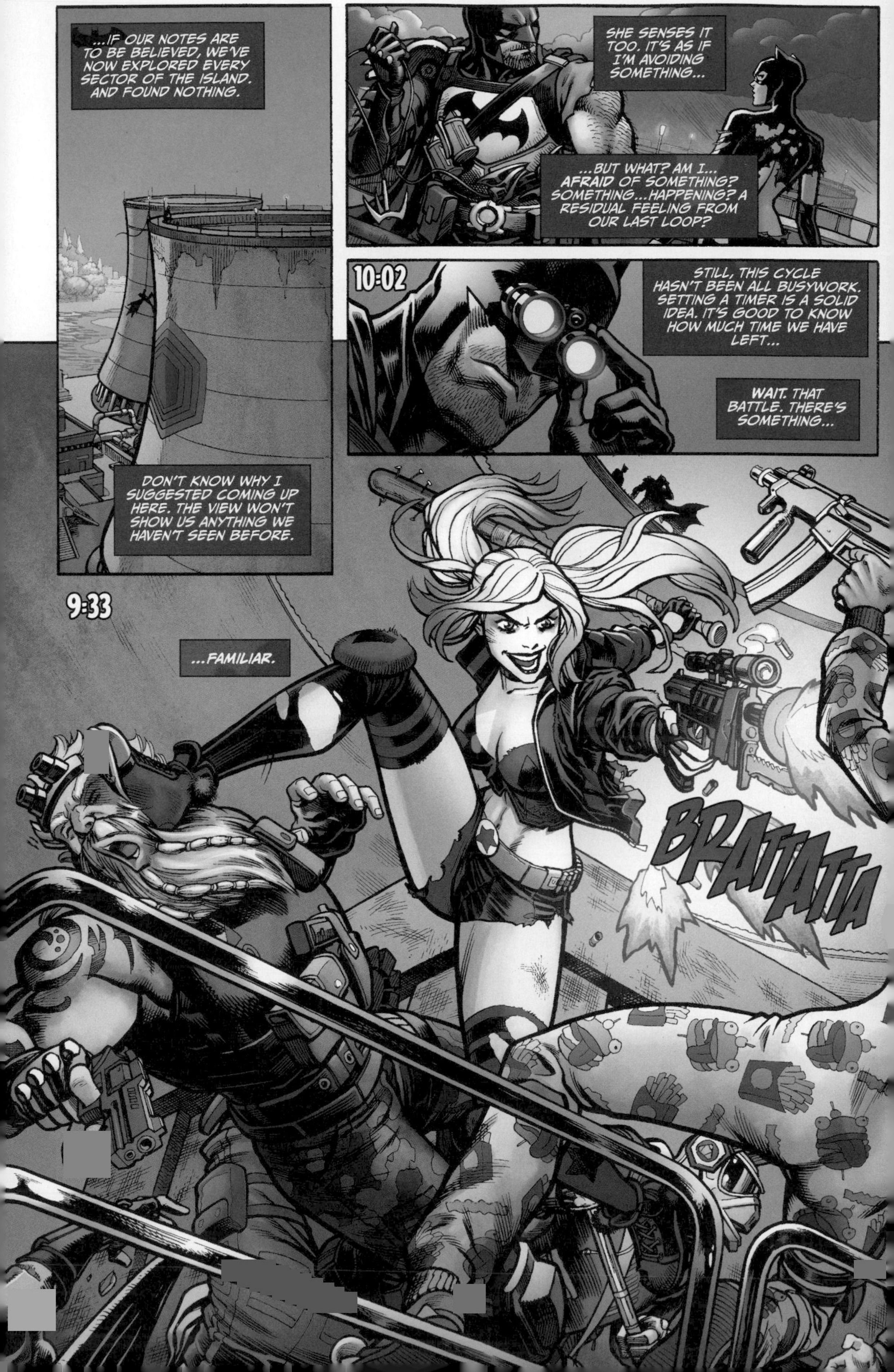
...IF OUR NOTES ARE TO BE BELIEVED, WE'VE NOW EXPLORED EVERY SECTOR OF THE ISLAND. AND FOUND NOTHING.
DON'T KNOW WHY I SUGGESTED COMING UP HERE. THE VIEW WON'T SHOW US ANYTHING WE HAVEN'T SEEN BEFORE.
SHE SENSES IT TOO. IT'S AS IF I'M AVOIDING SOMETHING...
...BUT WHAT? AM I... AFRAID OF SOMETHING? SOMETHING...HAPPENING? A RESIDUAL FEELING FROM OUR LAST LOOP?
10:02
STILL, THIS CYCLE HASN'T BEEN ALL BUSYWORK. SETTING A TIMER IS A SOLID IDEA. IT'S GOOD TO KNOW HOW MUCH TIME WE HAVE LEFT...
WAIT. THAT BATTLE. THERE'S SOMETHING...
9:33
...FAMILIAR.
BRATATATA

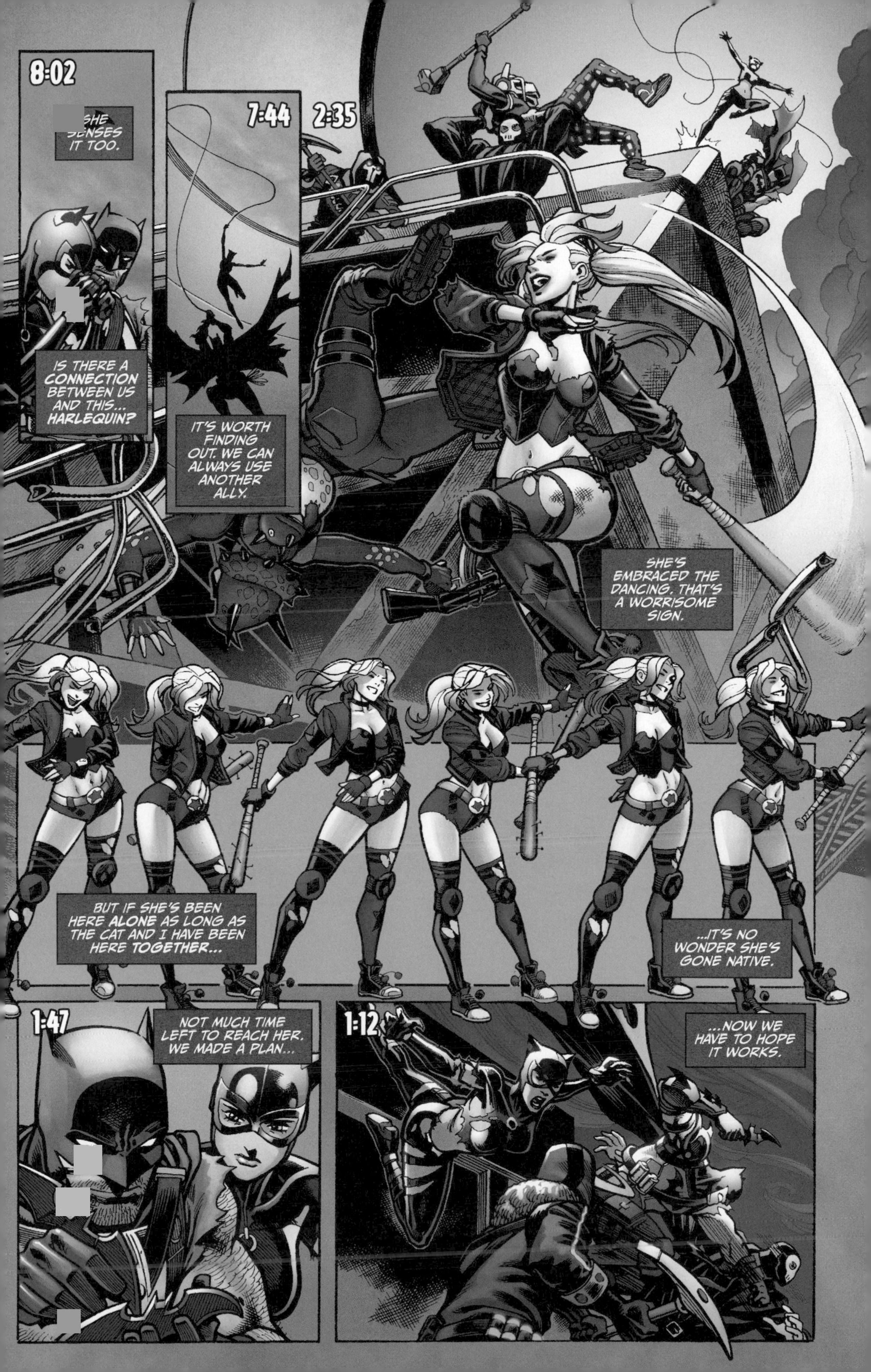
8:02
SHE SENSES IT TOO.
IS THERE A CONNECTION BETWEEN US AND THIS... HARLEQUIN?
7:44
IT'S WORTH FINDING OUT. WE CAN ALWAYS USE ANOTHER ALLY.
2:35
SHE'S EMBRACED THE DANCING. THAT'S A WORRISOME SIGN.
BUT IF SHE'S BEEN HERE ALONE AS LONG AS THE CAT AND I HAVE BEEN HERE TOGETHER...
...IT'S NO WONDER SHE'S GONE NATIVE.
1:47
NOT MUCH TIME LEFT TO REACH HER. WE MADE A PLAN...
1:12
...NOW WE HAVE TO HOPE IT WORKS.

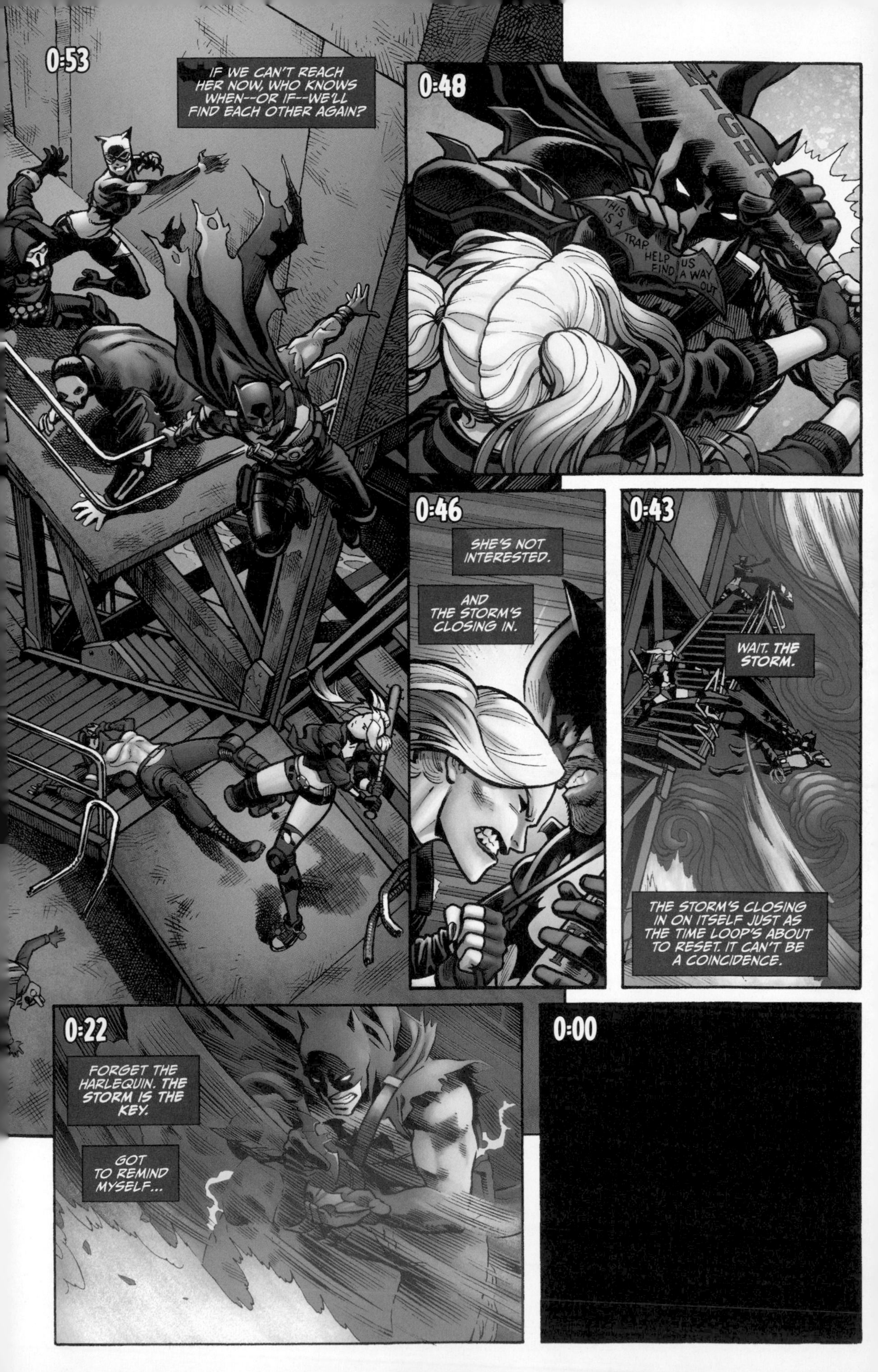
0:53
IF WE CAN'T REACH HER NOW, WHO KNOWS WHEN--OR IF--WE'LL FIND EACH OTHER AGAIN?
0:48
THIS IS A TRAP HELP US FIND A WAY OUT
0:46
SHE'S NOT INTERESTED.
AND THE STORM'S CLOSING IN.
0:43
WAIT. THE STORM.
THE STORM'S CLOSING IN ON ITSELF JUST AS THE TIME LOOP'S ABOUT TO RESET. IT CAN'T BE A COINCIDENCE.
0:22
FORGET THE HARLEQUIN. THE STORM IS THE KEY.
GOT TO REMIND MYSELF...
0:00

1:54

REDUKTION TIME: 240-210

I'VE BEEN CALCULATING THE MOVEMENTS OF THE STORM...FOR SOME TIME NOW, IT SEEMS.

$C = \pi d$

PHASE	TIME	WAIT	SHORT
1	0:00	3:20	3:00
2	6:20	2:00	2:20
3	10:20	1:30	1:30
4	13:20	1:20	1:10
5	15:50	0:50	1:00
6	17:40	0:30	1:00
7	19:10	0:00	0:55

$C = 2\pi r$

$S = V_i t + \frac{1}{2} A T$

ITS SPEED, CIRCUMFERENCE OF THE "EYE" AT DIFFERENT POINTS IN TIME...

...AND I THINK I UNDERSTAND WHY. ACCORDING TO MY NOTES, THE STORM'S CENTER RELOCATES EACH CYCLE.

1:12

IN A PLACE WHERE EVERY NONLIVING THING REMAINS CONSTANT, THE STORM CHANGES. ITS CENTER CHANGES. THAT'S SIGNIFICANT.

I'VE BEEN DEVELOPING A WAY TO FIND THE EXACT EPICENTER IN A GIVEN CYCLE. BASED ON MY DATA, THIS TIME AROUND, THIS IS IT...

0:39

...BUT WHAT'S ITS SIGNIFICANCE?

THE CAT'S ANNOYED. SHE DOESN'T UNDERSTAND WHAT I'M DOING. SHE...

0:34

...WAIT. SHE DOES UNDERSTAND.

AND SHE'S ONE STEP AHEAD OF ME.

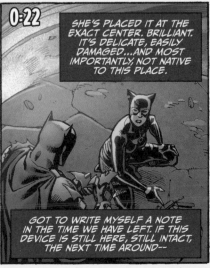

0:22

SHE'S PLACED IT AT THE EXACT CENTER. BRILLIANT. IT'S DELICATE, EASILY DAMAGED...AND MOST IMPORTANTLY, NOT NATIVE TO THIS PLACE.

GOT TO WRITE MYSELF A NOTE IN THE TIME WE HAVE LEFT. IF THIS DEVICE IS STILL HERE, STILL INTACT, THE NEXT TIME AROUND--

0:00

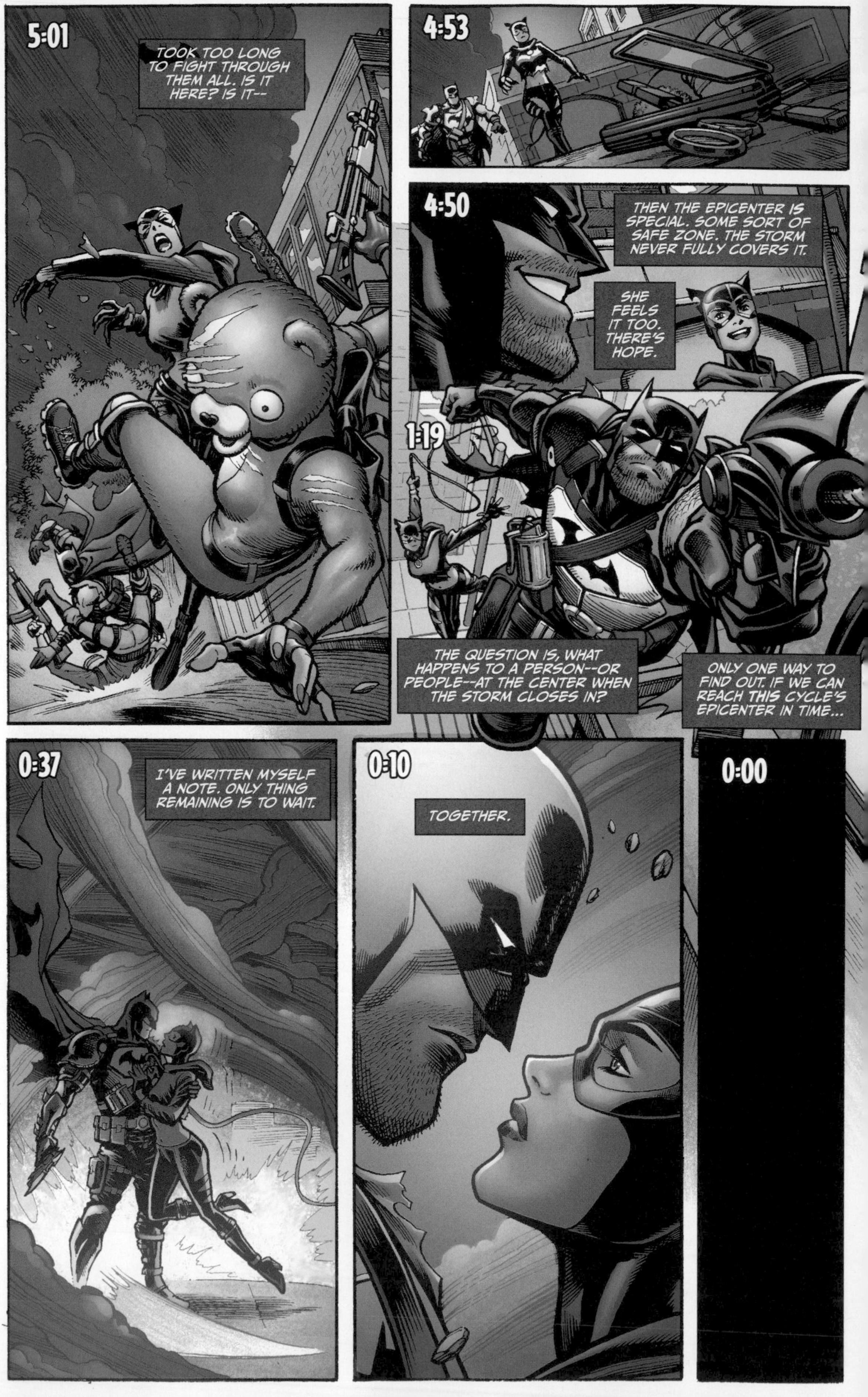
5:01
TOOK TOO LONG TO FIGHT THROUGH THEM ALL. IS IT HERE? IS IT--
4:53
4:50
THEN THE EPICENTER IS SPECIAL. SOME SORT OF SAFE ZONE. THE STORM NEVER FULLY COVERS IT.
SHE FEELS IT TOO. THERE'S HOPE.
1:19
THE QUESTION IS, WHAT HAPPENS TO A PERSON--OR PEOPLE--AT THE CENTER WHEN THE STORM CLOSES IN?
ONLY ONE WAY TO FIND OUT. IF WE CAN REACH THIS CYCLE'S EPICENTER IN TIME...
0:37
I'VE WRITTEN MYSELF A NOTE. ONLY THING REMAINING IS TO WAIT.
0:10
TOGETHER.
0:00

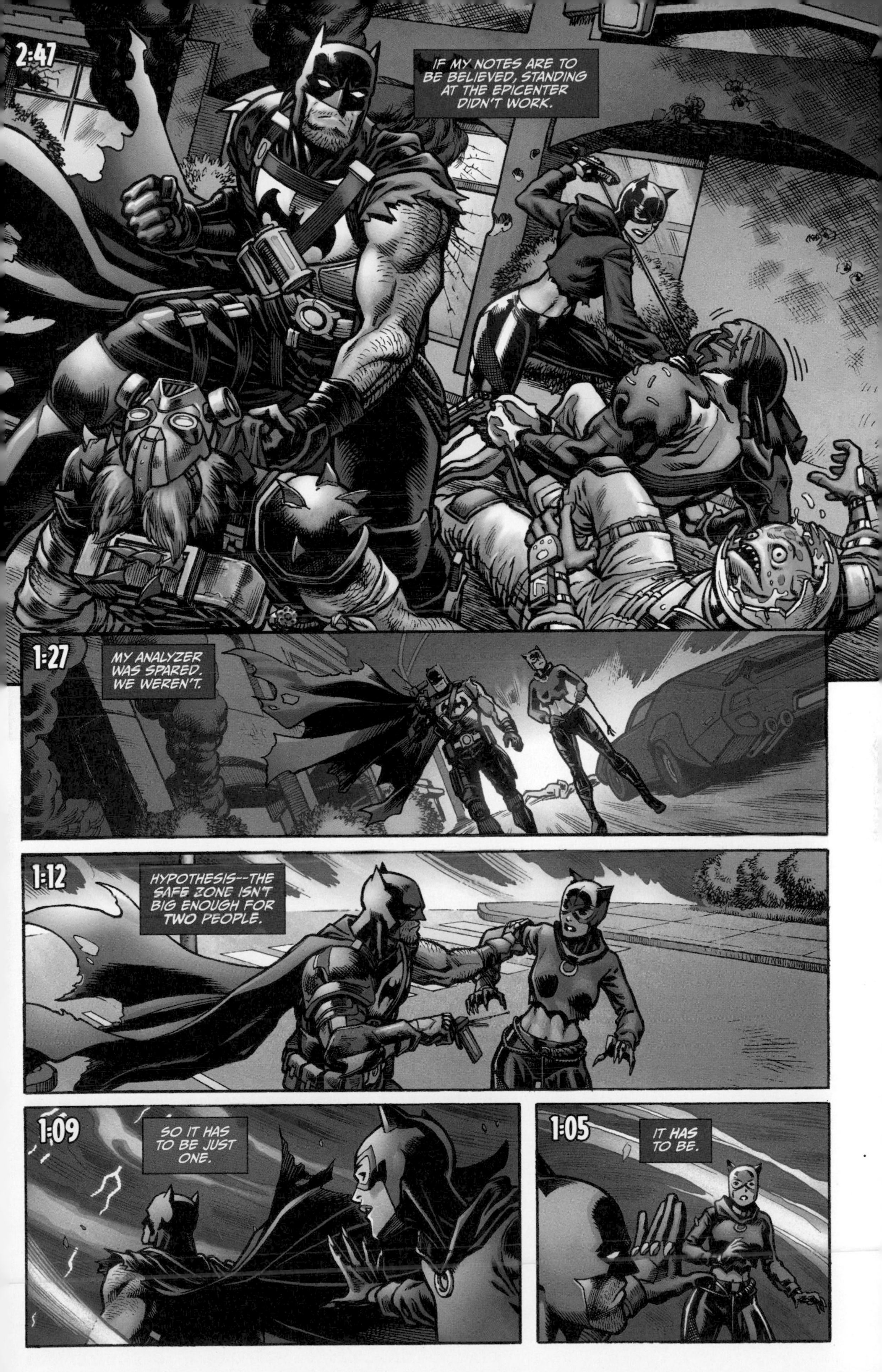
2:47
IF MY NOTES ARE TO BE BELIEVED, STANDING AT THE EPICENTER DIDN'T WORK.
1:27
MY ANALYZER WAS SPARED. WE WEREN'T.
1:12
HYPOTHESIS--THE SAFE ZONE ISN'T BIG ENOUGH FOR TWO PEOPLE.
1:09
SO IT HAS TO BE JUST ONE.
1:05
IT HAS TO BE.

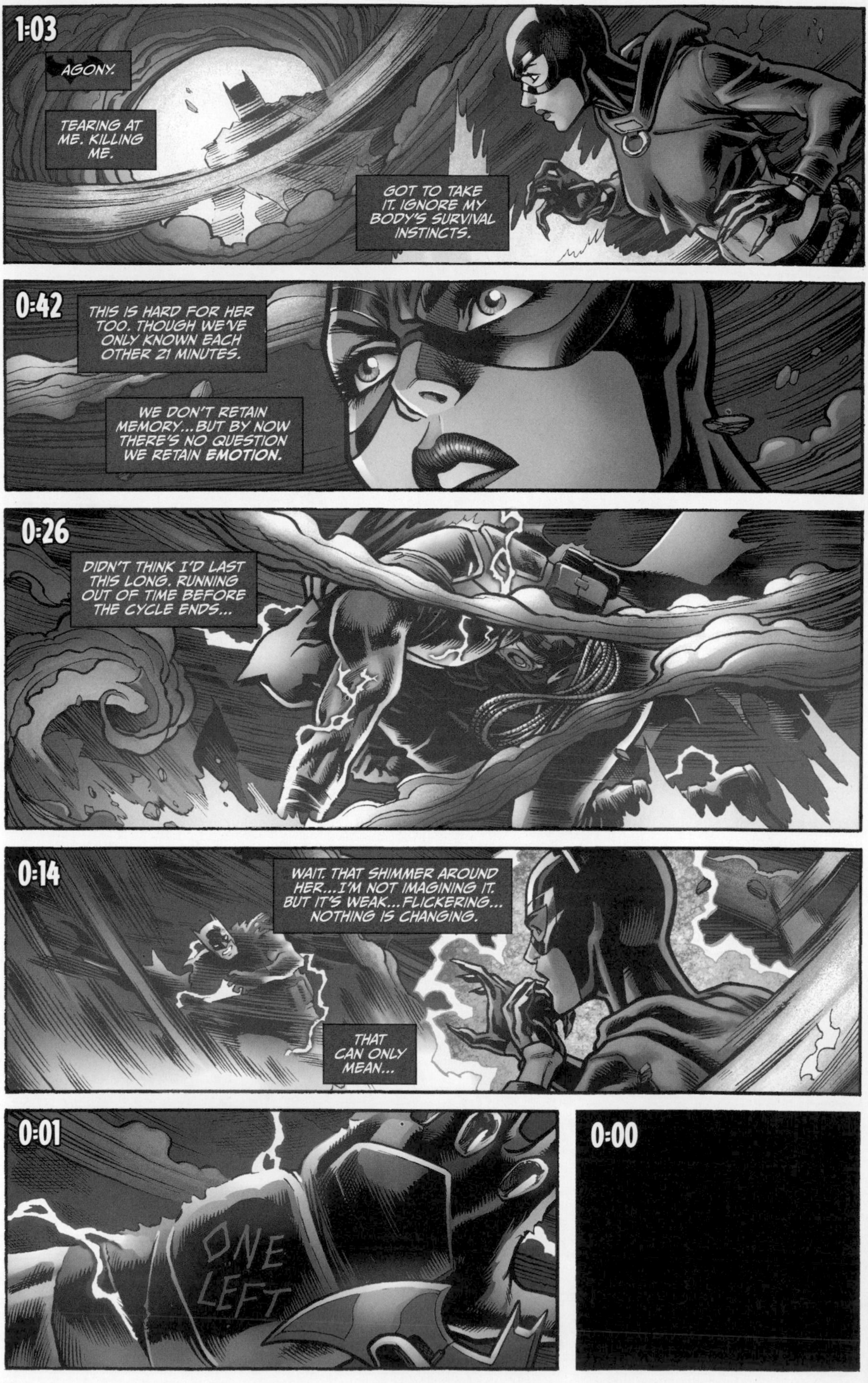
1:03
AGONY.
TEARING AT ME. KILLING ME.
GOT TO TAKE IT. IGNORE MY BODY'S SURVIVAL INSTINCTS.
0:42
THIS IS HARD FOR HER TOO. THOUGH WE'VE ONLY KNOWN EACH OTHER 21 MINUTES.
WE DON'T RETAIN MEMORY...BUT BY NOW THERE'S NO QUESTION WE RETAIN EMOTION.
0:26
DIDN'T THINK I'D LAST THIS LONG. RUNNING OUT OF TIME BEFORE THE CYCLE ENDS...
0:14
WAIT. THAT SHIMMER AROUND HER...I'M NOT IMAGINING IT. BUT IT'S WEAK...FLICKERING... NOTHING IS CHANGING.
THAT CAN ONLY MEAN...
0:01
ONE LEFT
0:00

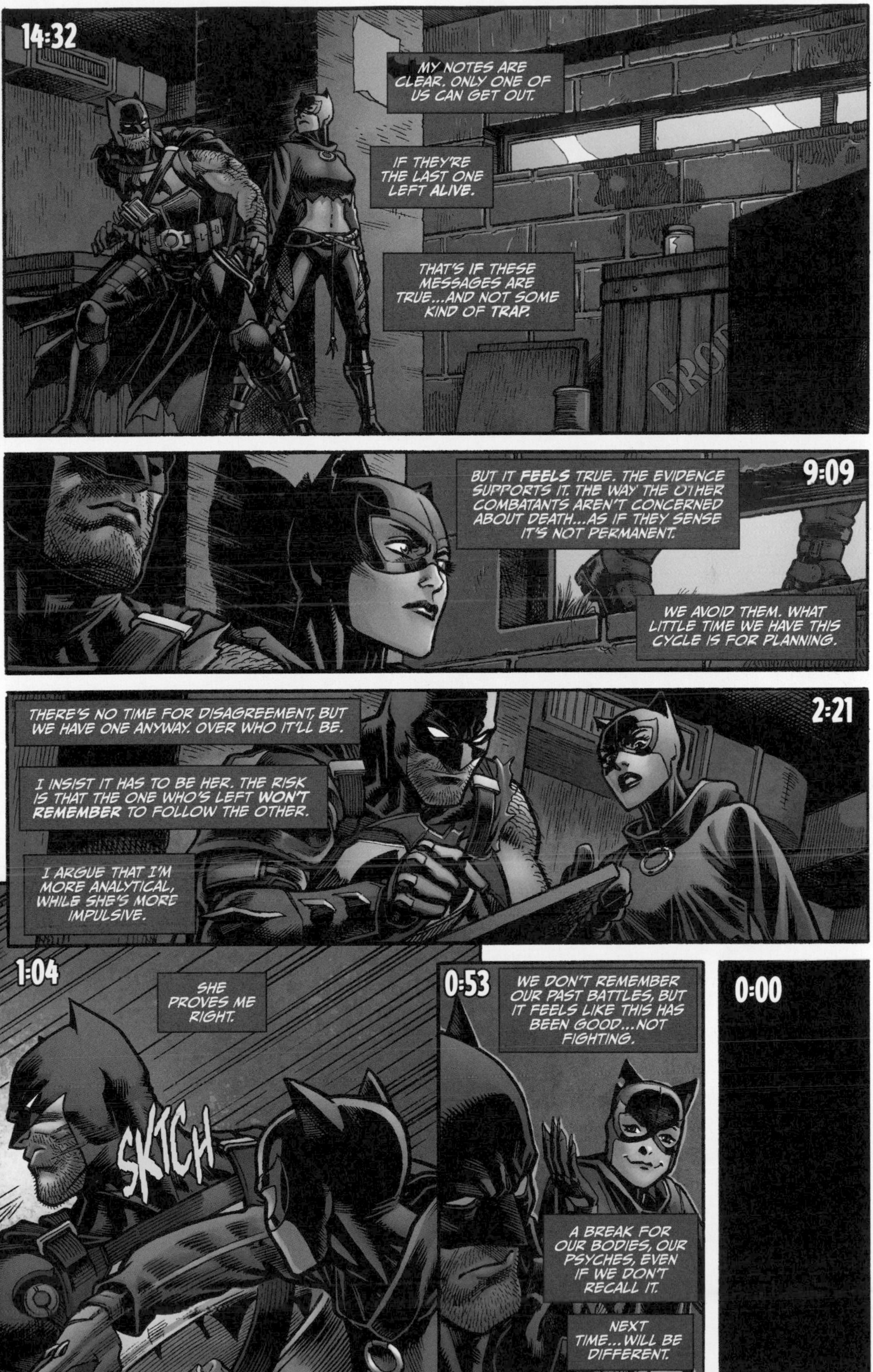
14:32
MY NOTES ARE CLEAR. ONLY ONE OF US CAN GET OUT.
IF THEY'RE THE LAST ONE LEFT ALIVE.
THAT'S IF THESE MESSAGES ARE TRUE...AND NOT SOME KIND OF TRAP.
9:09
BUT IT FEELS TRUE. THE EVIDENCE SUPPORTS IT. THE WAY THE OTHER COMBATANTS AREN'T CONCERNED ABOUT DEATH...AS IF THEY SENSE IT'S NOT PERMANENT.
WE AVOID THEM. WHAT LITTLE TIME WE HAVE THIS CYCLE IS FOR PLANNING.
2:21
THERE'S NO TIME FOR DISAGREEMENT, BUT WE HAVE ONE ANYWAY. OVER WHO IT'LL BE.
I INSIST IT HAS TO BE HER. THE RISK IS THAT THE ONE WHO'S LEFT WON'T REMEMBER TO FOLLOW THE OTHER.
I ARGUE THAT I'M MORE ANALYTICAL, WHILE SHE'S MORE IMPULSIVE.
1:04
SHE PROVES ME RIGHT.
SKTCH
0:53
WE DON'T REMEMBER OUR PAST BATTLES, BUT IT FEELS LIKE THIS HAS BEEN GOOD...NOT FIGHTING.
A BREAK FOR OUR BODIES, OUR PSYCHES, EVEN IF WE DON'T RECALL IT.
NEXT TIME...WILL BE DIFFERENT.
0:00

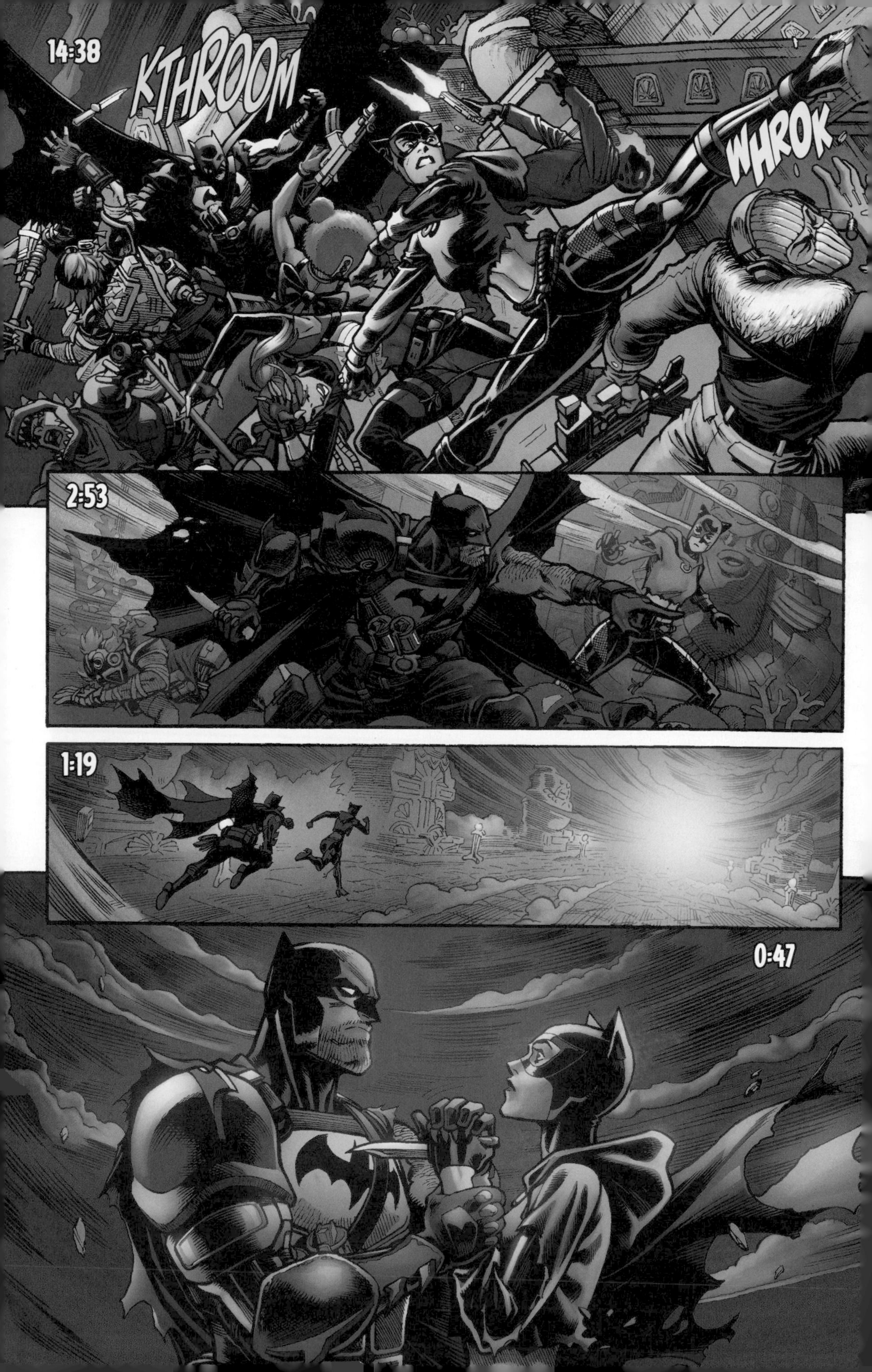
14:38
KTHROOM
WHROK
2:53
1:19
0:47

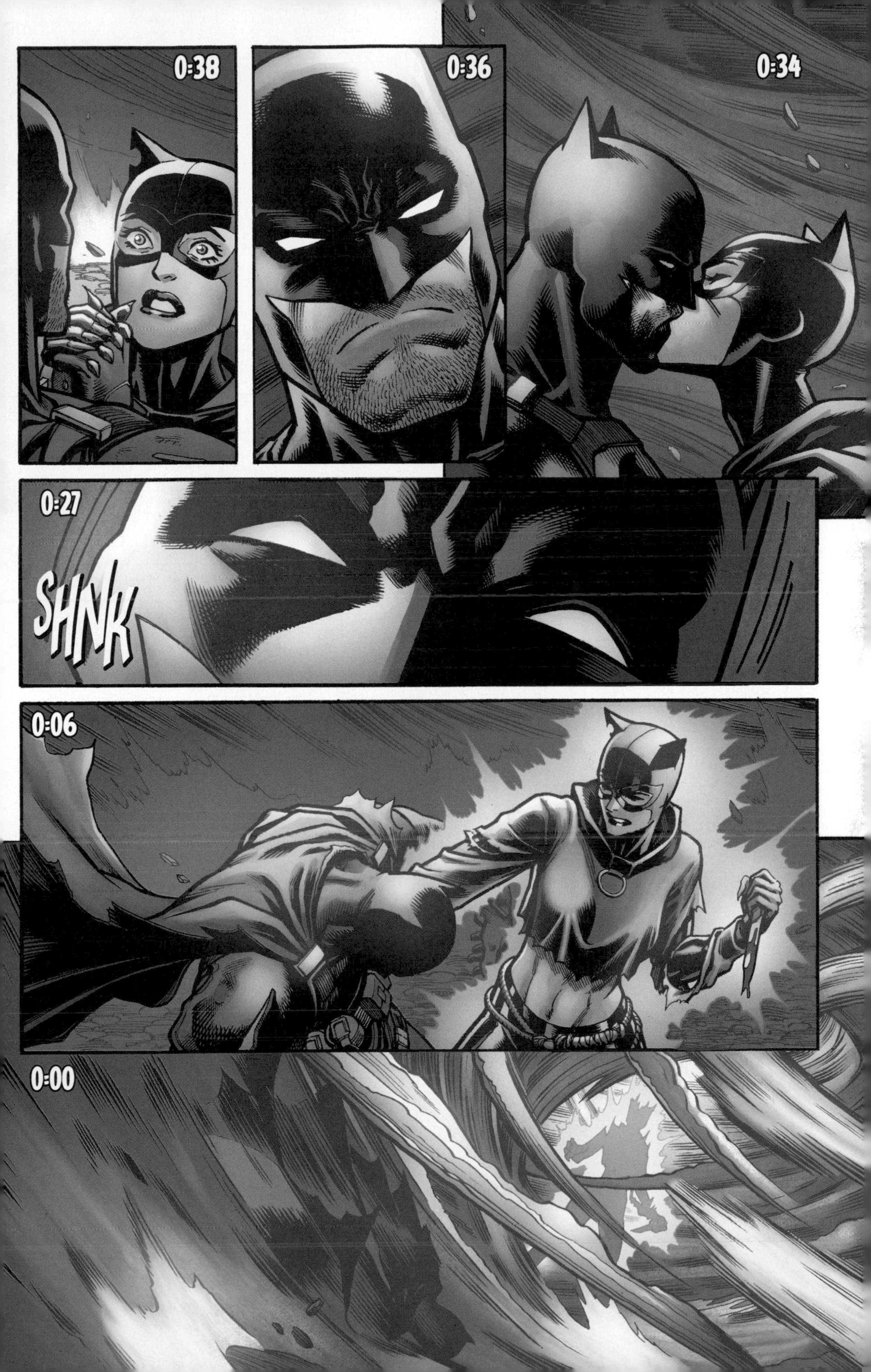
0:38
0:36
0:34
0:27
SHNK
0:06
0:00

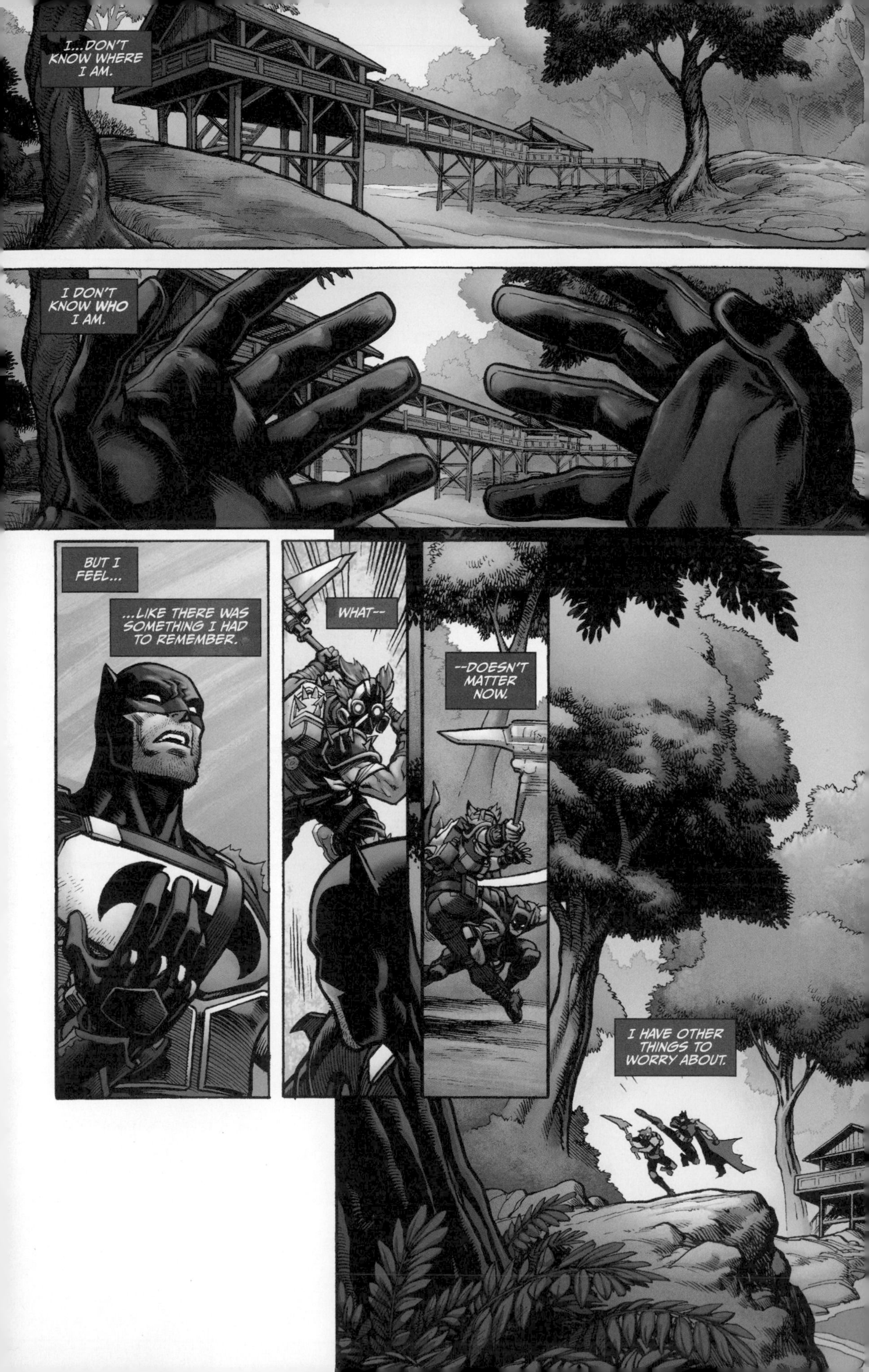
I...DON'T KNOW WHERE I AM.
I DON'T KNOW WHO I AM.
BUT I FEEL...
...LIKE THERE WAS SOMETHING I HAD TO REMEMBER.
WHAT--
--DOESN'T MATTER NOW.
I HAVE OTHER THINGS TO WORRY ABOUT.

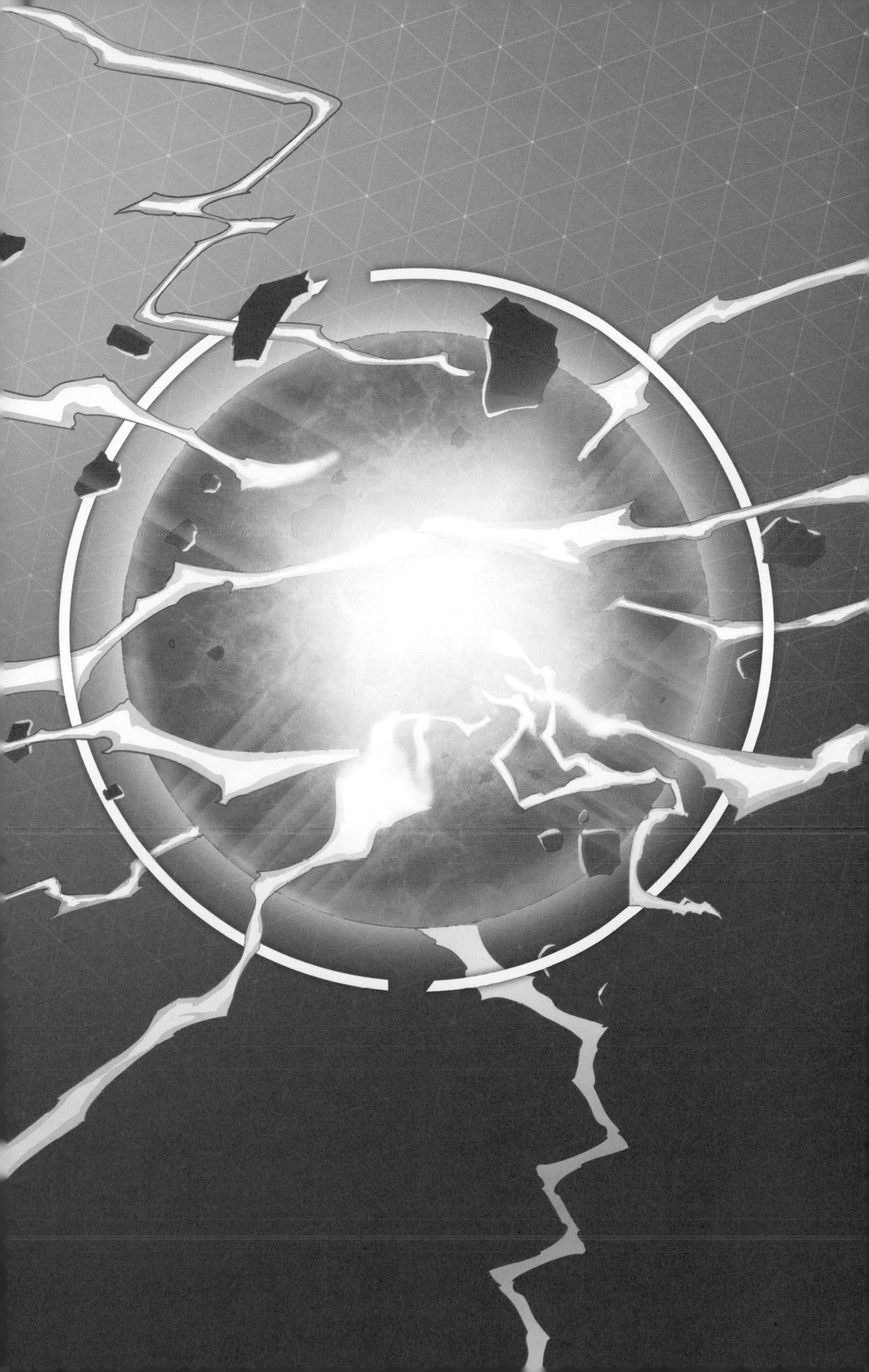

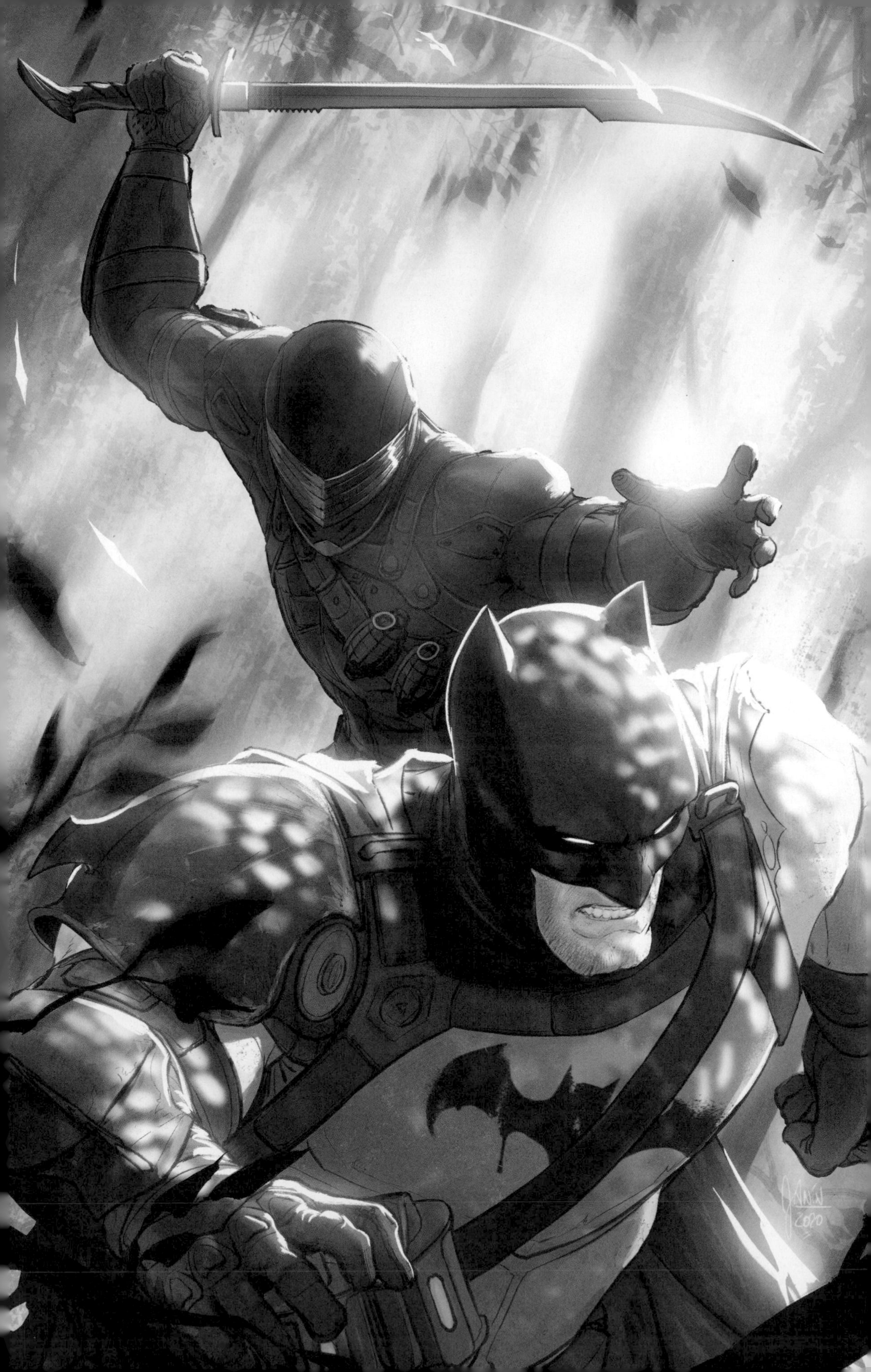

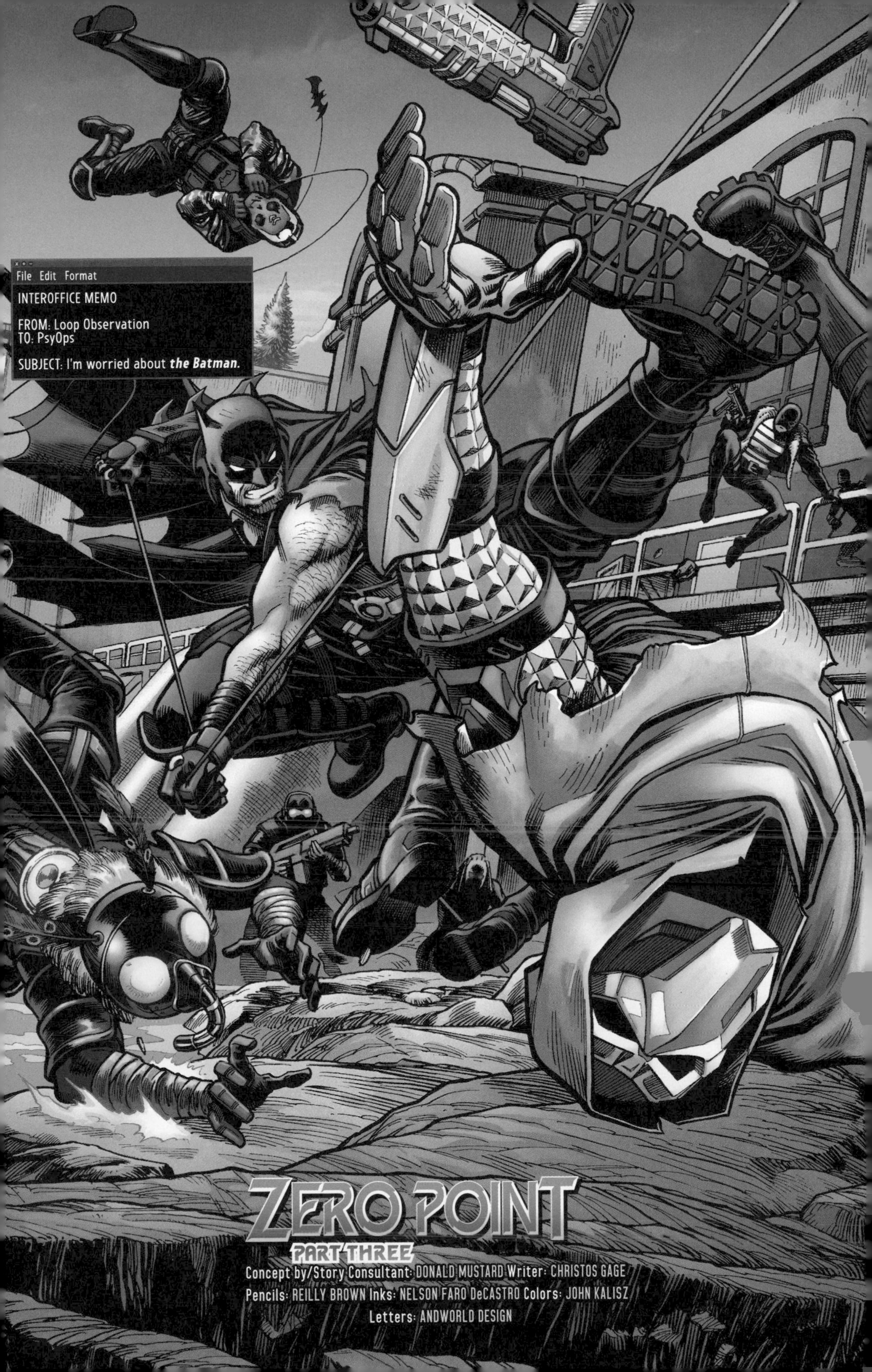
File Edit Format
INTEROFFICE MEMO
FROM: Loop Observation
TO: PsyOps
SUBJECT: I'm worried about ***the Batman.***
ZERO POINT
PART THREE
Concept by/Story Consultant: DONALD MUSTARD Writer: CHRISTOS GAGE
Pencils: REILLY BROWN Inks: NELSON FARO DeCASTRO Colors: JOHN KALISZ
Letters: ANDWORLD DESIGN

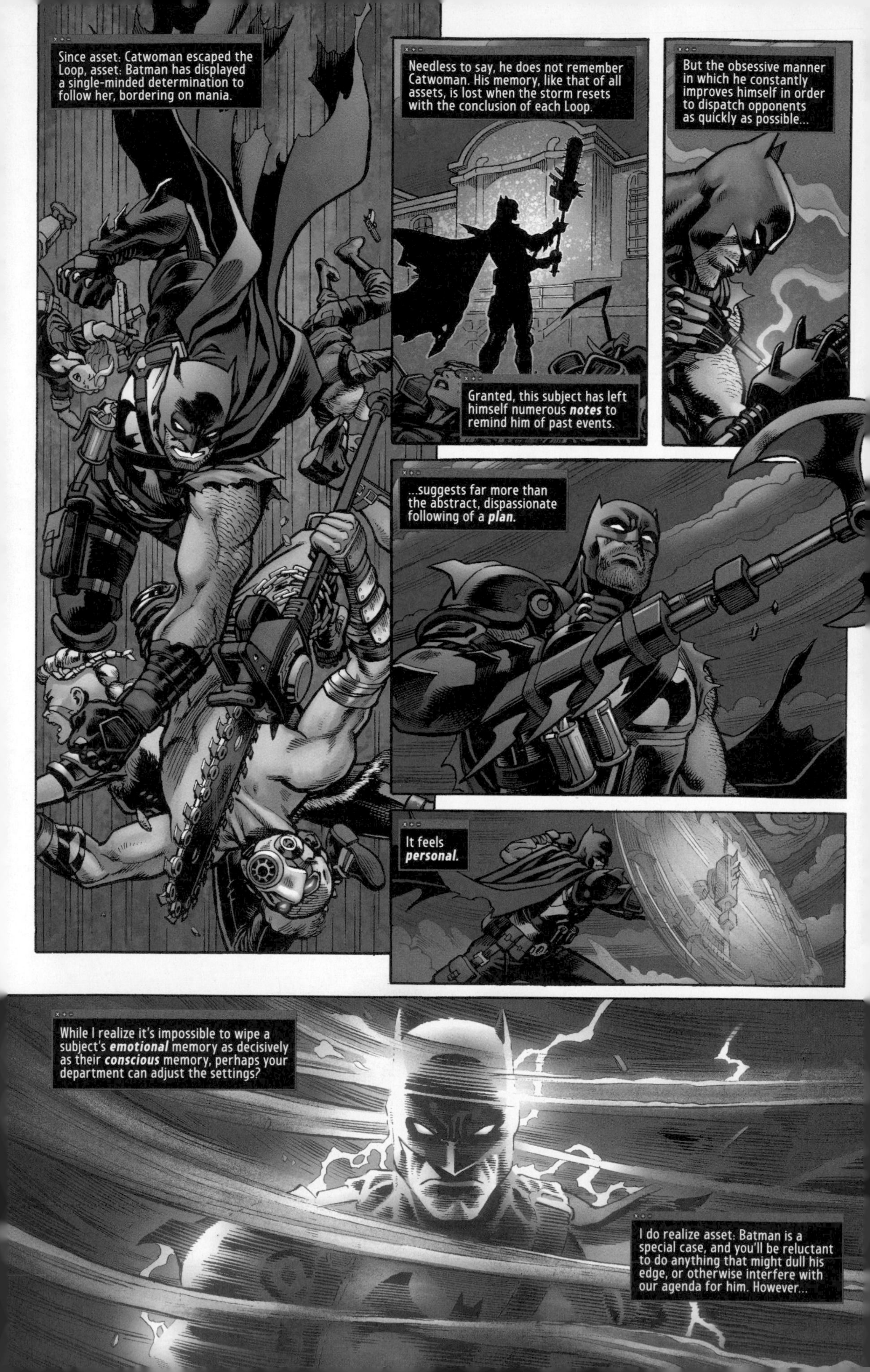
Since asset: Catwoman escaped the Loop, asset: Batman has displayed a single-minded determination to follow her, bordering on mania.
Needless to say, he does not remember Catwoman. His memory, like that of all assets, is lost when the storm resets with the conclusion of each Loop.
Granted, this subject has left himself numerous **notes** to remind him of past events.
But the obsessive manner in which he constantly improves himself in order to dispatch opponents as quickly as possible...
...suggests far more than the abstract, dispassionate following of a **plan.**
It feels **personal.**
While I realize it's impossible to wipe a subject's **emotional** memory as decisively as their **conscious** memory, perhaps your department can adjust the settings?
I do realize asset: Batman is a special case, and you'll be reluctant to do anything that might dull his edge, or otherwise interfere with our agenda for him. However...

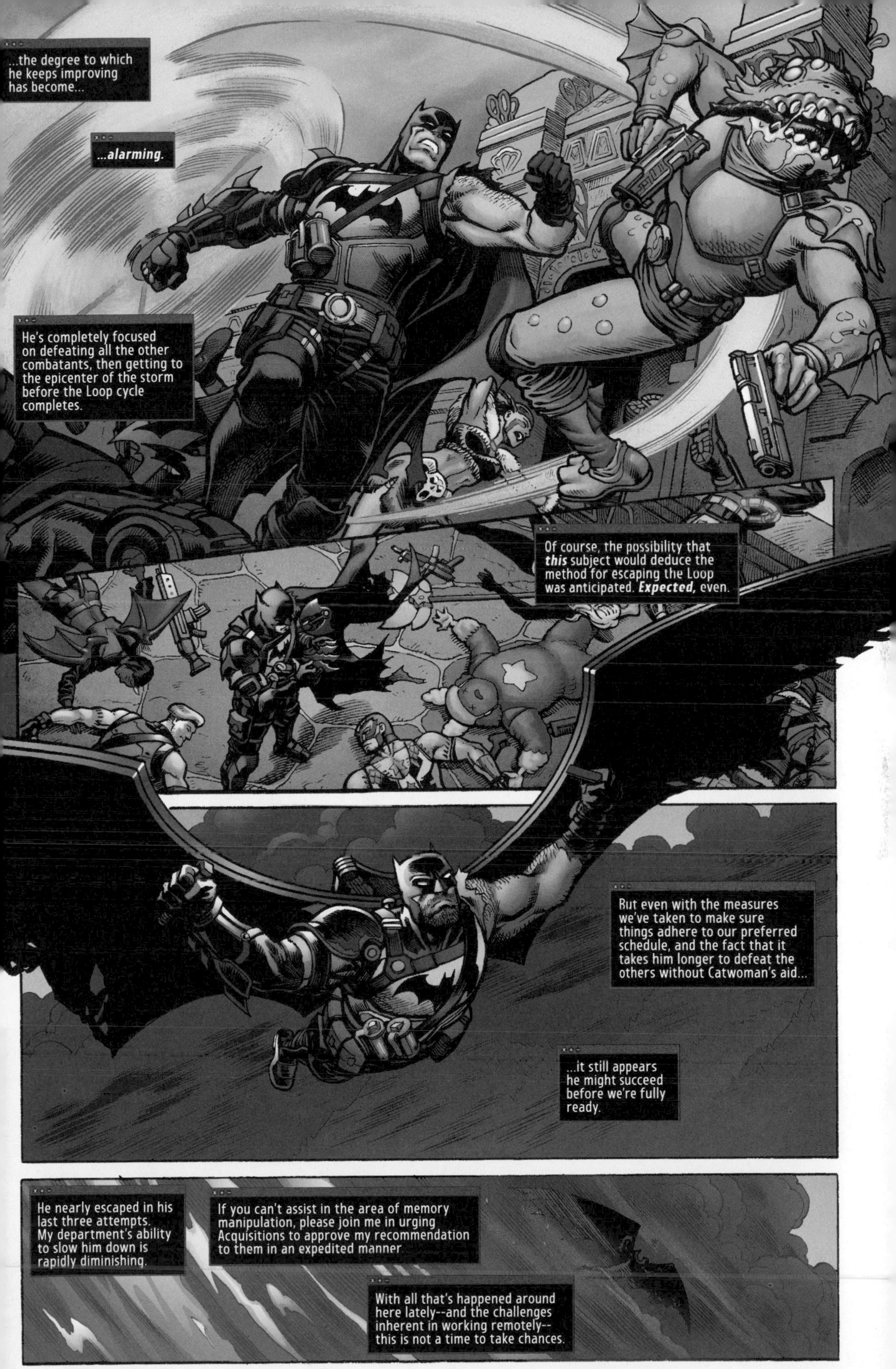
...the degree to which he keeps improving has become...
...alarming.
He's completely focused on defeating all the other combatants, then getting to the epicenter of the storm before the Loop cycle completes.
Of course, the possibility that this subject would deduce the method for escaping the Loop was anticipated. Expected, even.
But even with the measures we've taken to make sure things adhere to our preferred schedule, and the fact that it takes him longer to defeat the others without Catwoman's aid...
...it still appears he might succeed before we're fully ready.
He nearly escaped in his last three attempts. My department's ability to slow him down is rapidly diminishing.
If you can't assist in the area of memory manipulation, please join me in urging Acquisitions to approve my recommendation to them in an expedited manner.
With all that's happened around here lately--and the challenges inherent in working remotely--this is not a time to take chances.

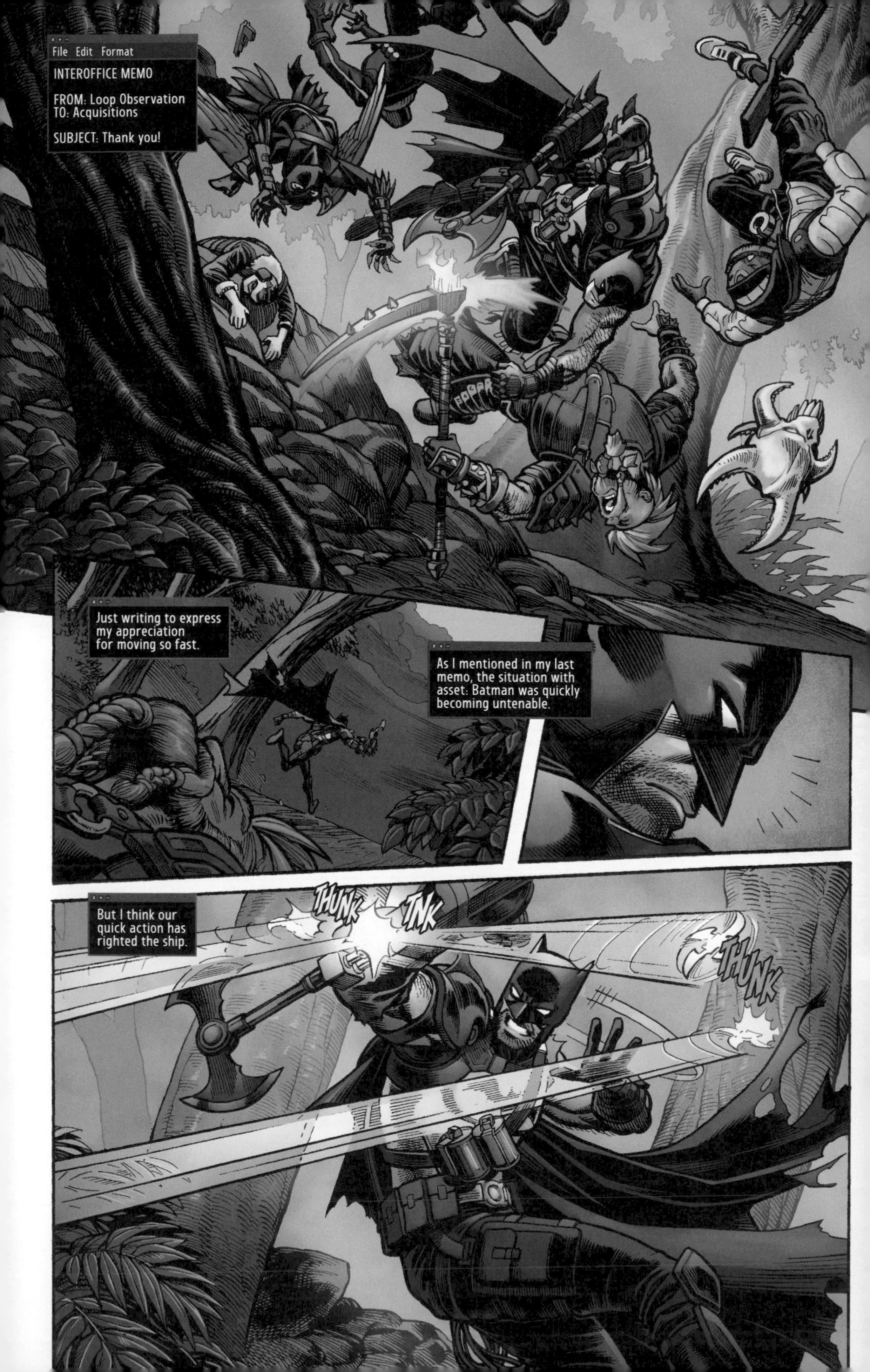

File Edit Format
INTEROFFICE MEMO
FROM: Loop Observation
TO: Acquisitions
SUBJECT: Thank you!
Just writing to express my appreciation for moving so fast.
As I mentioned in my last memo, the situation with asset: Batman was quickly becoming untenable.
But I think our quick action has righted the ship.
THUNK
TNK
THUNK

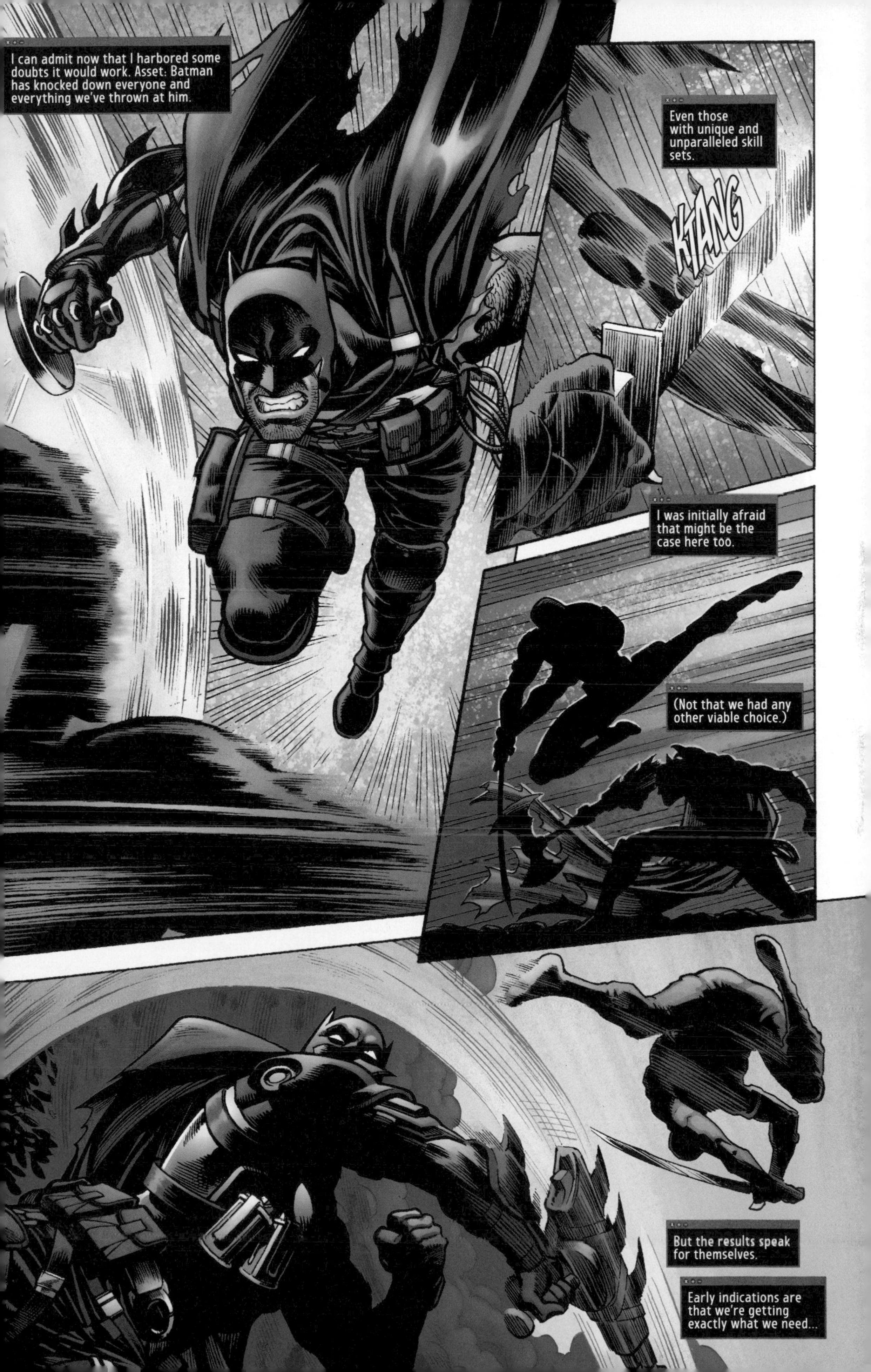
I can admit now that I harbored some doubts it would work. Asset: Batman has knocked down everyone and everything we've thrown at him.
Even those with unique and unparalleled skill sets.
KTANG
I was initially afraid that might be the case here too.
(Not that we had any other viable choice.)
But the results speak for themselves.
Early indications are that we're getting exactly what we need...

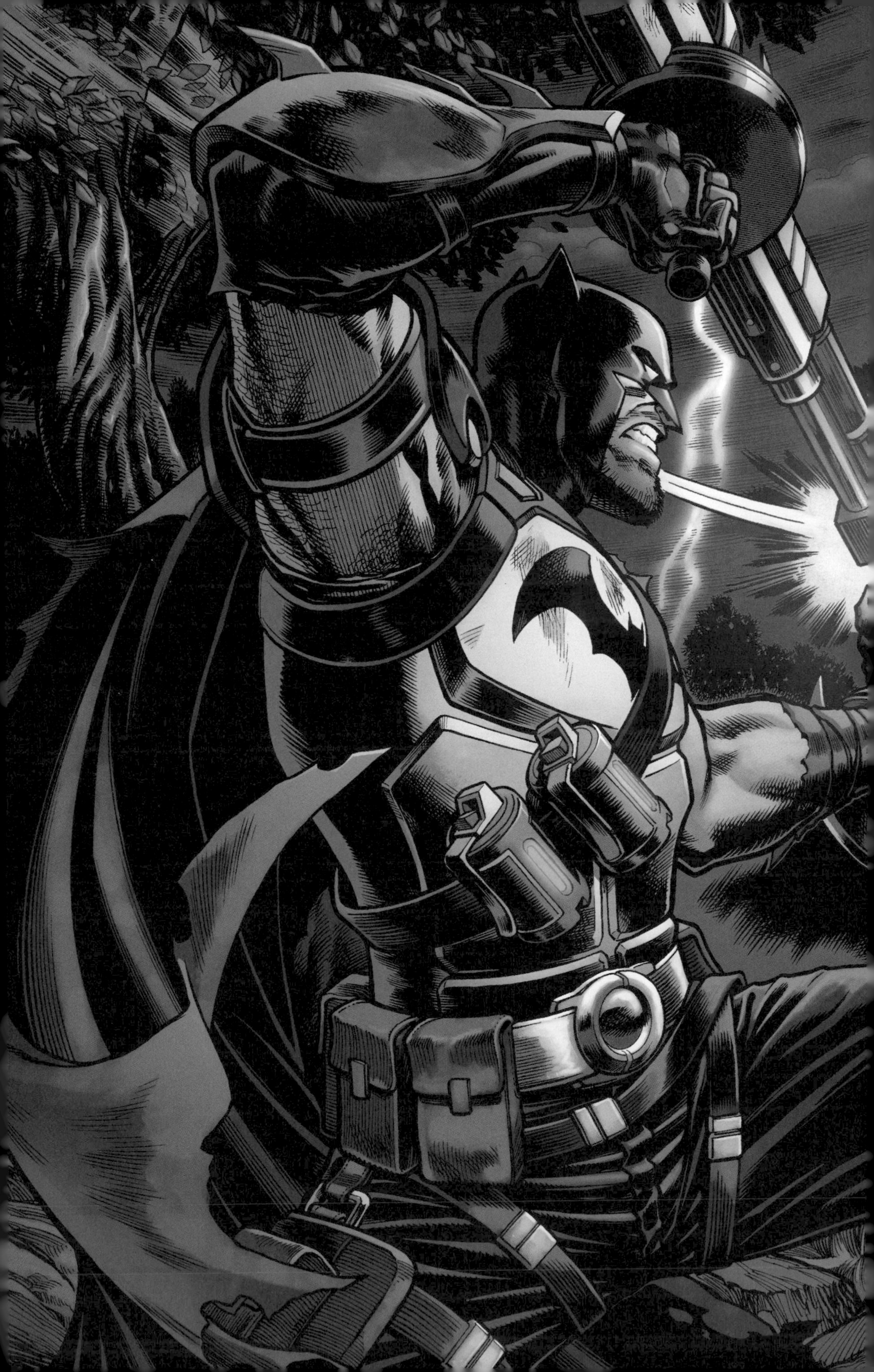

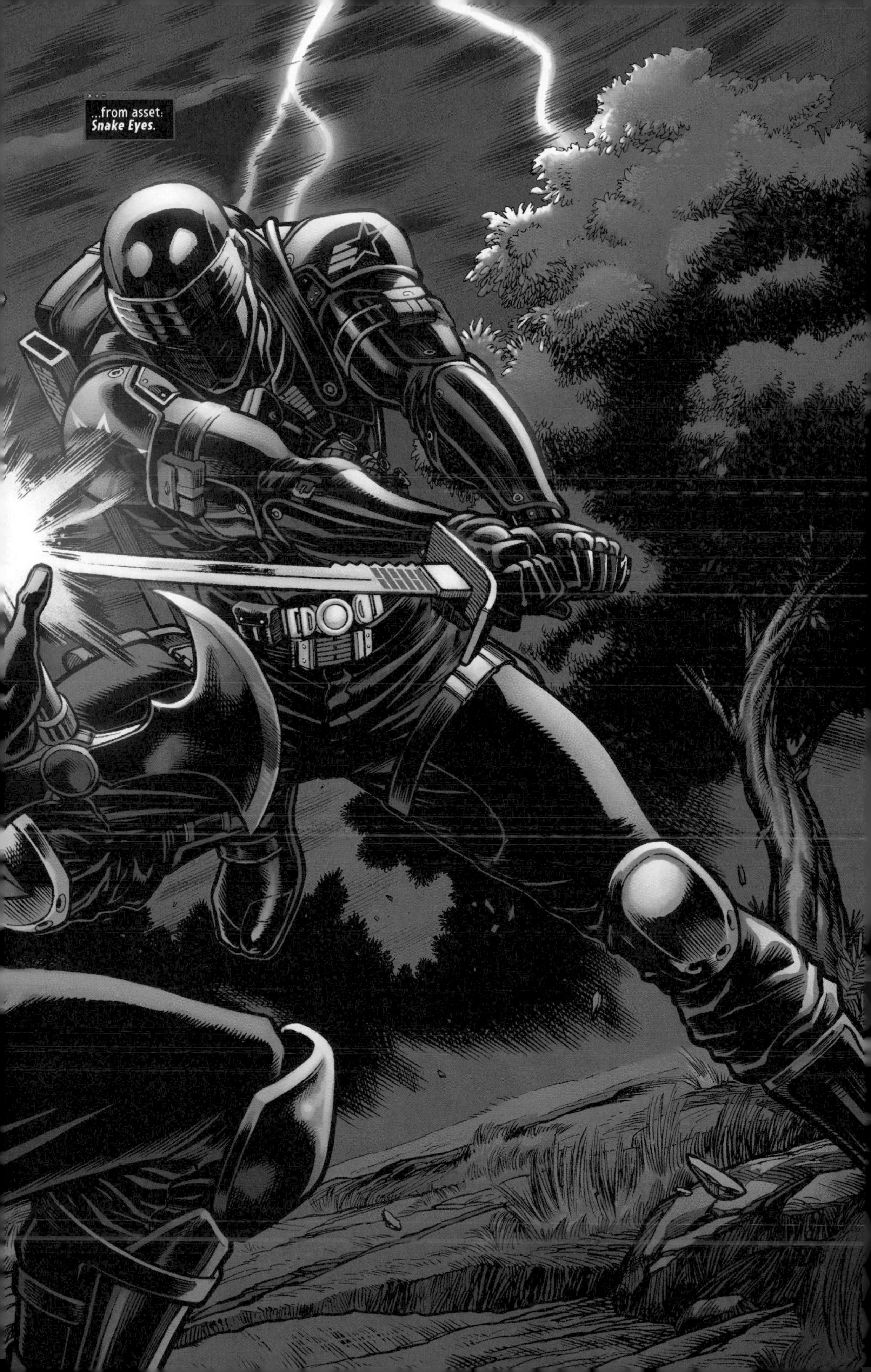
...from asset:
Snake Eyes.

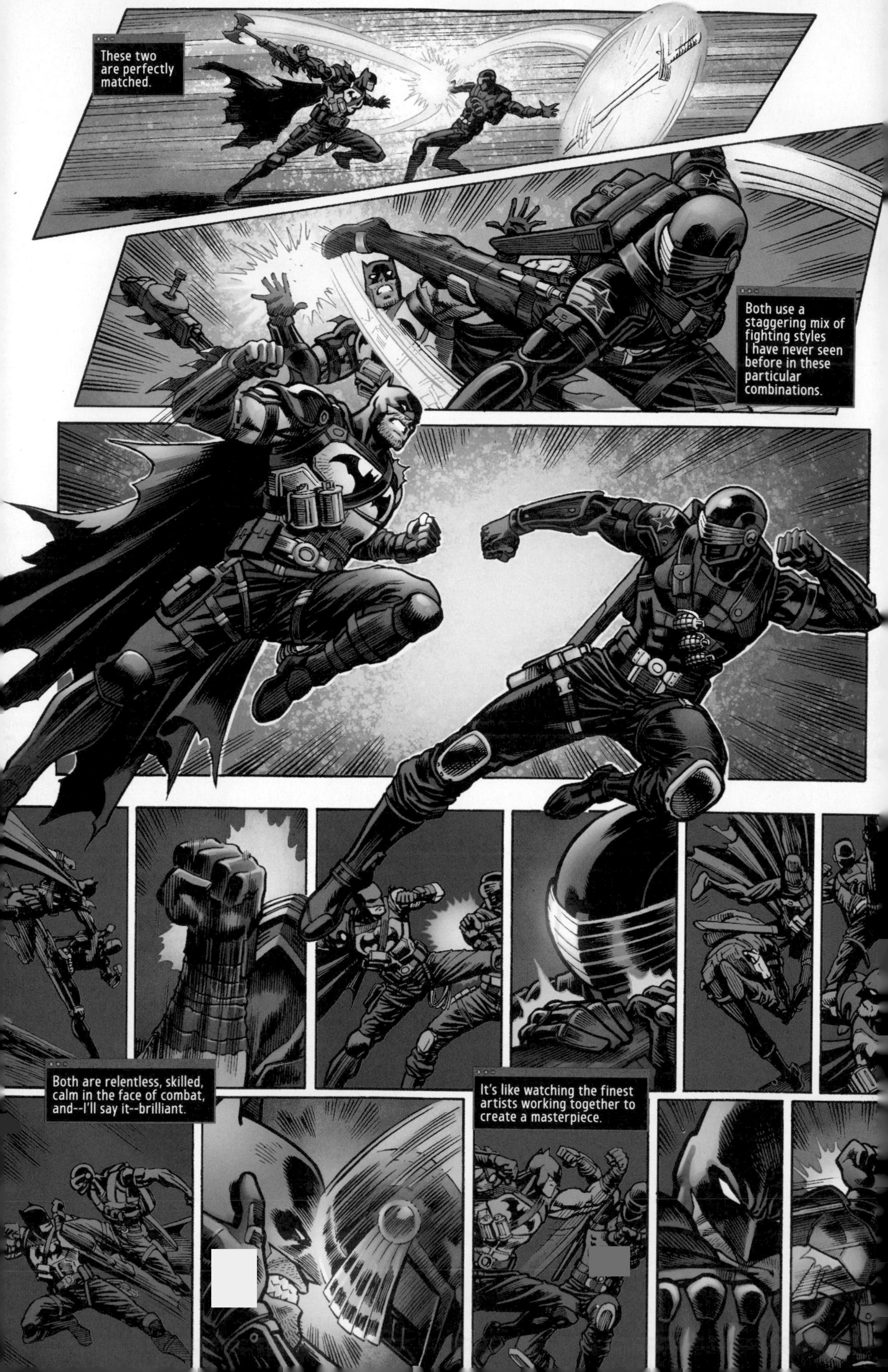
These two are perfectly matched.
Both use a staggering mix of fighting styles I have never seen before in these particular combinations.
Both are relentless, skilled, calm in the face of combat, and--I'll say it--brilliant.
It's like watching the finest artists working together to create a masterpiece.

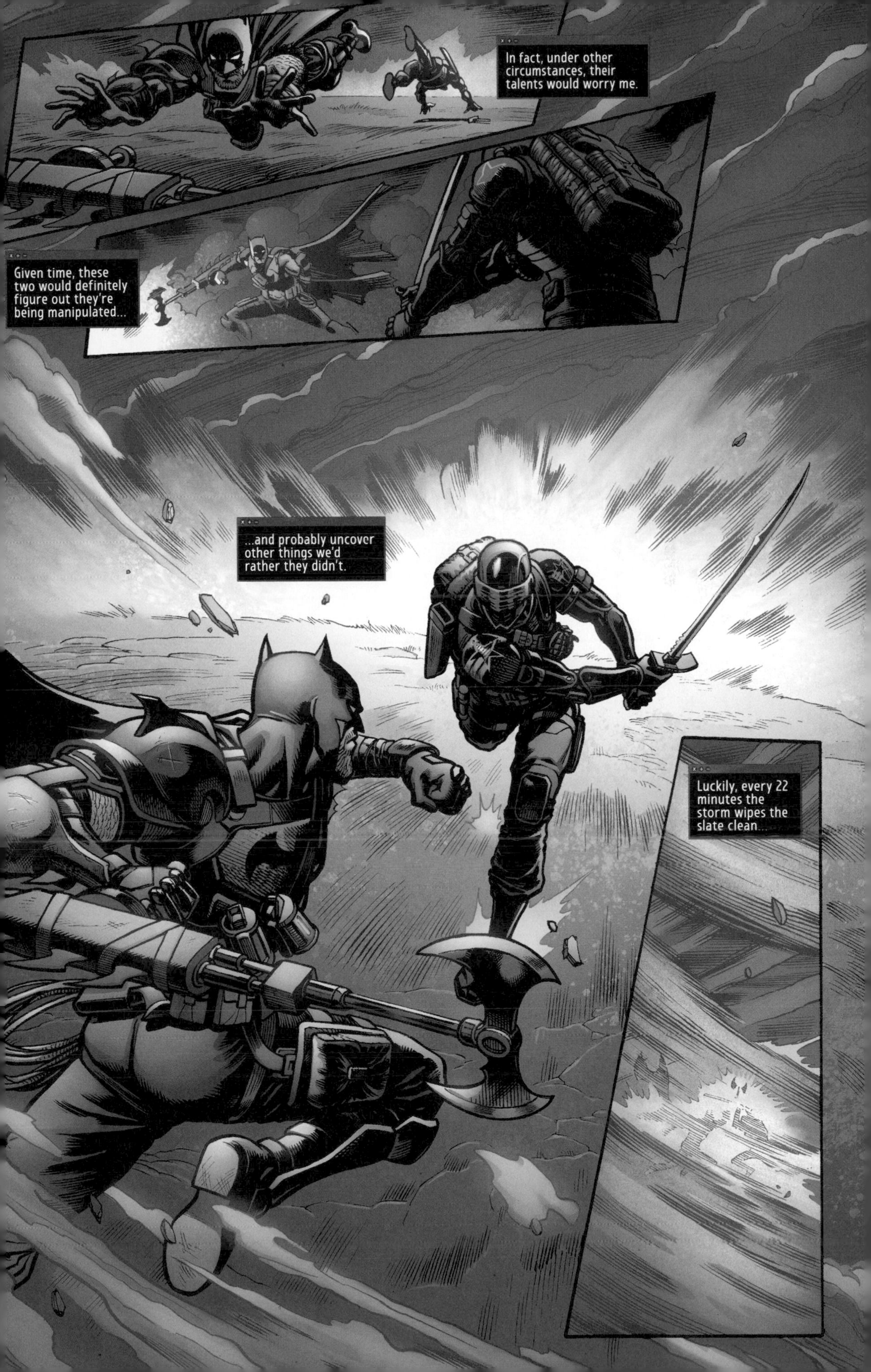
In fact, under other circumstances, their talents would worry me.
Given time, these two would definitely figure out they're being manipulated...
...and probably uncover other things we'd rather they didn't.
Luckily, every 22 minutes the storm wipes the slate clean...

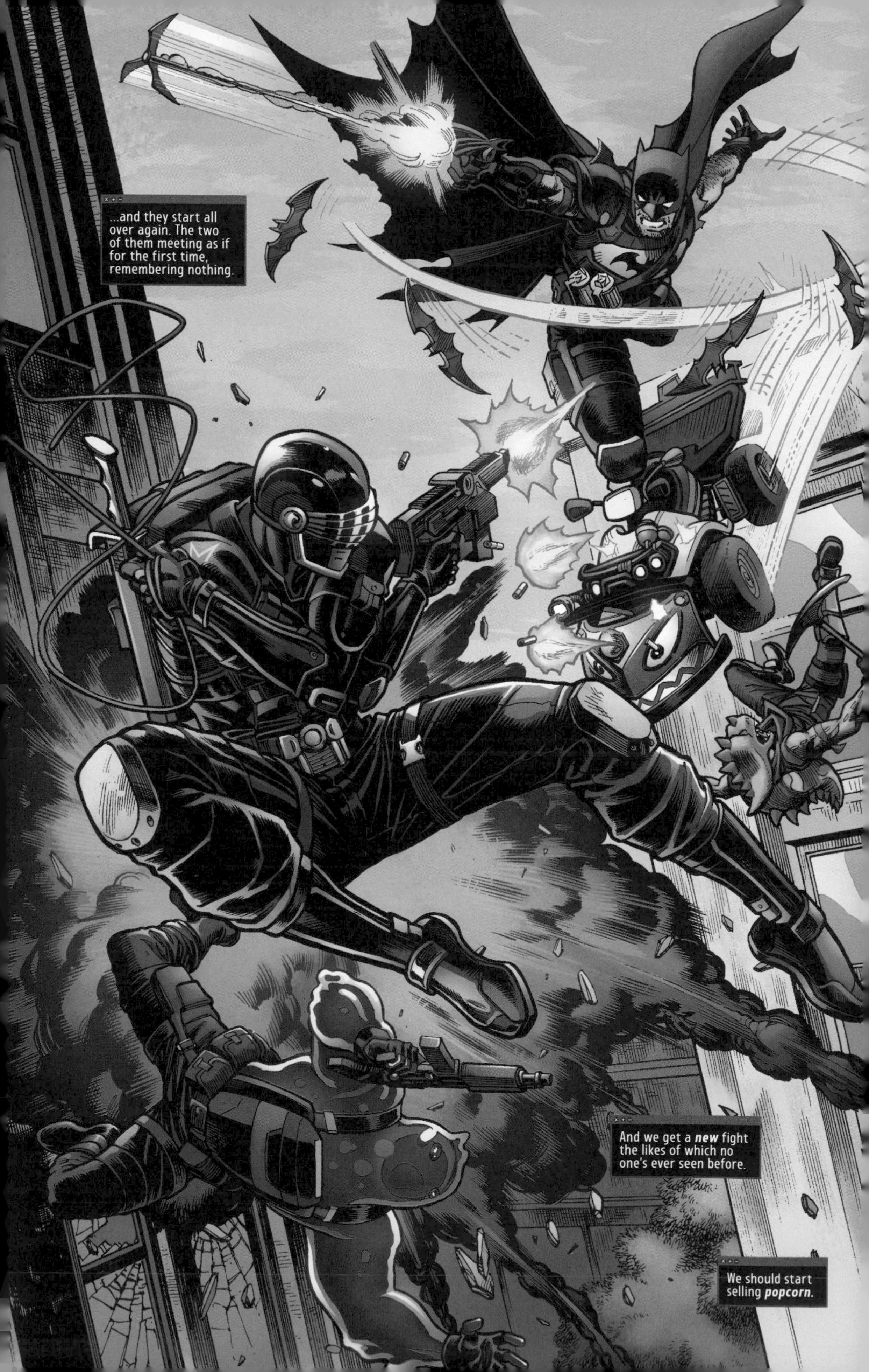
...and they start all over again. The two of them meeting as if for the first time, remembering nothing.
And we get a ***new*** fight the likes of which no one's ever seen before.
We should start selling ***popcorn.***

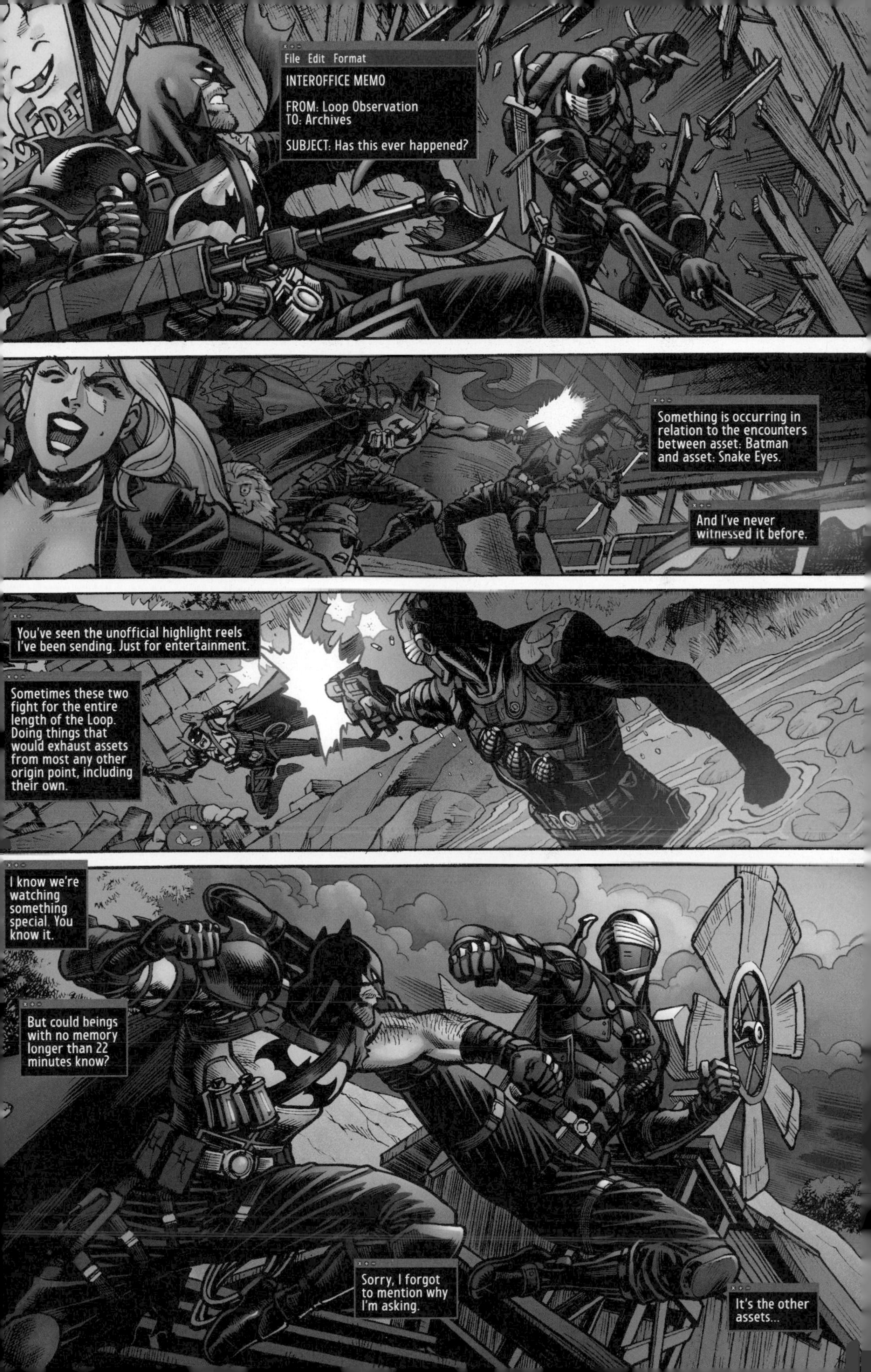
File Edit Format
INTEROFFICE MEMO
FROM: Loop Observation
TO: Archives
SUBJECT: Has this ever happened?
Something is occurring in relation to the encounters between asset: Batman and asset: Snake Eyes.
And I've never witnessed it before.
You've seen the unofficial highlight reels I've been sending. Just for entertainment.
Sometimes these two fight for the entire length of the Loop. Doing things that would exhaust assets from most any other origin point, including their own.
I know we're watching something special. You know it.
But could beings with no memory longer than 22 minutes know?
Sorry, I forgot to mention why I'm asking.
It's the other assets...

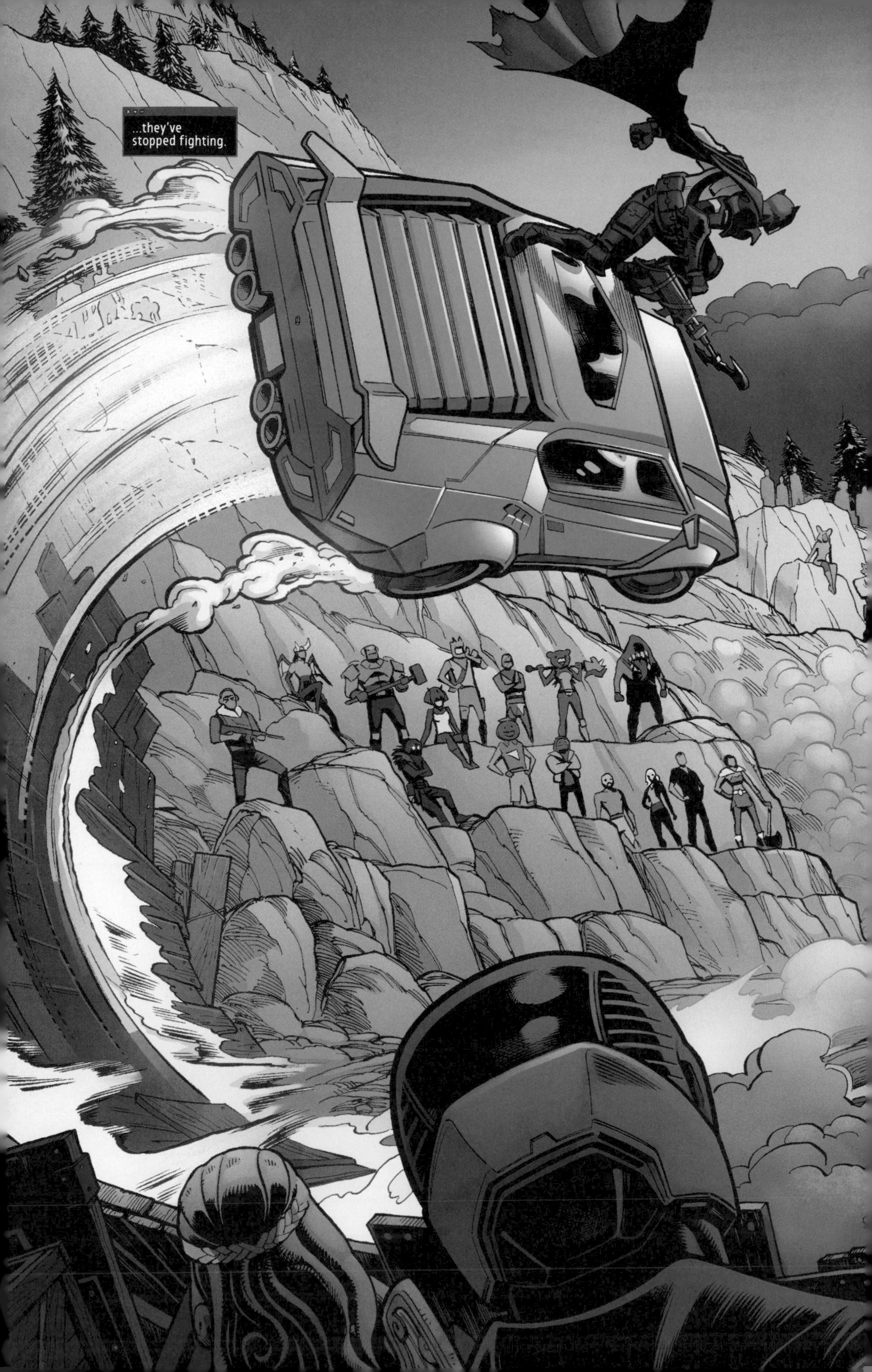
...they've
stopped fighting.

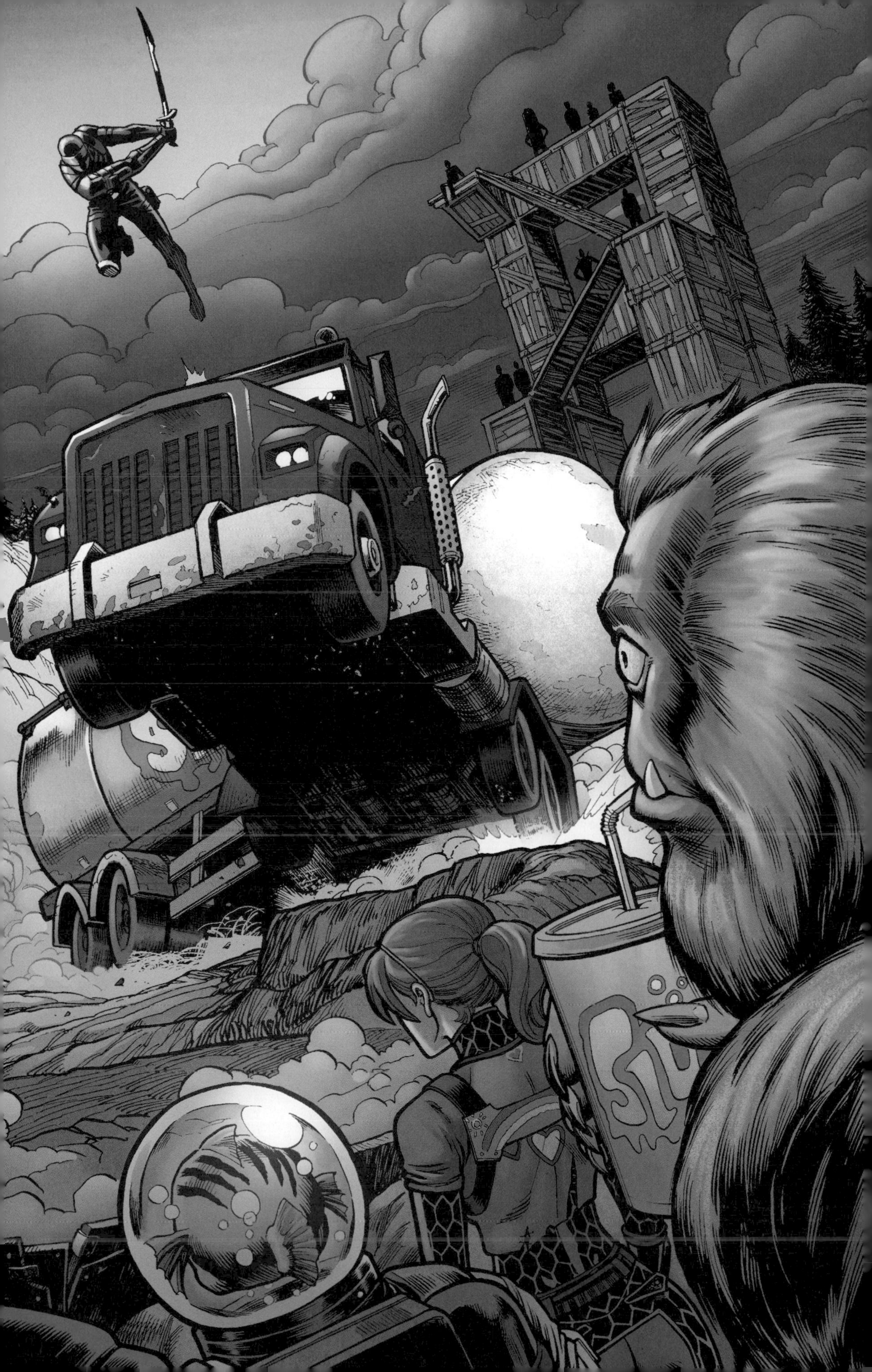

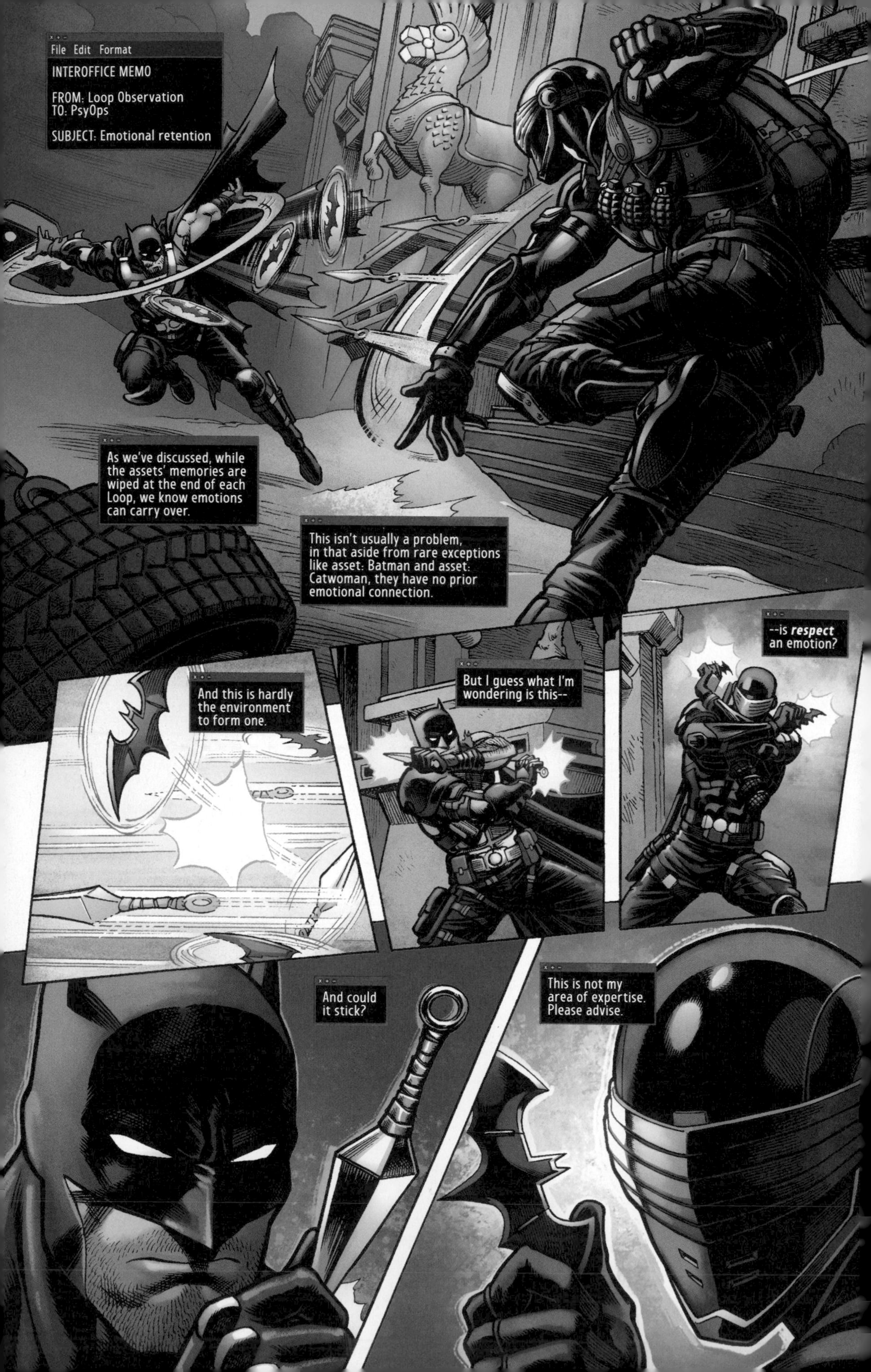

File Edit Format
INTEROFFICE MEMO
FROM: Loop Observation
TO: PsyOps
SUBJECT: Emotional retention
As we've discussed, while the assets' memories are wiped at the end of each Loop, we know emotions can carry over.
This isn't usually a problem, in that aside from rare exceptions like asset: Batman and asset: Catwoman, they have no prior emotional connection.
And this is hardly the environment to form one.
But I guess what I'm wondering is this--
--is ***respect*** an emotion?
And could it stick?
This is not my area of expertise. Please advise.

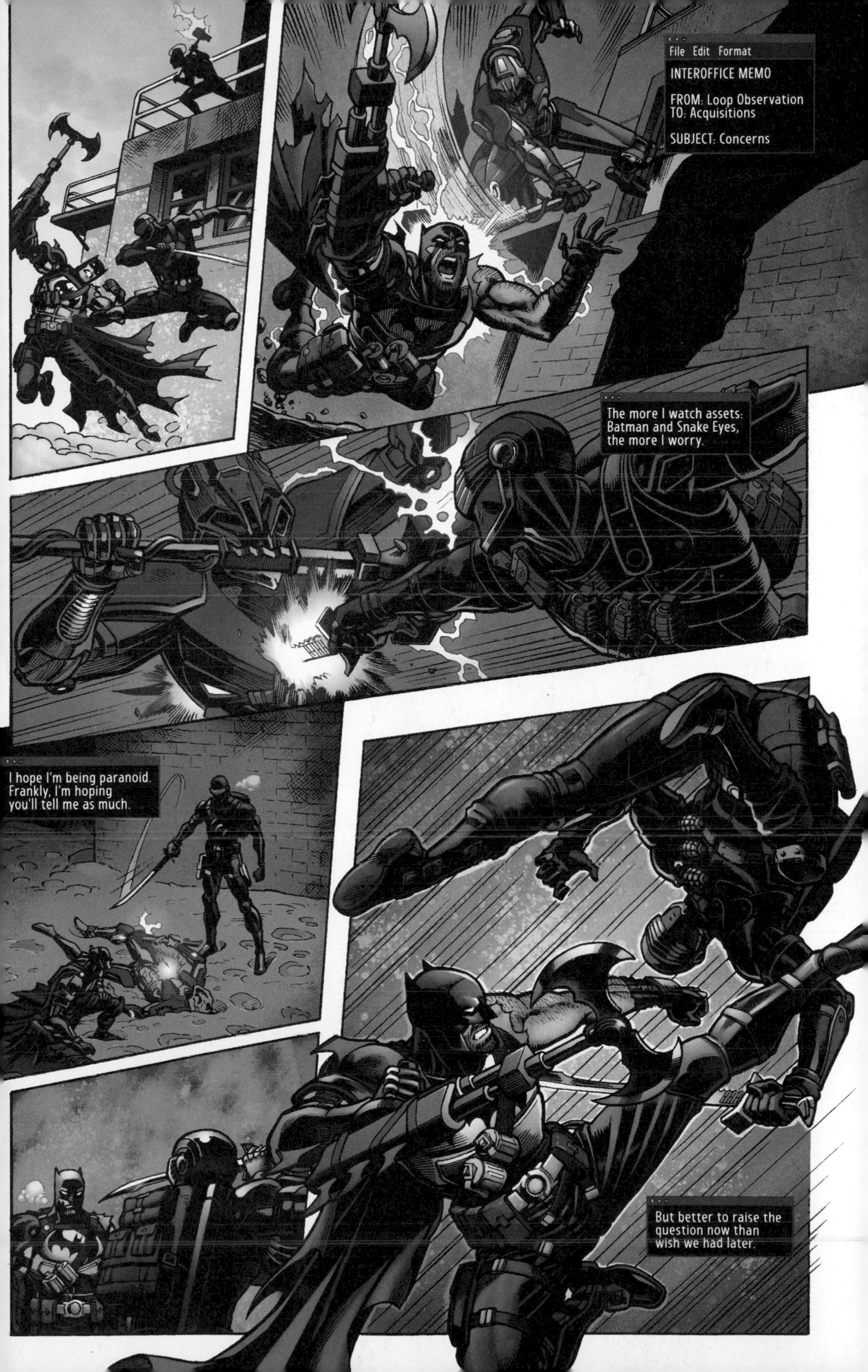
File Edit Format
INTEROFFICE MEMO
FROM: Loop Observation
TO: Acquisitions
SUBJECT: Concerns
The more I watch assets: Batman and Snake Eyes, the more I worry.
I hope I'm being paranoid. Frankly, I'm hoping you'll tell me as much.
But better to raise the question now than wish we had later.

We're all aware that assets often band together for the sake of convenience...

...but these alliances are ephemeral. When it comes to being the last one standing at the end of a Loop--

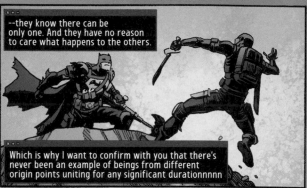

--they know there can be only one. And they have no reason to care what happens to the others.

Which is why I want to confirm with you that there's never been an example of beings from different origin points uniting for any significant durationnnnn

oaredjik0[=

MESSAGE DELETED

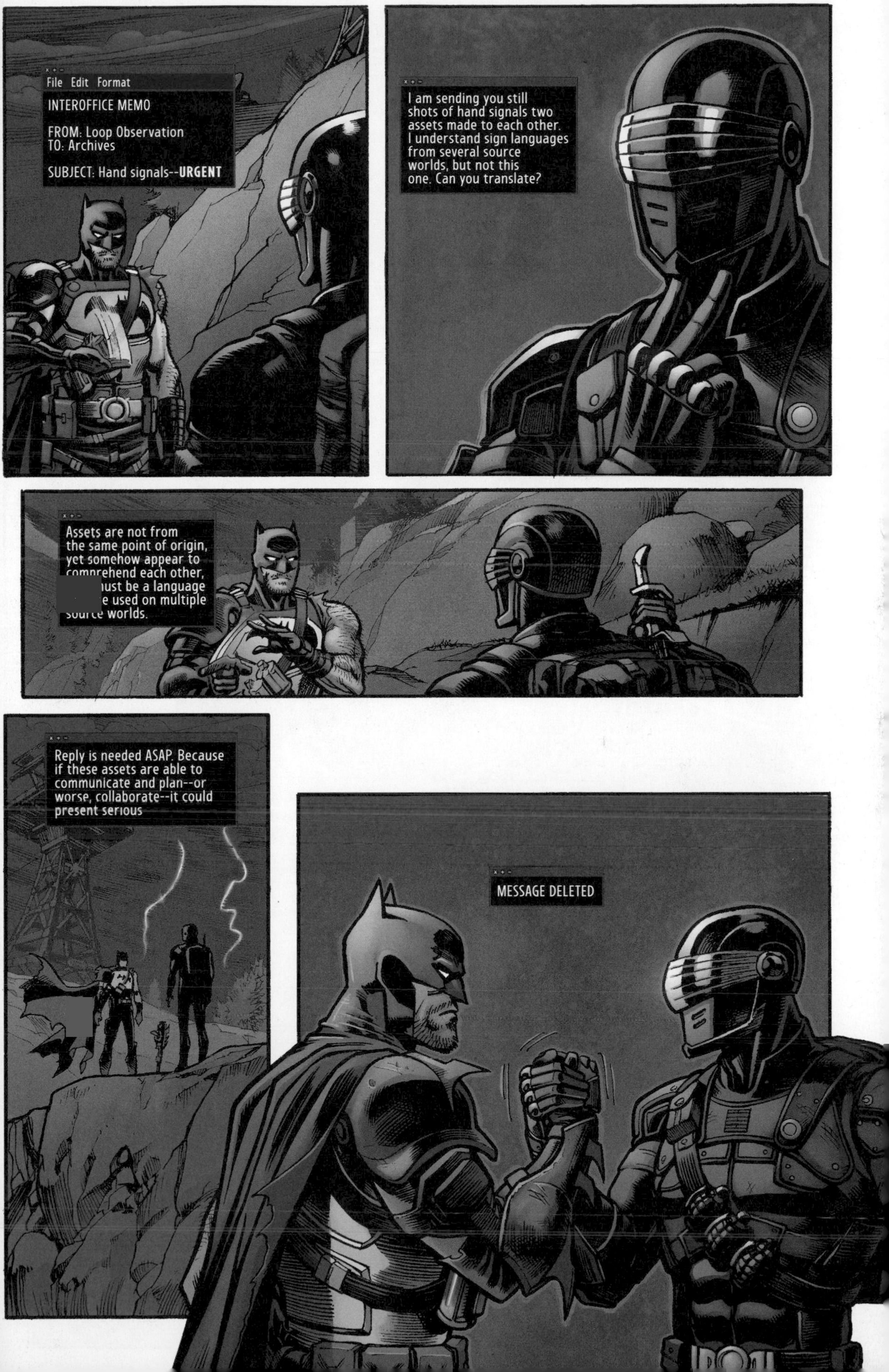

File Edit Format
INTEROFFICE MEMO
FROM: Loop Observation
TO: Archives
SUBJECT: Hand signals--**URGENT**
I am sending you still shots of hand signals two assets made to each other. I understand sign languages from several source worlds, but not this one. Can you translate?
Assets are not from the same point of origin, yet somehow appear to comprehend each other, [redacted]ust be a language [redacted]e used on multiple source worlds.
Reply is needed ASAP. Because if these assets are able to communicate and plan--or worse, collaborate--it could present serious
MESSAGE DELETED

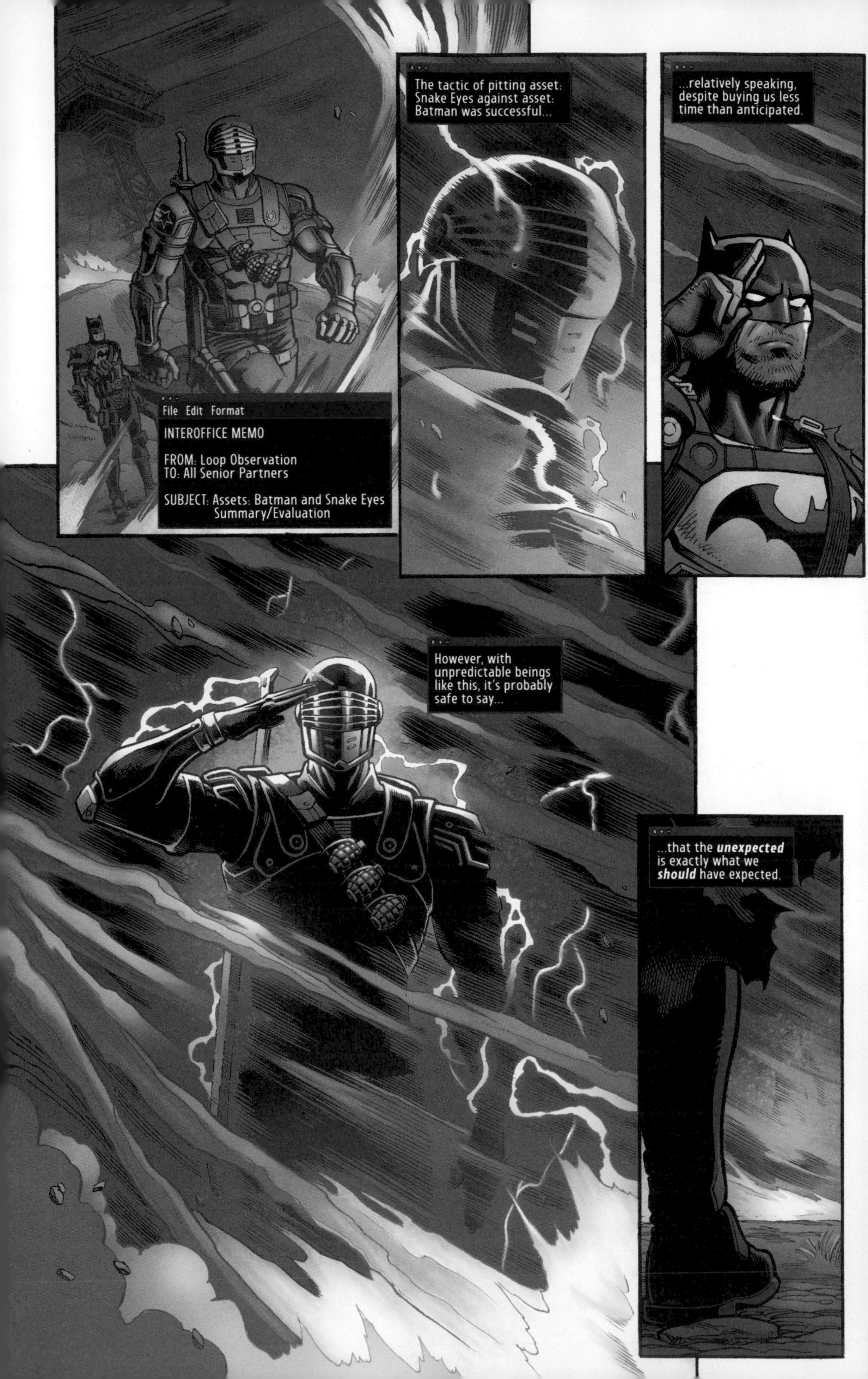
File Edit Format
INTEROFFICE MEMO
FROM: Loop Observation
TO: All Senior Partners
SUBJECT: Assets: Batman and Snake Eyes Summary/Evaluation
The tactic of pitting asset: Snake Eyes against asset: Batman was successful...
...relatively speaking, despite buying us less time than anticipated.
However, with unpredictable beings like this, it's probably safe to say...
...that the *unexpected* is exactly what we *should* have expected.

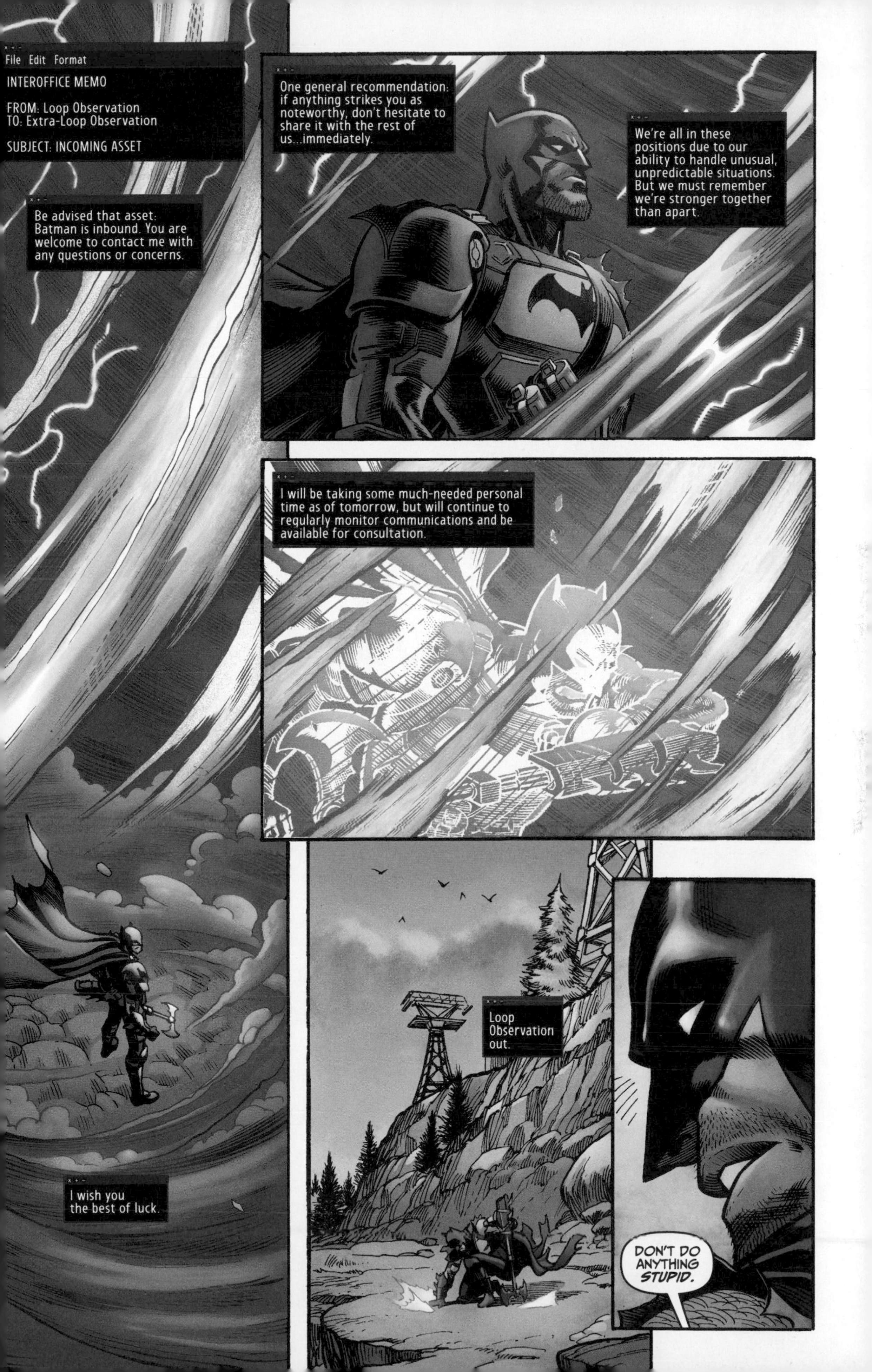
File Edit Format
INTEROFFICE MEMO
FROM: Loop Observation
TO: Extra-Loop Observation
SUBJECT: INCOMING ASSET
Be advised that asset: Batman is inbound. You are welcome to contact me with any questions or concerns.
One general recommendation: if anything strikes you as noteworthy, don't hesitate to share it with the rest of us...immediately.
We're all in these positions due to our ability to handle unusual, unpredictable situations. But we must remember we're stronger together than apart.
I will be taking some much-needed personal time as of tomorrow, but will continue to regularly monitor communications and be available for consultation.
I wish you the best of luck.
Loop Observation out.
DON'T DO ANYTHING STUPID.

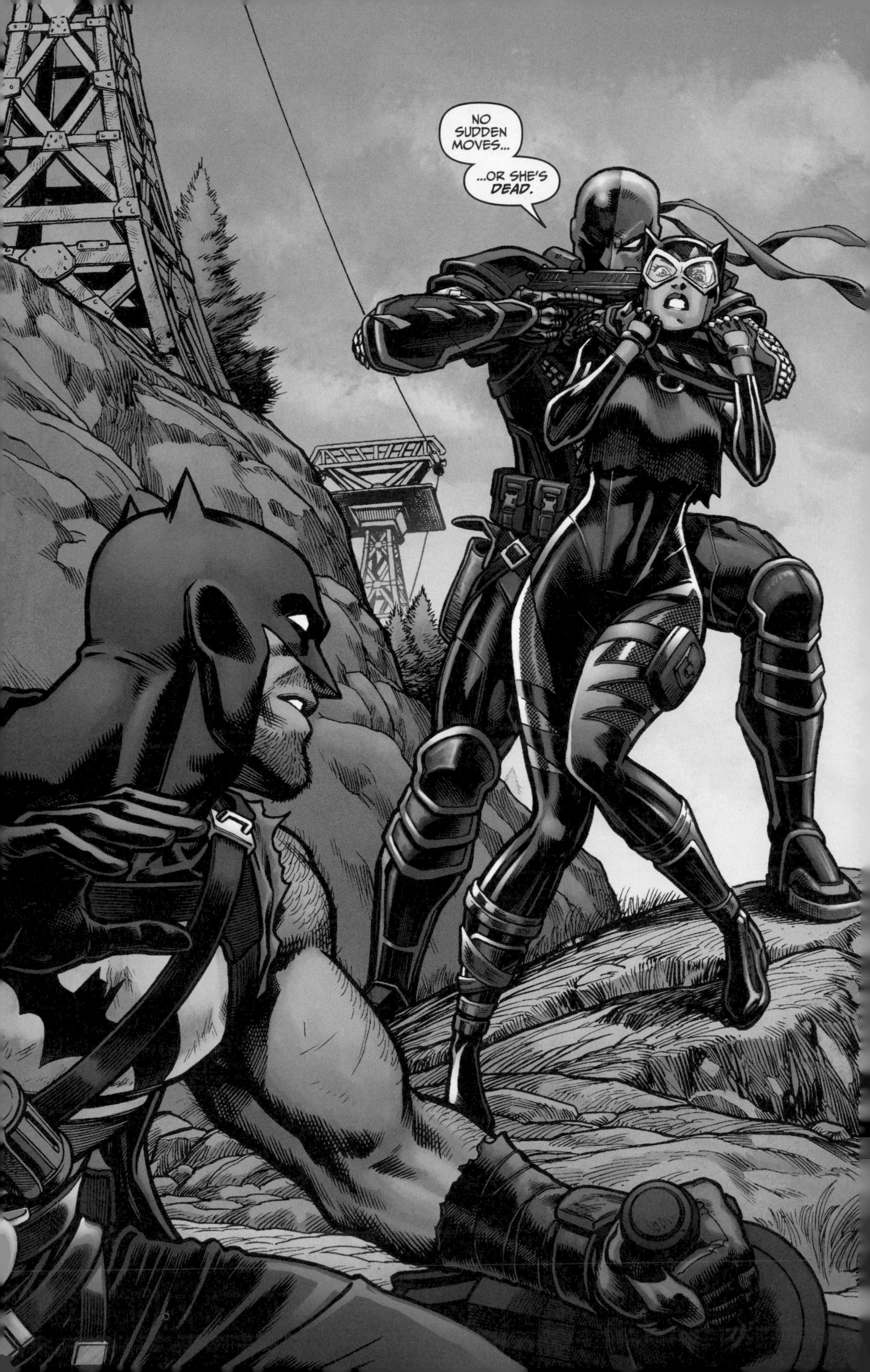
NO SUDDEN MOVES...
...OR SHE'S *DEAD.*

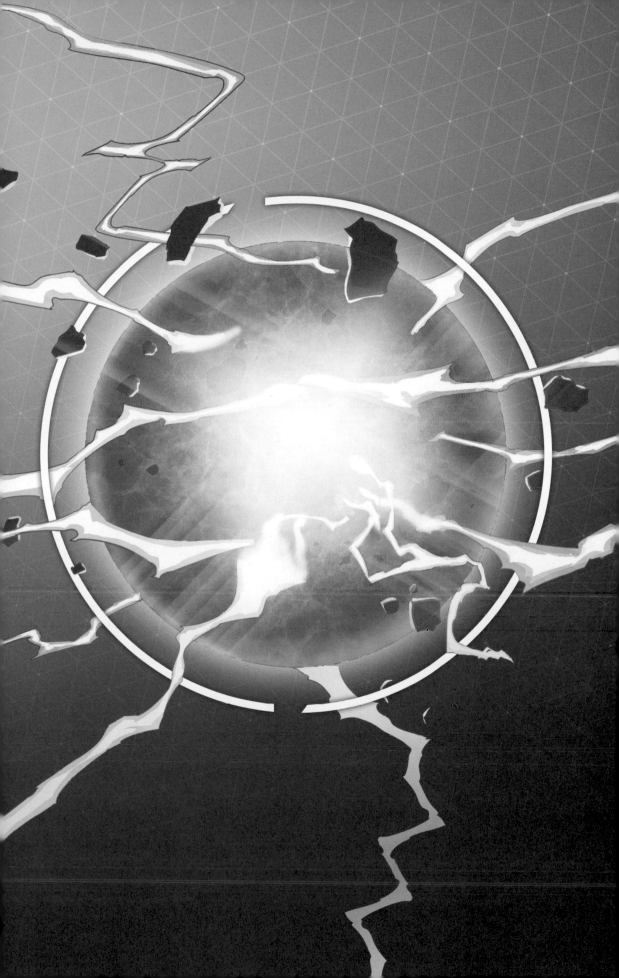

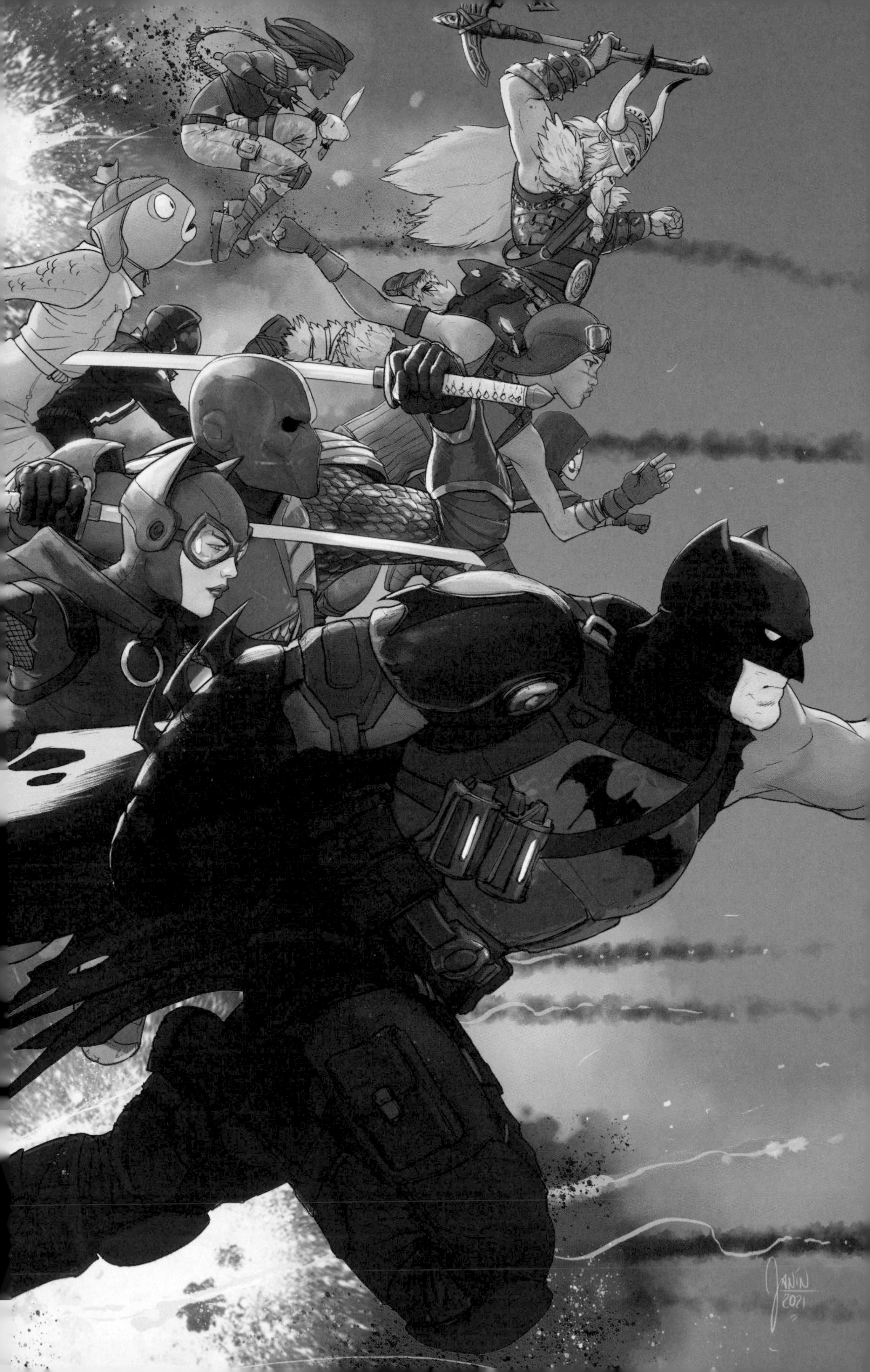
Janín
2021

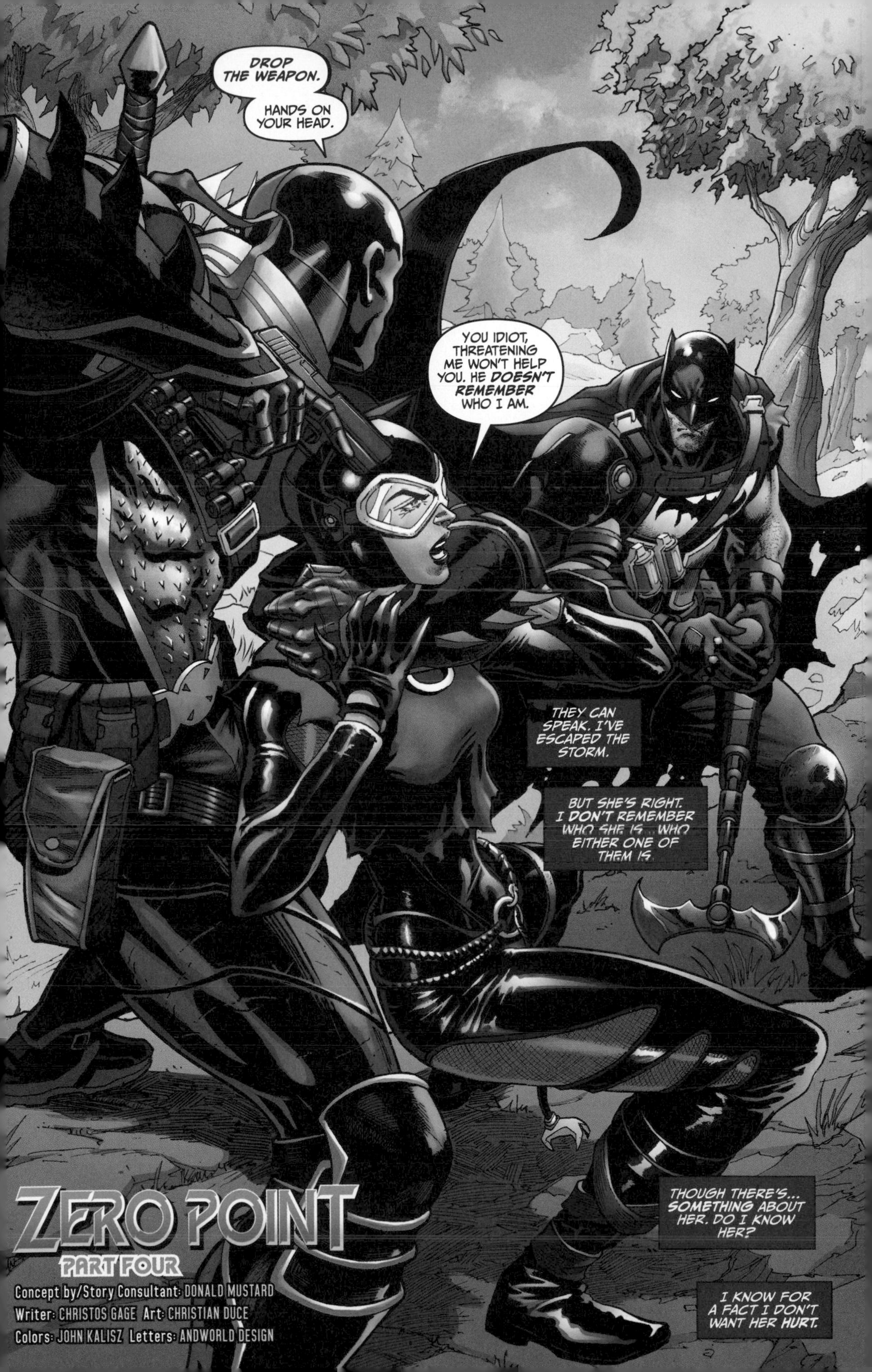
DROP THE WEAPON.
HANDS ON YOUR HEAD.
YOU IDIOT, THREATENING ME WON'T HELP YOU. HE DOESN'T REMEMBER WHO I AM.
THEY CAN SPEAK. I'VE ESCAPED THE STORM.
BUT SHE'S RIGHT. I DON'T REMEMBER WHO SHE IS... WHO EITHER ONE OF THEM IS.
THOUGH THERE'S... SOMETHING ABOUT HER. DO I KNOW HER?
I KNOW FOR A FACT I DON'T WANT HER HURT.
ZERO POINT
PART FOUR
Concept by/Story Consultant: DONALD MUSTARD
Writer: CHRISTOS GAGE Art: CHRISTIAN DUCE
Colors: JOHN KALISZ Letters: ANDWORLD DESIGN

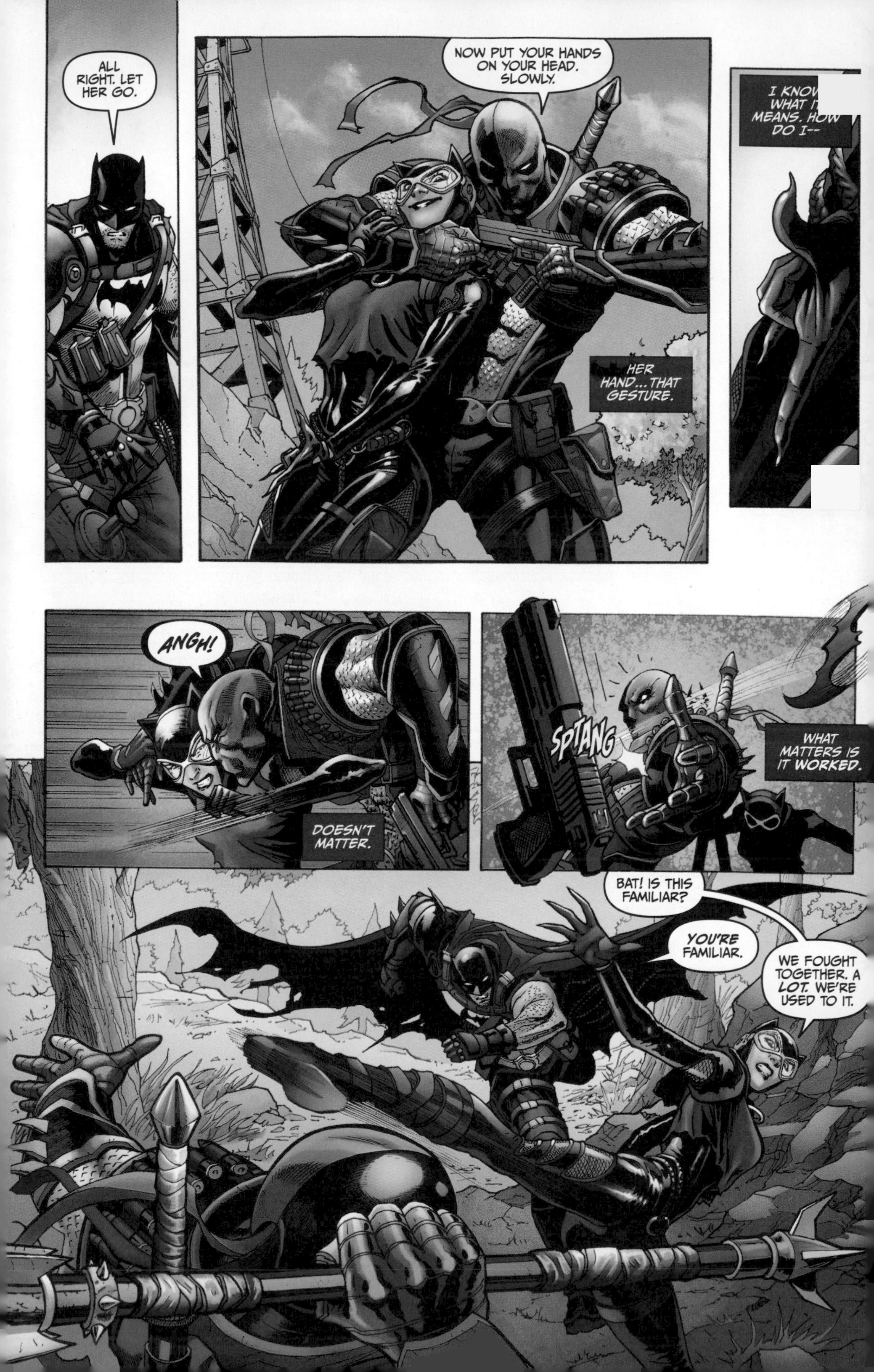
ALL RIGHT. LET HER GO.
NOW PUT YOUR HANDS ON YOUR HEAD. SLOWLY.
HER HAND...THAT GESTURE.
I KNOW WHAT IT MEANS. HOW DO I--
ANGH!
DOESN'T MATTER.
SPTANG
WHAT MATTERS IS IT WORKED.
BAT! IS THIS FAMILIAR?
YOU'RE FAMILIAR.
WE FOUGHT TOGETHER. A LOT. WE'RE USED TO IT.

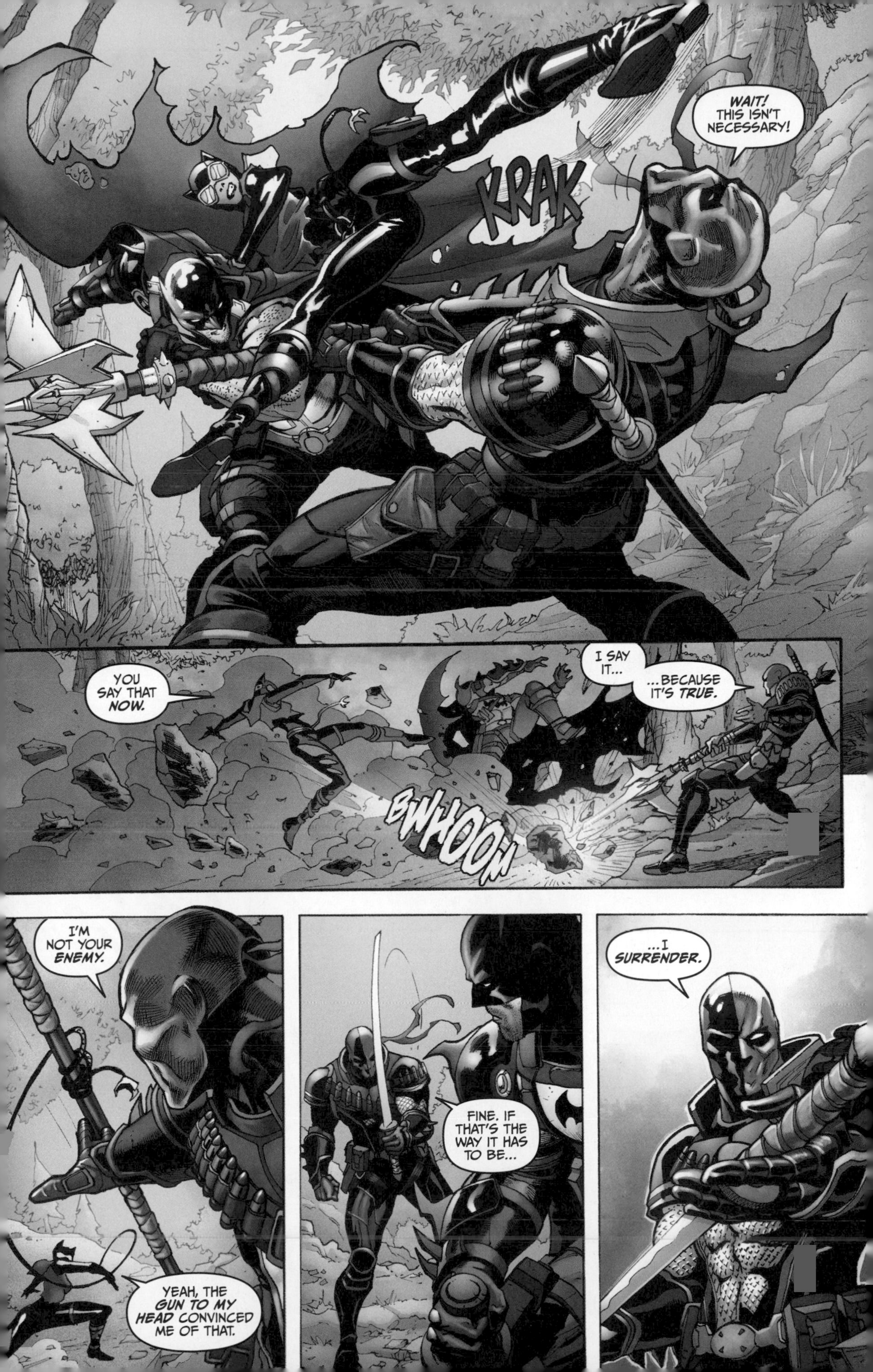
WAIT! THIS ISN'T NECESSARY!
KRAK
YOU SAY THAT NOW.
I SAY IT...
...BECAUSE IT'S TRUE.
BWHOOM
I'M NOT YOUR ENEMY.
YEAH, THE GUN TO MY HEAD CONVINCED ME OF THAT.
FINE. IF THAT'S THE WAY IT HAS TO BE...
...I SURRENDER.

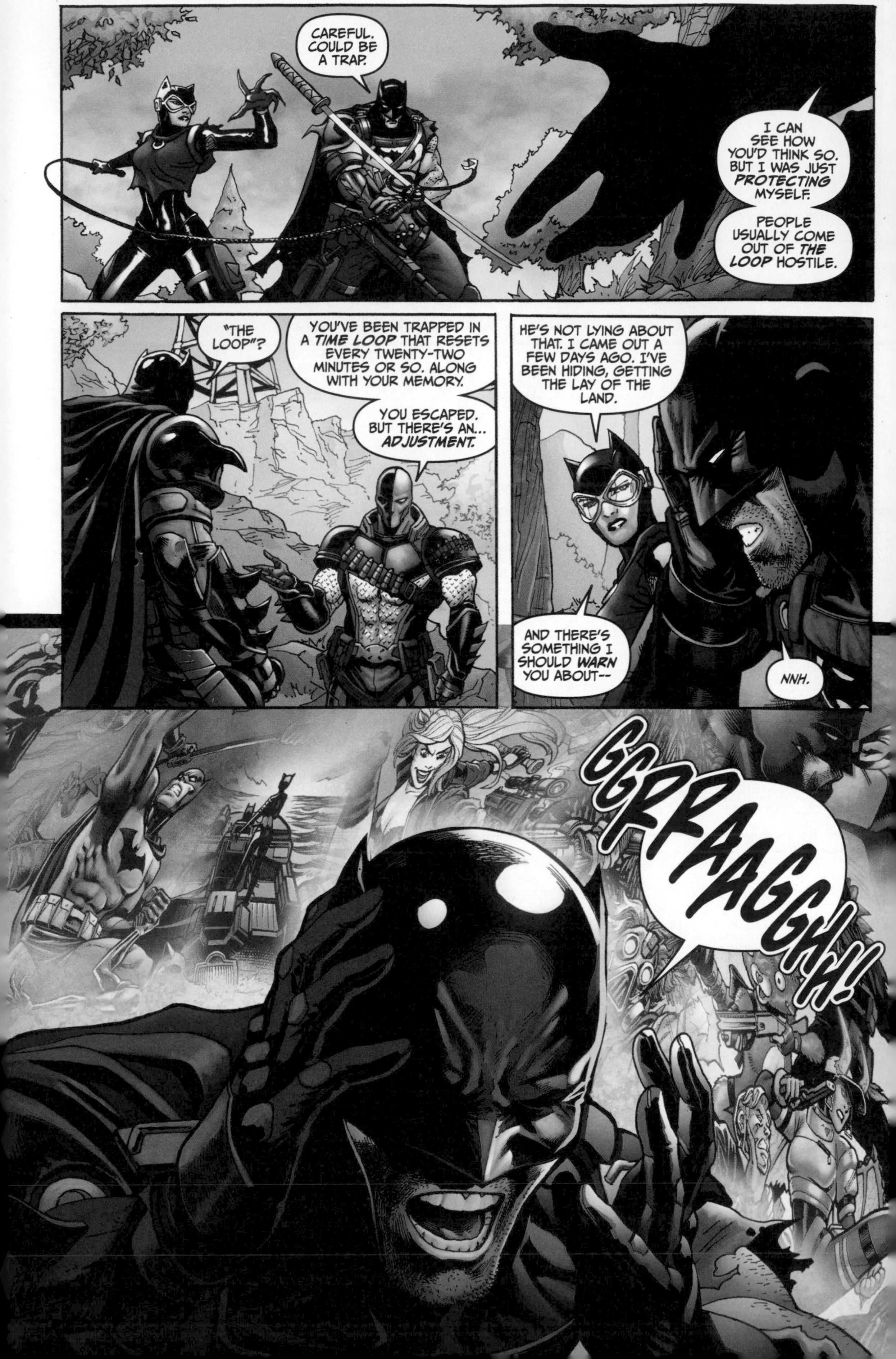
CAREFUL. COULD BE A TRAP.
I CAN SEE HOW YOU'D THINK SO. BUT I WAS JUST PROTECTING MYSELF.
PEOPLE USUALLY COME OUT OF THE LOOP HOSTILE.
"THE LOOP"?
YOU'VE BEEN TRAPPED IN A TIME LOOP THAT RESETS EVERY TWENTY-TWO MINUTES OR SO. ALONG WITH YOUR MEMORY.
YOU ESCAPED. BUT THERE'S AN... ADJUSTMENT.
HE'S NOT LYING ABOUT THAT. I CAME OUT A FEW DAYS AGO. I'VE BEEN HIDING, GETTING THE LAY OF THE LAND.
AND THERE'S SOMETHING I SHOULD WARN YOU ABOUT--
NNH.
GGRRAAGGHH!

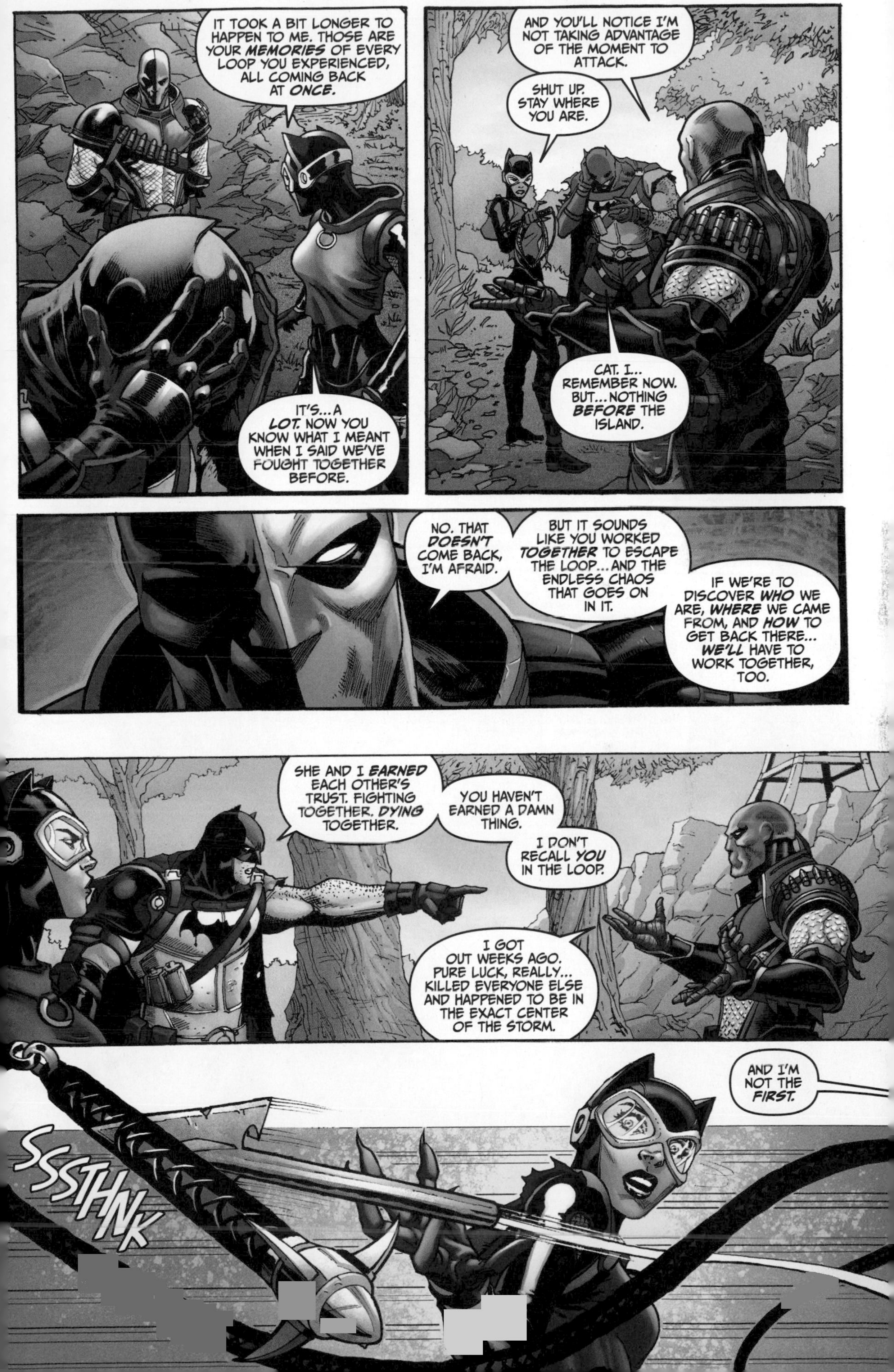
IT TOOK A BIT LONGER TO HAPPEN TO ME. THOSE ARE YOUR MEMORIES OF EVERY LOOP YOU EXPERIENCED, ALL COMING BACK AT ONCE.
IT'S...A LOT. NOW YOU KNOW WHAT I MEANT WHEN I SAID WE'VE FOUGHT TOGETHER BEFORE.
AND YOU'LL NOTICE I'M NOT TAKING ADVANTAGE OF THE MOMENT TO ATTACK.
SHUT UP. STAY WHERE YOU ARE.
CAT. I... REMEMBER NOW. BUT...NOTHING BEFORE THE ISLAND.
NO. THAT DOESN'T COME BACK, I'M AFRAID.
BUT IT SOUNDS LIKE YOU WORKED TOGETHER TO ESCAPE THE LOOP...AND THE ENDLESS CHAOS THAT GOES ON IN IT.
IF WE'RE TO DISCOVER WHO WE ARE, WHERE WE CAME FROM, AND HOW TO GET BACK THERE... WE'LL HAVE TO WORK TOGETHER, TOO.
SHE AND I EARNED EACH OTHER'S TRUST. FIGHTING TOGETHER. DYING TOGETHER.
YOU HAVEN'T EARNED A DAMN THING.
I DON'T RECALL YOU IN THE LOOP.
I GOT OUT WEEKS AGO. PURE LUCK, REALLY... KILLED EVERYONE ELSE AND HAPPENED TO BE IN THE EXACT CENTER OF THE STORM.
AND I'M NOT THE FIRST.
SSSTHNK

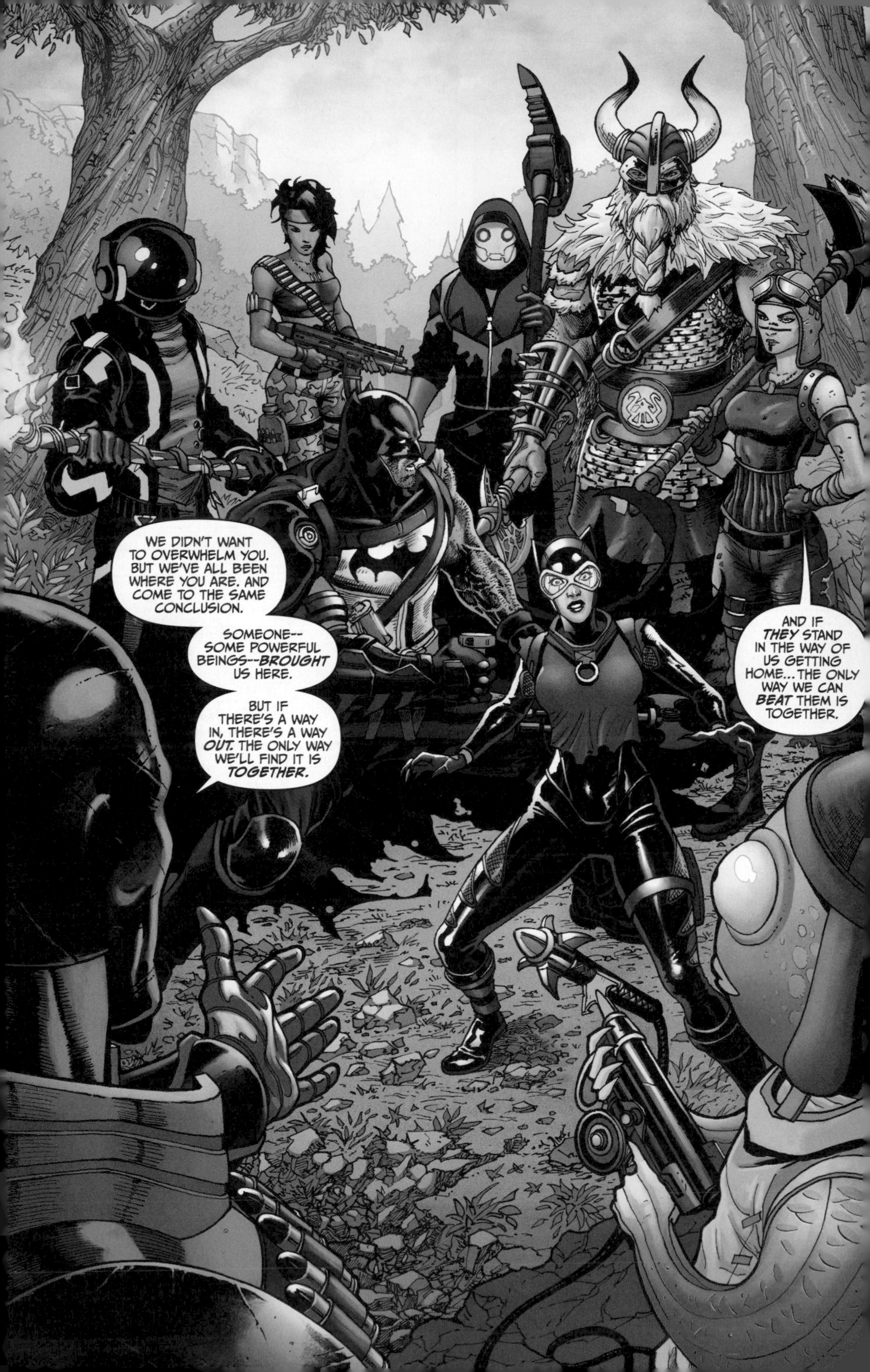
WE DIDN'T WANT TO OVERWHELM YOU. BUT WE'VE ALL BEEN WHERE YOU ARE. AND COME TO THE SAME CONCLUSION.
SOMEONE-- SOME POWERFUL BEINGS--BROUGHT US HERE.
BUT IF THERE'S A WAY IN, THERE'S A WAY OUT. THE ONLY WAY WE'LL FIND IT IS TOGETHER.
AND IF THEY STAND IN THE WAY OF US GETTING HOME... THE ONLY WAY WE CAN BEAT THEM IS TOGETHER.

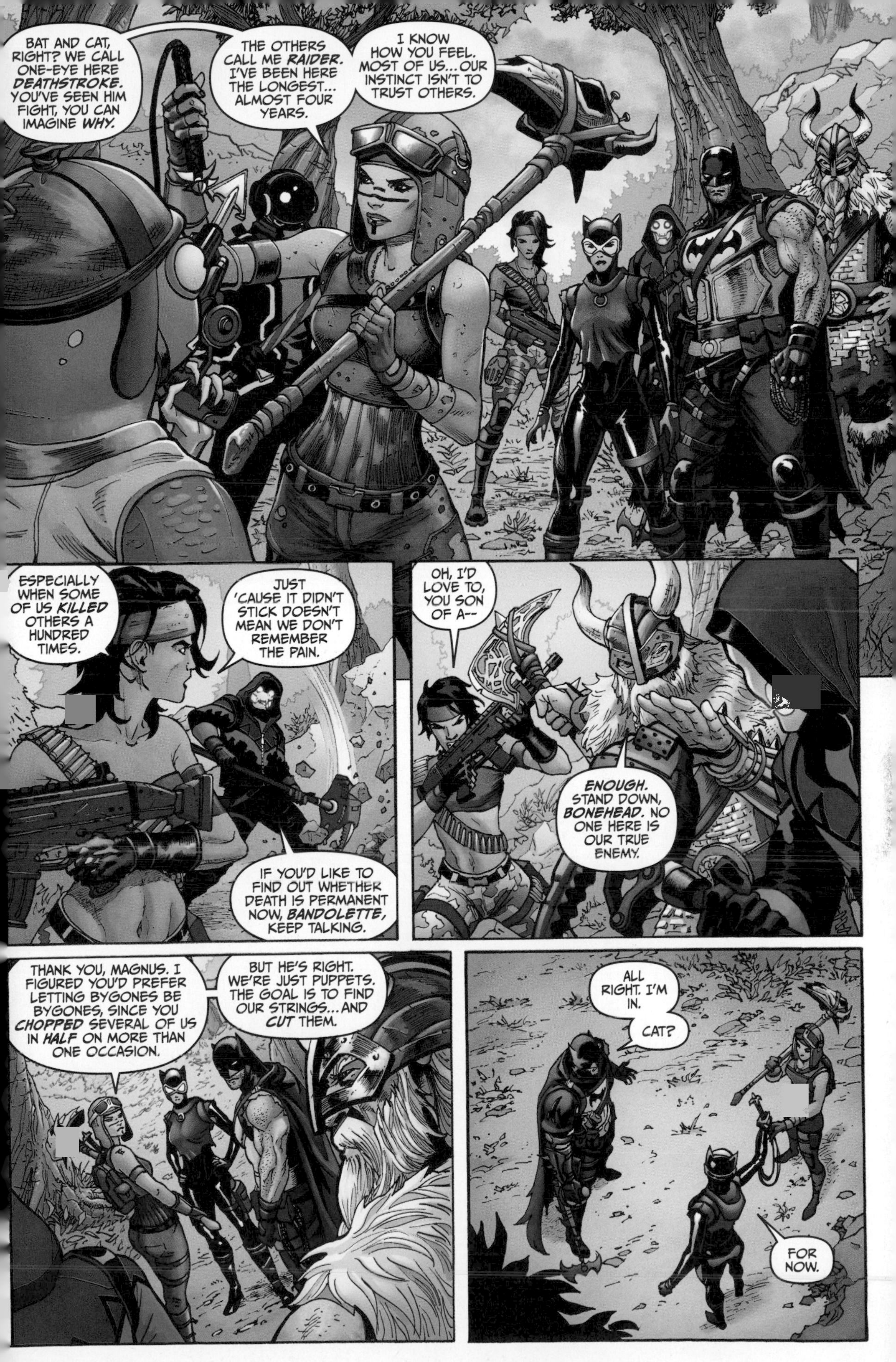
BAT AND CAT, RIGHT? WE CALL ONE-EYE HERE DEATHSTROKE. YOU'VE SEEN HIM FIGHT, YOU CAN IMAGINE WHY.
THE OTHERS CALL ME RAIDER. I'VE BEEN HERE THE LONGEST... ALMOST FOUR YEARS.
I KNOW HOW YOU FEEL. MOST OF US...OUR INSTINCT ISN'T TO TRUST OTHERS.
ESPECIALLY WHEN SOME OF US KILLED OTHERS A HUNDRED TIMES.
JUST 'CAUSE IT DIDN'T STICK DOESN'T MEAN WE DON'T REMEMBER THE PAIN.
IF YOU'D LIKE TO FIND OUT WHETHER DEATH IS PERMANENT NOW, BANDOLETTE, KEEP TALKING.
OH, I'D LOVE TO, YOU SON OF A--
ENOUGH. STAND DOWN, BONEHEAD. NO ONE HERE IS OUR TRUE ENEMY.
THANK YOU, MAGNUS. I FIGURED YOU'D PREFER LETTING BYGONES BE BYGONES, SINCE YOU CHOPPED SEVERAL OF US IN HALF ON MORE THAN ONE OCCASION.
BUT HE'S RIGHT. WE'RE JUST PUPPETS. THE GOAL IS TO FIND OUR STRINGS...AND CUT THEM.
ALL RIGHT. I'M IN.
CAT?
FOR NOW.

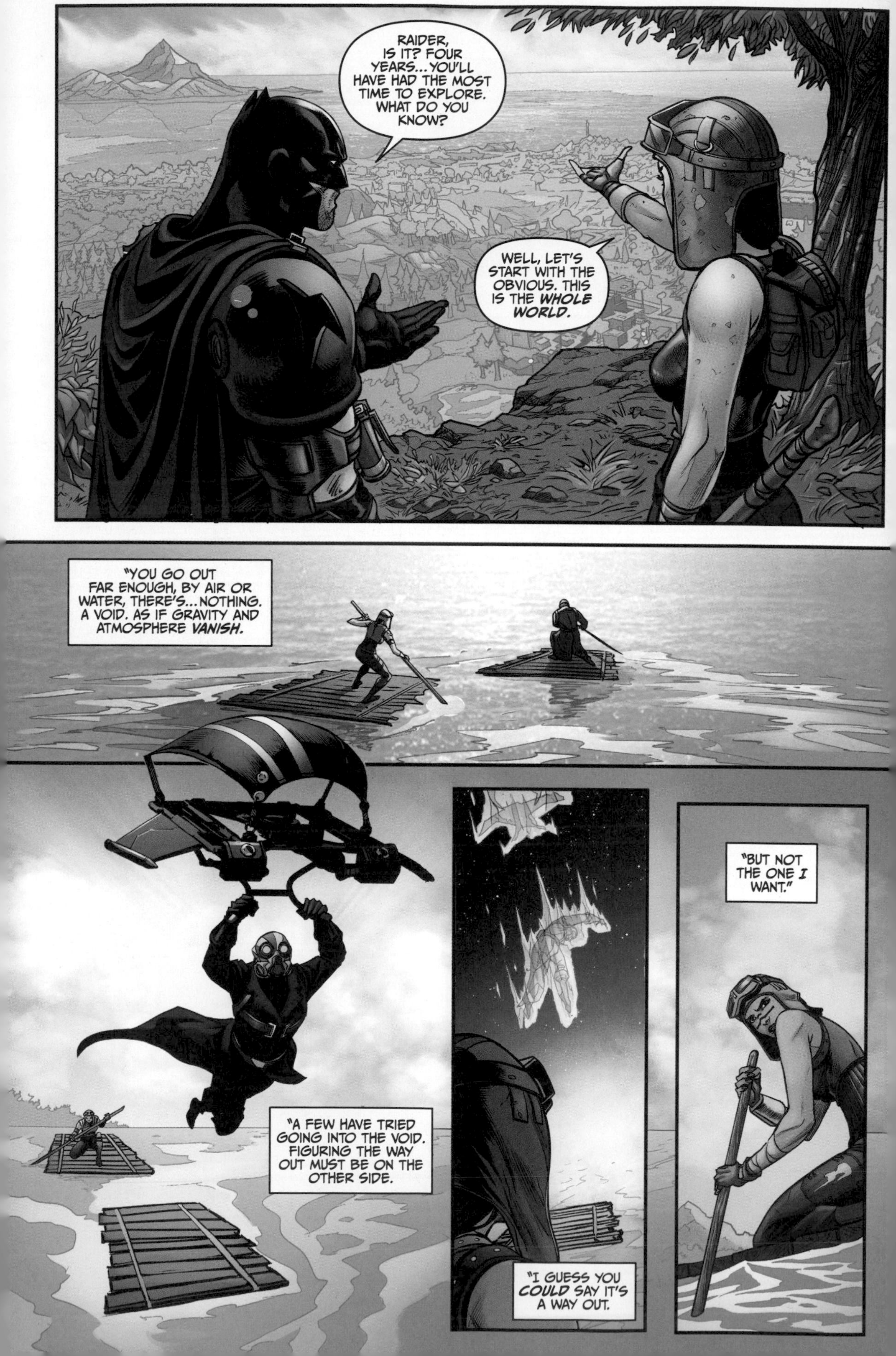
RAIDER, IS IT? FOUR YEARS...YOU'LL HAVE HAD THE MOST TIME TO EXPLORE. WHAT DO YOU KNOW?
WELL, LET'S START WITH THE OBVIOUS. THIS IS THE *WHOLE WORLD.*
"YOU GO OUT FAR ENOUGH, BY AIR OR WATER, THERE'S...NOTHING. A VOID. AS IF GRAVITY AND ATMOSPHERE *VANISH.*
"A FEW HAVE TRIED GOING INTO THE VOID. FIGURING THE WAY OUT MUST BE ON THE OTHER SIDE.
"I GUESS YOU *COULD* SAY IT'S A WAY OUT.
"BUT NOT THE ONE *I* WANT."

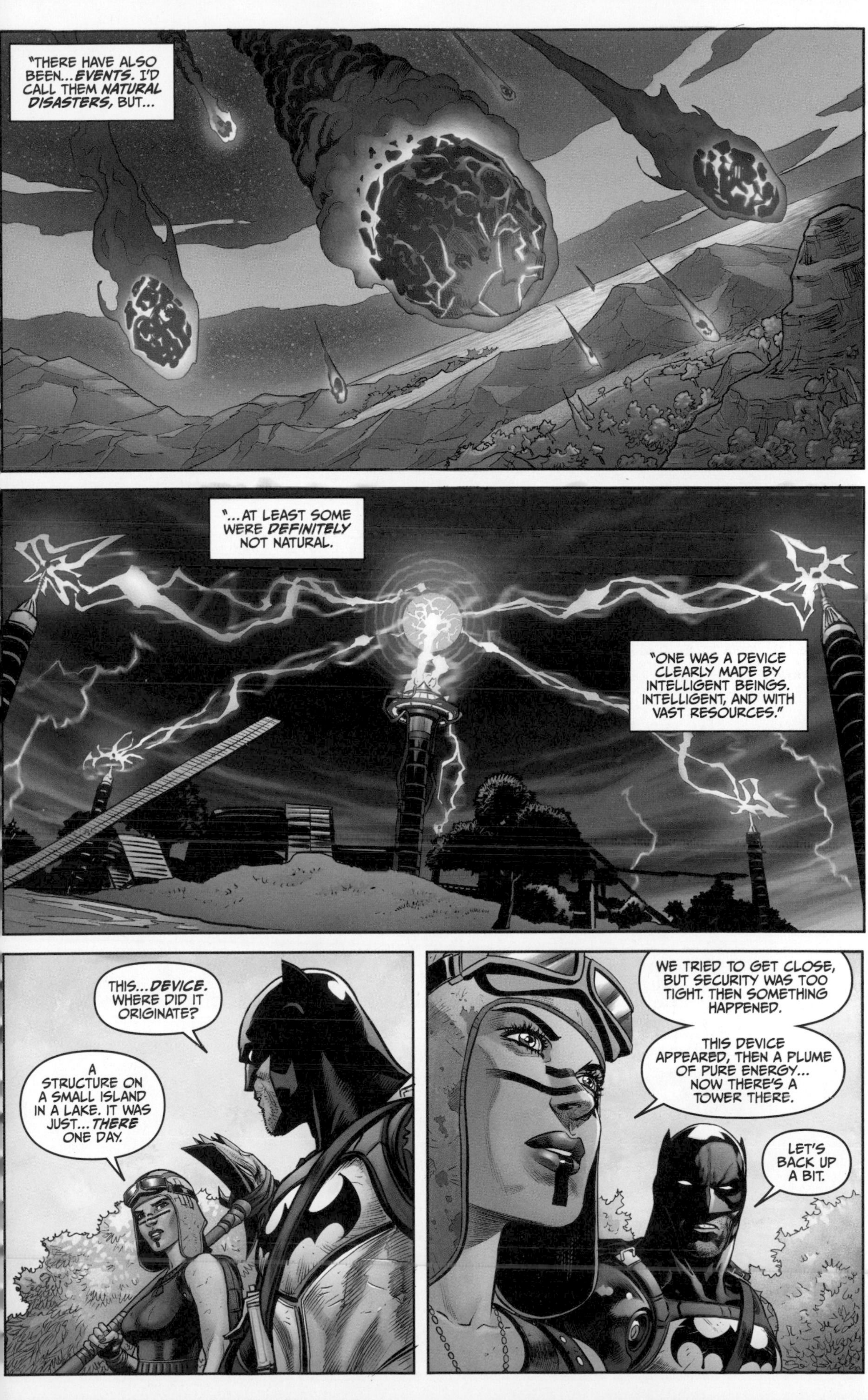
"THERE HAVE ALSO BEEN...EVENTS. I'D CALL THEM NATURAL DISASTERS, BUT...
"...AT LEAST SOME WERE DEFINITELY NOT NATURAL.
"ONE WAS A DEVICE CLEARLY MADE BY INTELLIGENT BEINGS. INTELLIGENT, AND WITH VAST RESOURCES."
THIS...DEVICE. WHERE DID IT ORIGINATE?
A STRUCTURE ON A SMALL ISLAND IN A LAKE. IT WAS JUST...THERE ONE DAY.
WE TRIED TO GET CLOSE, BUT SECURITY WAS TOO TIGHT. THEN SOMETHING HAPPENED.
THIS DEVICE APPEARED, THEN A PLUME OF PURE ENERGY... NOW THERE'S A TOWER THERE.
LET'S BACK UP A BIT.

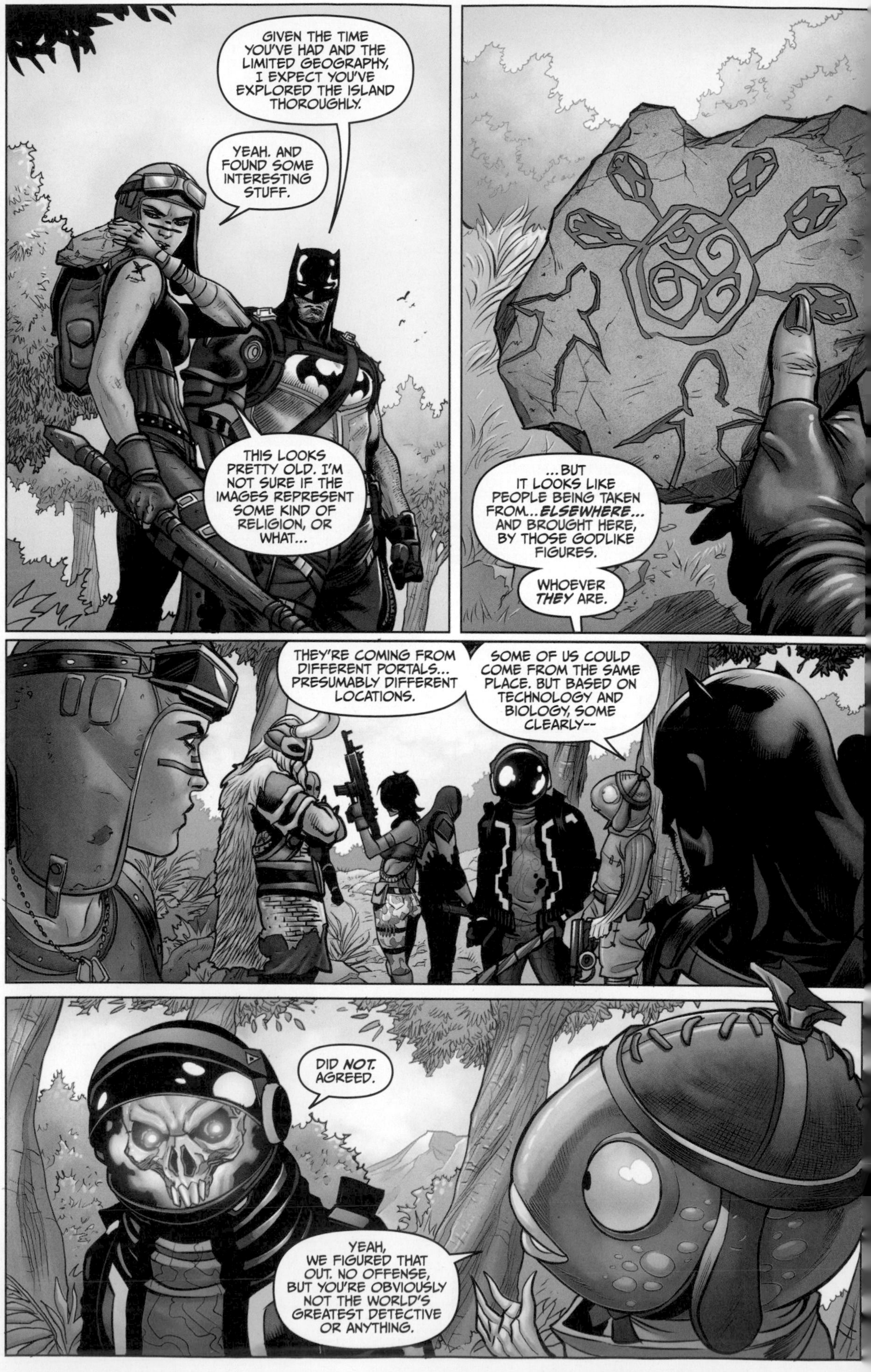
GIVEN THE TIME YOU'VE HAD AND THE LIMITED GEOGRAPHY, I EXPECT YOU'VE EXPLORED THE ISLAND THOROUGHLY.
YEAH. AND FOUND SOME INTERESTING STUFF.
THIS LOOKS PRETTY OLD. I'M NOT SURE IF THE IMAGES REPRESENT SOME KIND OF RELIGION, OR WHAT...
...BUT IT LOOKS LIKE PEOPLE BEING TAKEN FROM...*ELSEWHERE*... AND BROUGHT HERE, BY THOSE GODLIKE FIGURES.
WHOEVER *THEY* ARE.
THEY'RE COMING FROM DIFFERENT PORTALS... PRESUMABLY DIFFERENT LOCATIONS.
SOME OF US COULD COME FROM THE SAME PLACE. BUT BASED ON TECHNOLOGY AND BIOLOGY, SOME CLEARLY--
DID *NOT.* AGREED.
YEAH, WE FIGURED THAT OUT. NO OFFENSE, BUT YOU'RE OBVIOUSLY NOT THE WORLD'S GREATEST DETECTIVE OR ANYTHING.

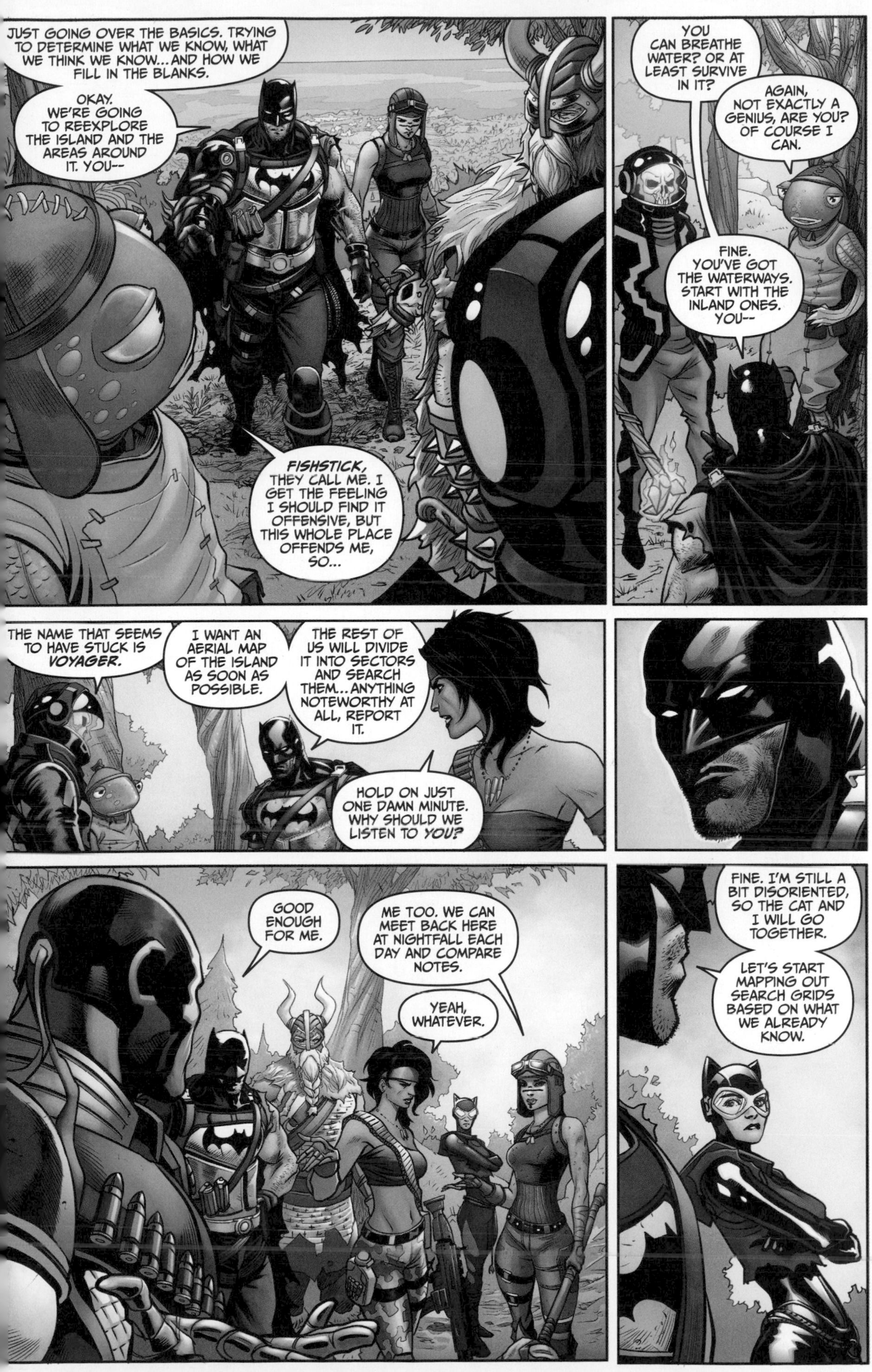
JUST GOING OVER THE BASICS. TRYING TO DETERMINE WHAT WE KNOW, WHAT WE THINK WE KNOW...AND HOW WE FILL IN THE BLANKS.
OKAY. WE'RE GOING TO REEXPLORE THE ISLAND AND THE AREAS AROUND IT. YOU--
FISHSTICK, THEY CALL ME. I GET THE FEELING I SHOULD FIND IT OFFENSIVE, BUT THIS WHOLE PLACE OFFENDS ME, SO...
YOU CAN BREATHE WATER? OR AT LEAST SURVIVE IN IT?
AGAIN, NOT EXACTLY A GENIUS, ARE YOU? OF COURSE I CAN.
FINE. YOU'VE GOT THE WATERWAYS. START WITH THE INLAND ONES. YOU--
THE NAME THAT SEEMS TO HAVE STUCK IS *VOYAGER.*
I WANT AN AERIAL MAP OF THE ISLAND AS SOON AS POSSIBLE.
THE REST OF US WILL DIVIDE IT INTO SECTORS AND SEARCH THEM...ANYTHING NOTEWORTHY AT ALL, REPORT IT.
HOLD ON JUST ONE DAMN MINUTE. WHY SHOULD WE LISTEN TO *YOU?*
GOOD ENOUGH FOR ME.
ME TOO. WE CAN MEET BACK HERE AT NIGHTFALL EACH DAY AND COMPARE NOTES.
YEAH, WHATEVER.
FINE. I'M STILL A BIT DISORIENTED, SO THE CAT AND I WILL GO TOGETHER.
LET'S START MAPPING OUT SEARCH GRIDS BASED ON WHAT WE ALREADY KNOW.

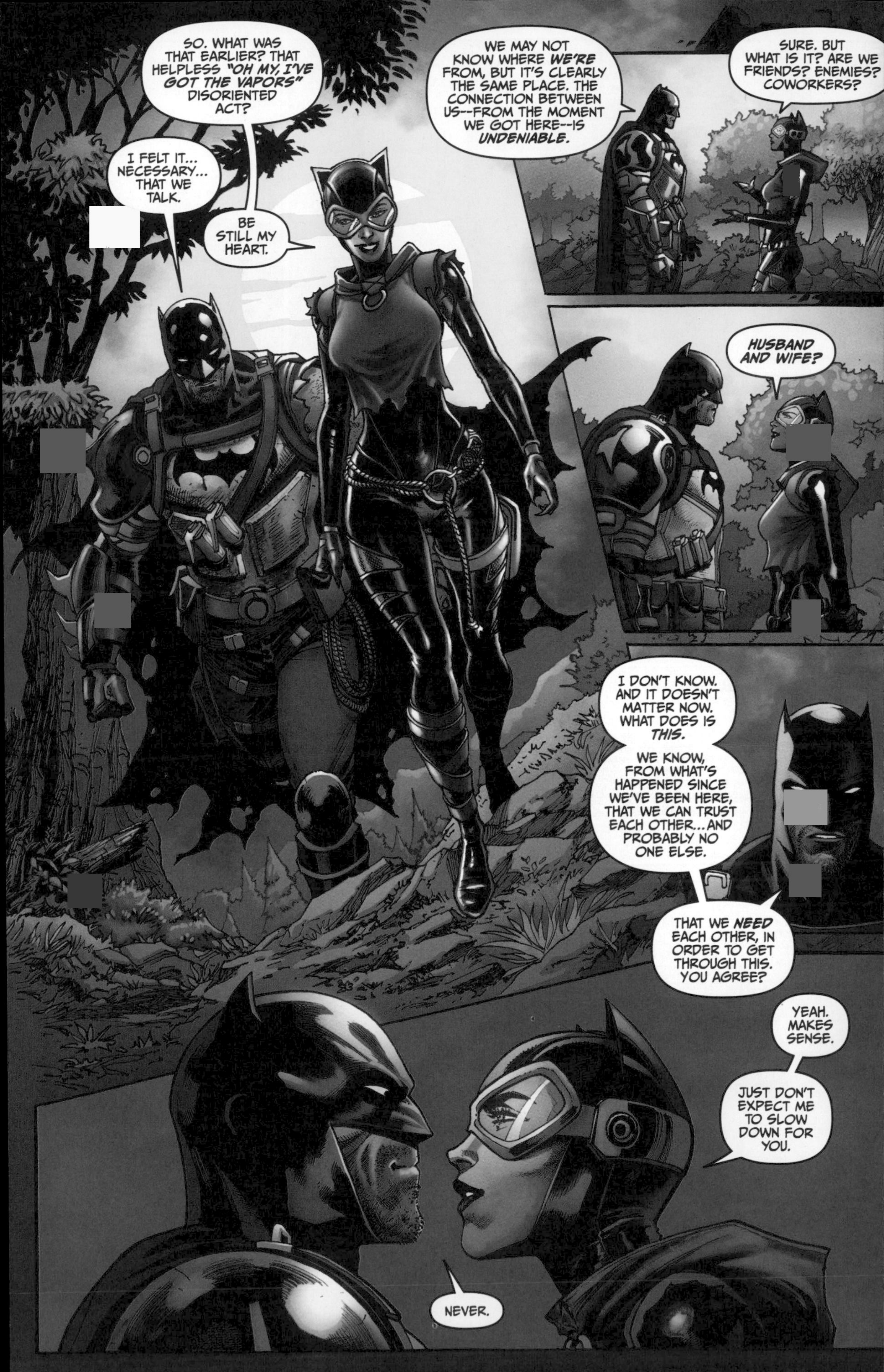
SO. WHAT WAS THAT EARLIER? THAT HELPLESS *"OH MY, I'VE GOT THE VAPORS"* DISORIENTED ACT?
I FELT IT... NECESSARY... THAT WE TALK.
BE STILL MY HEART.
WE MAY NOT KNOW WHERE *WE'RE* FROM, BUT IT'S CLEARLY THE SAME PLACE. THE CONNECTION BETWEEN US--FROM THE MOMENT WE GOT HERE--IS *UNDENIABLE.*
SURE. BUT WHAT IS IT? ARE WE FRIENDS? ENEMIES? COWORKERS?
HUSBAND AND WIFE?
I DON'T KNOW. AND IT DOESN'T MATTER NOW. WHAT DOES IS *THIS.*
WE KNOW, FROM WHAT'S HAPPENED SINCE WE'VE BEEN HERE, THAT WE CAN TRUST EACH OTHER...AND PROBABLY NO ONE ELSE.
THAT WE *NEED* EACH OTHER, IN ORDER TO GET THROUGH THIS. YOU AGREE?
YEAH. MAKES SENSE.
JUST DON'T EXPECT ME TO SLOW DOWN FOR YOU.
NEVER.

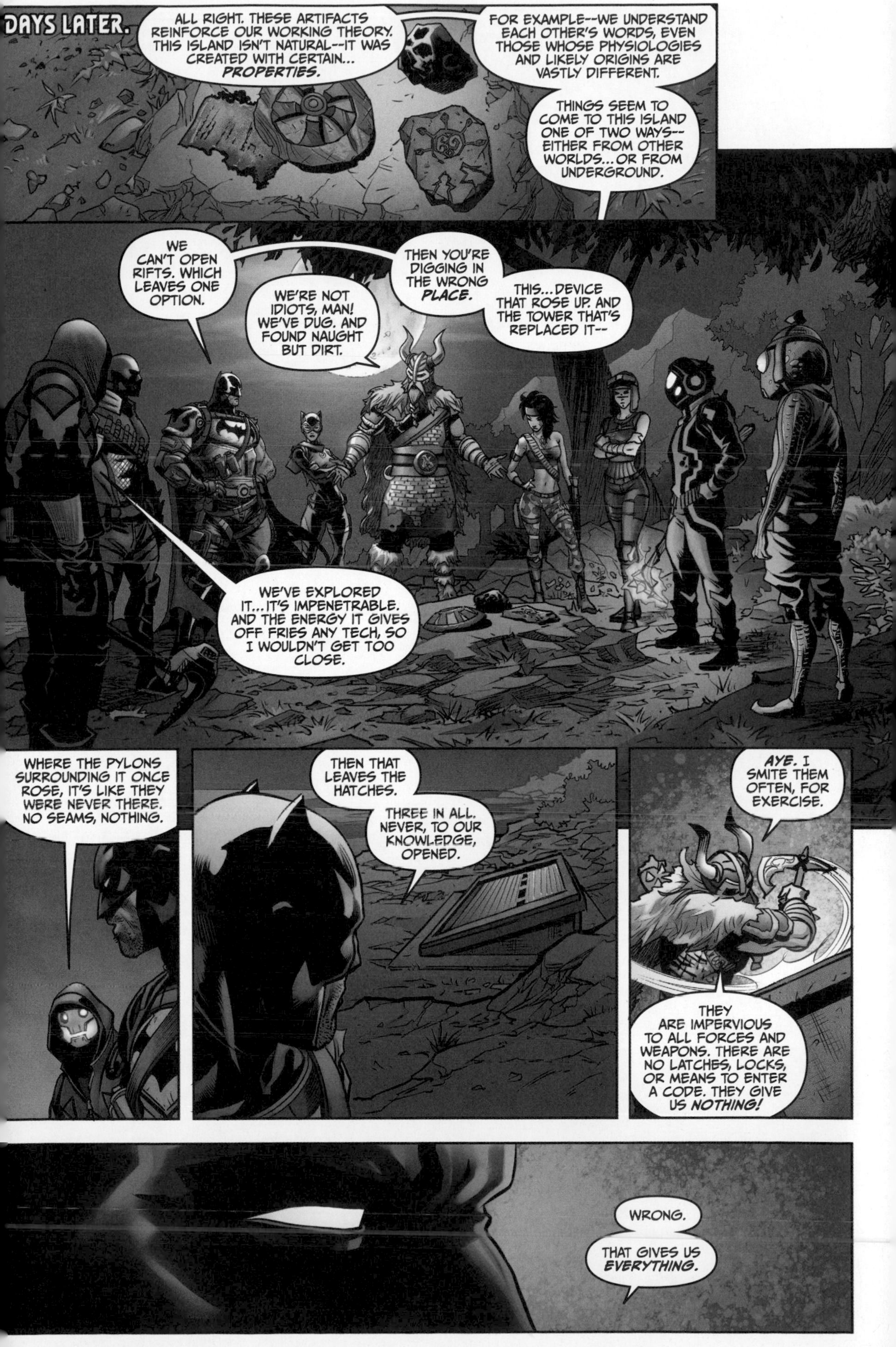
DAYS LATER.
ALL RIGHT. THESE ARTIFACTS REINFORCE OUR WORKING THEORY. THIS ISLAND ISN'T NATURAL--IT WAS CREATED WITH CERTAIN... PROPERTIES.
FOR EXAMPLE--WE UNDERSTAND EACH OTHER'S WORDS, EVEN THOSE WHOSE PHYSIOLOGIES AND LIKELY ORIGINS ARE VASTLY DIFFERENT.
THINGS SEEM TO COME TO THIS ISLAND ONE OF TWO WAYS--EITHER FROM OTHER WORLDS...OR FROM UNDERGROUND.
WE CAN'T OPEN RIFTS. WHICH LEAVES ONE OPTION.
WE'RE NOT IDIOTS, MAN! WE'VE DUG. AND FOUND NAUGHT BUT DIRT.
THEN YOU'RE DIGGING IN THE WRONG PLACE.
THIS...DEVICE THAT ROSE UP. AND THE TOWER THAT'S REPLACED IT--
WE'VE EXPLORED IT...IT'S IMPENETRABLE. AND THE ENERGY IT GIVES OFF FRIES ANY TECH, SO I WOULDN'T GET TOO CLOSE.
WHERE THE PYLONS SURROUNDING IT ONCE ROSE, IT'S LIKE THEY WERE NEVER THERE. NO SEAMS, NOTHING.
THEN THAT LEAVES THE HATCHES.
THREE IN ALL. NEVER, TO OUR KNOWLEDGE, OPENED.
AYE. I SMITE THEM OFTEN, FOR EXERCISE.
THEY ARE IMPERVIOUS TO ALL FORCES AND WEAPONS. THERE ARE NO LATCHES, LOCKS, OR MEANS TO ENTER A CODE. THEY GIVE US NOTHING!
WRONG.
THAT GIVES US EVERYTHING.

WHOEVER CONTROLS THIS PLACE SEEMS UNLIKELY TO HAVE DESIGNED HATCHES THAT ONLY OPEN FROM *ONE SIDE*.

HOW THE HELL DO *YOU* KNOW?

MY DEVICE CAN ANALYZE AND REPLICATE ENERGY FREQUENCIES. IF WE THEORIZE THAT THE HATCHES ARE DESIGNED TO OPEN FOR WHOEVER "THEY" ARE, AND NOT US...

...THERE'S SOMETHING ABOUT *THEM* THEY RECOGNIZE. WE NEED TO FIND IT.

PATTERNS OF BEHAVIOR ARE... SOMETHING I FEEL I'VE STUDIED. OUR PUPPET MASTERS WOULDN'T CHANCE GETTING TRAPPED OUT HERE.

"WE'RE GOING TO COLLECT ENERGY TRACES FROM VARIOUS LOCATIONS. LIKE THE PLACES THE PYLONS ROSE FROM.

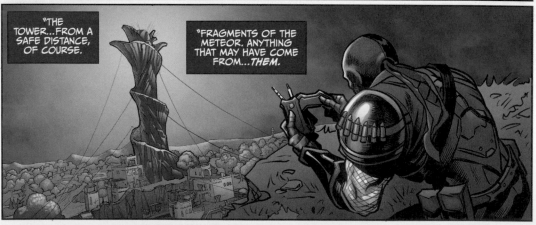

"THE TOWER...FROM A SAFE DISTANCE, OF COURSE.

"FRAGMENTS OF THE METEOR. ANYTHING THAT MAY HAVE COME FROM...*THEM*.

"AND WE'LL TRY EACH PARTICULAR ENERGY SIGNATURE ON THE HATCH. EVEN IF IT TAKES DOZENS, HUNDREDS... *THOUSANDS*.

"IN THE HOPE THAT ONE...

"...IS THE KEY."

CLICK

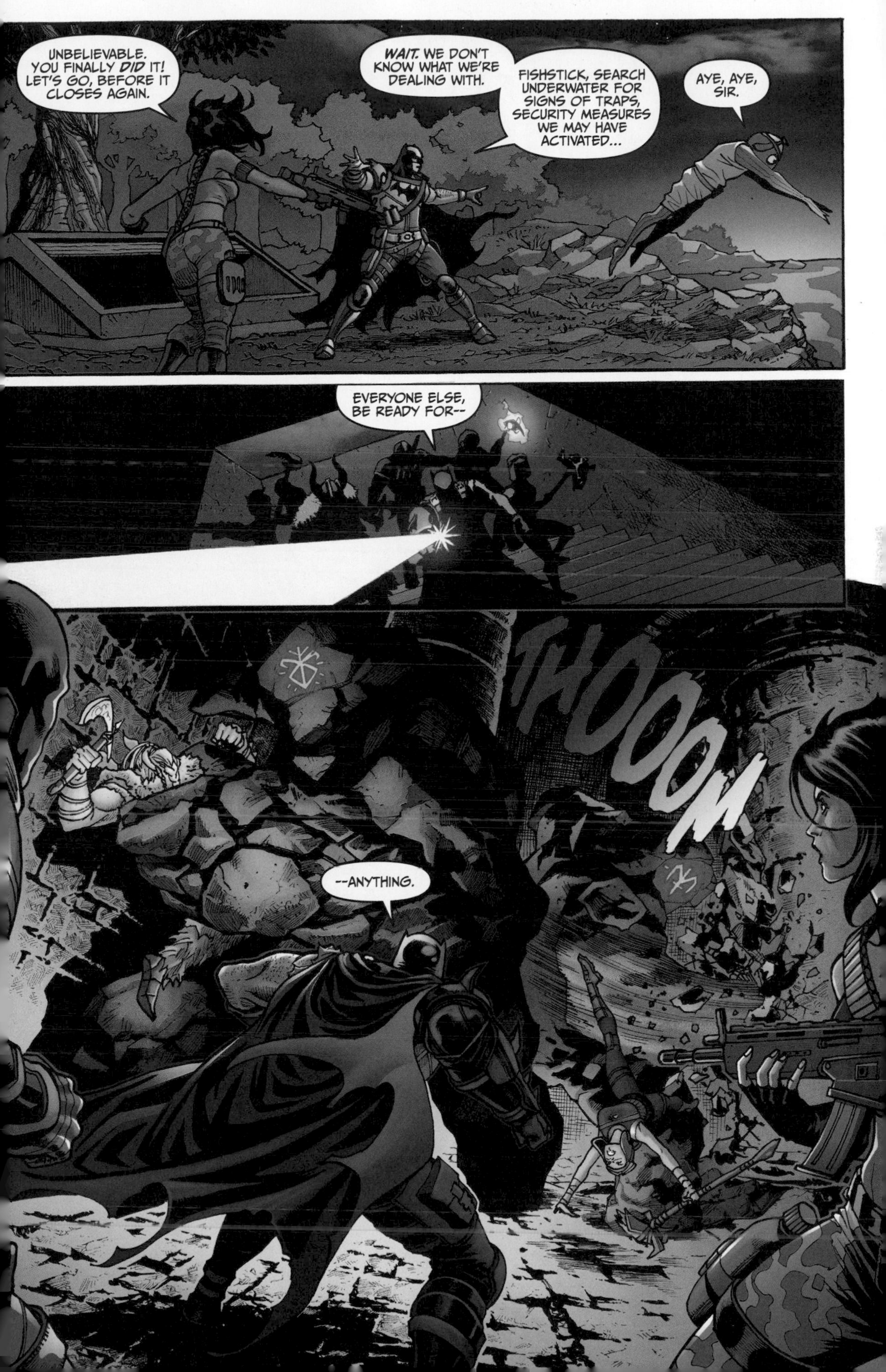
UNBELIEVABLE. YOU FINALLY *DID* IT! LET'S GO, BEFORE IT CLOSES AGAIN.
WAIT. WE DON'T KNOW WHAT WE'RE DEALING WITH.
FISHSTICK, SEARCH UNDERWATER FOR SIGNS OF TRAPS, SECURITY MEASURES WE MAY HAVE ACTIVATED...
AYE, AYE, SIR.
EVERYONE ELSE, BE READY FOR--
THOOOM
--ANYTHING.

KTRNCH
WE'RE JUST CHIPPING OFF PIECES! THE GLOWING RUNES--IN THEIR FOREHEADS--
--TARGET THOSE!
BLAM BLAM
DONE.
IF THIS DOESN'T WORK, I AM GOING TO HAUNT YOU...
BTOOOM
NOT BAD. HOW'D YOU KNOW?
THEY DIDN'T FEEL PAIN OR OTHERWISE ACT *ALIVE.* WHICH MEANT SOMETHING WAS ANIMATING THEM, AND IDENTIFYING US AS INTRUDERS.
STAY ALERT. WE FAKED THE ENERGY SIGNATURE OF THEIR MASTERS TO OPEN THE HATCH, BUT IT'S NOT *IN* US, SO THIS COULD HAPPEN AGAIN.
I THINK I FOUND THE LIGHTS...

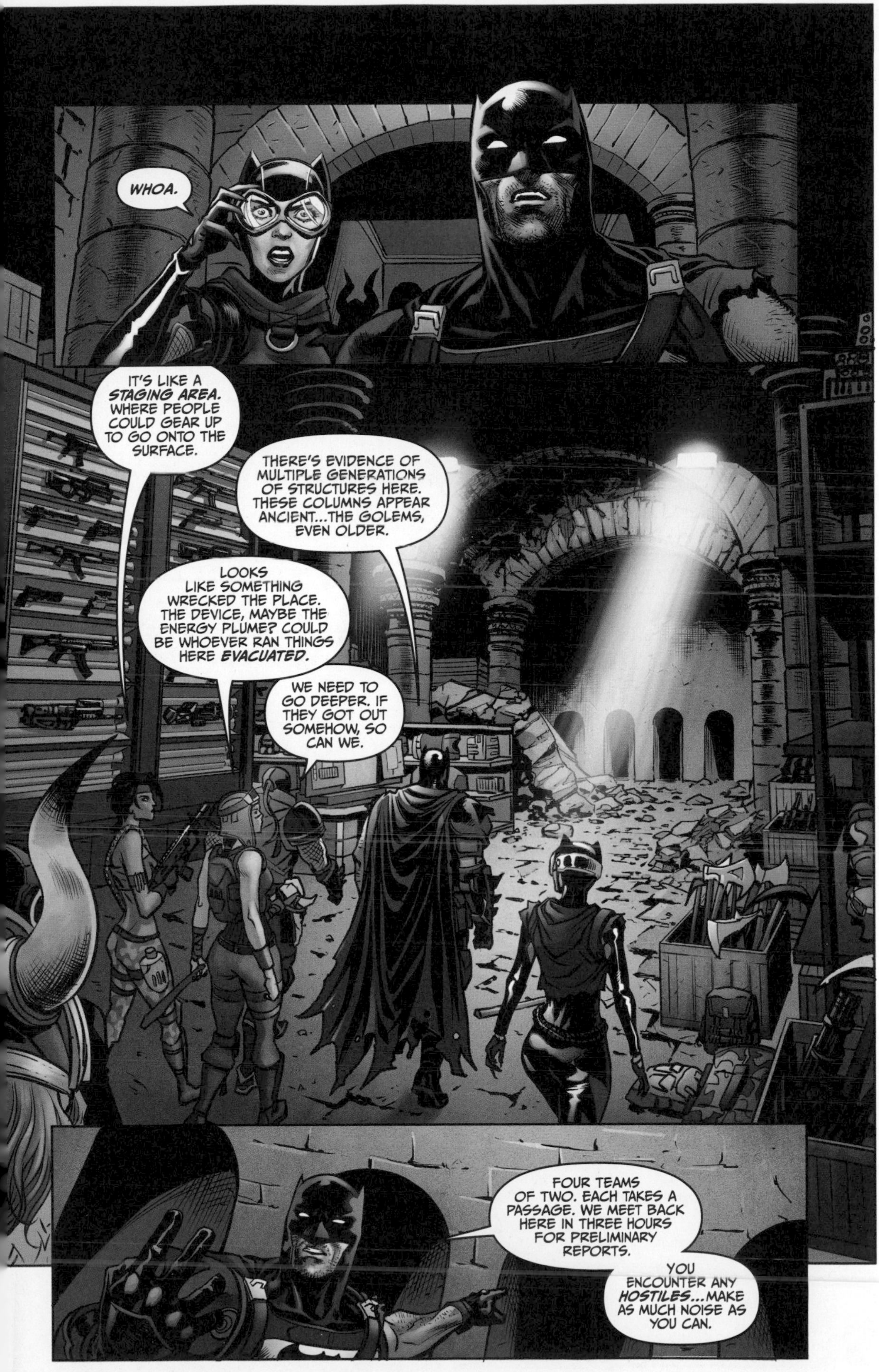
WHOA.
IT'S LIKE A STAGING AREA. WHERE PEOPLE COULD GEAR UP TO GO ONTO THE SURFACE.
THERE'S EVIDENCE OF MULTIPLE GENERATIONS OF STRUCTURES HERE. THESE COLUMNS APPEAR ANCIENT...THE GOLEMS, EVEN OLDER.
LOOKS LIKE SOMETHING WRECKED THE PLACE. THE DEVICE, MAYBE THE ENERGY PLUME? COULD BE WHOEVER RAN THINGS HERE EVACUATED.
WE NEED TO GO DEEPER. IF THEY GOT OUT SOMEHOW, SO CAN WE.
FOUR TEAMS OF TWO. EACH TAKES A PASSAGE. WE MEET BACK HERE IN THREE HOURS FOR PRELIMINARY REPORTS.
YOU ENCOUNTER ANY HOSTILES...MAKE AS MUCH NOISE AS YOU CAN.

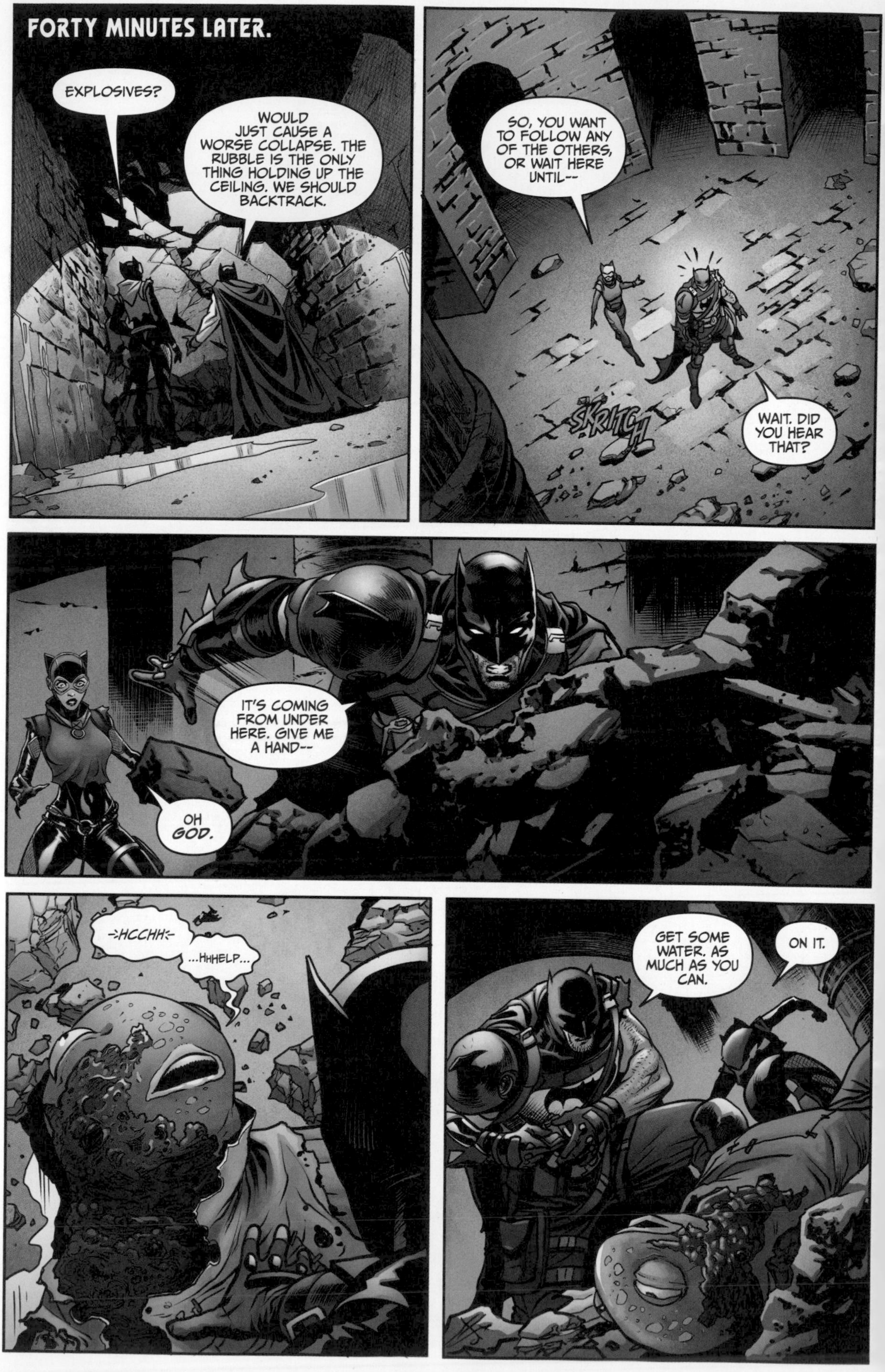
FORTY MINUTES LATER.
EXPLOSIVES?
WOULD JUST CAUSE A WORSE COLLAPSE. THE RUBBLE IS THE ONLY THING HOLDING UP THE CEILING. WE SHOULD BACKTRACK.
SO, YOU WANT TO FOLLOW ANY OF THE OTHERS, OR WAIT HERE UNTIL--
SKRITCH
WAIT. DID YOU HEAR THAT?
IT'S COMING FROM UNDER HERE. GIVE ME A HAND--
OH GOD.
-HCCHH-
...HHHELP...
GET SOME WATER. AS MUCH AS YOU CAN.
ON IT.

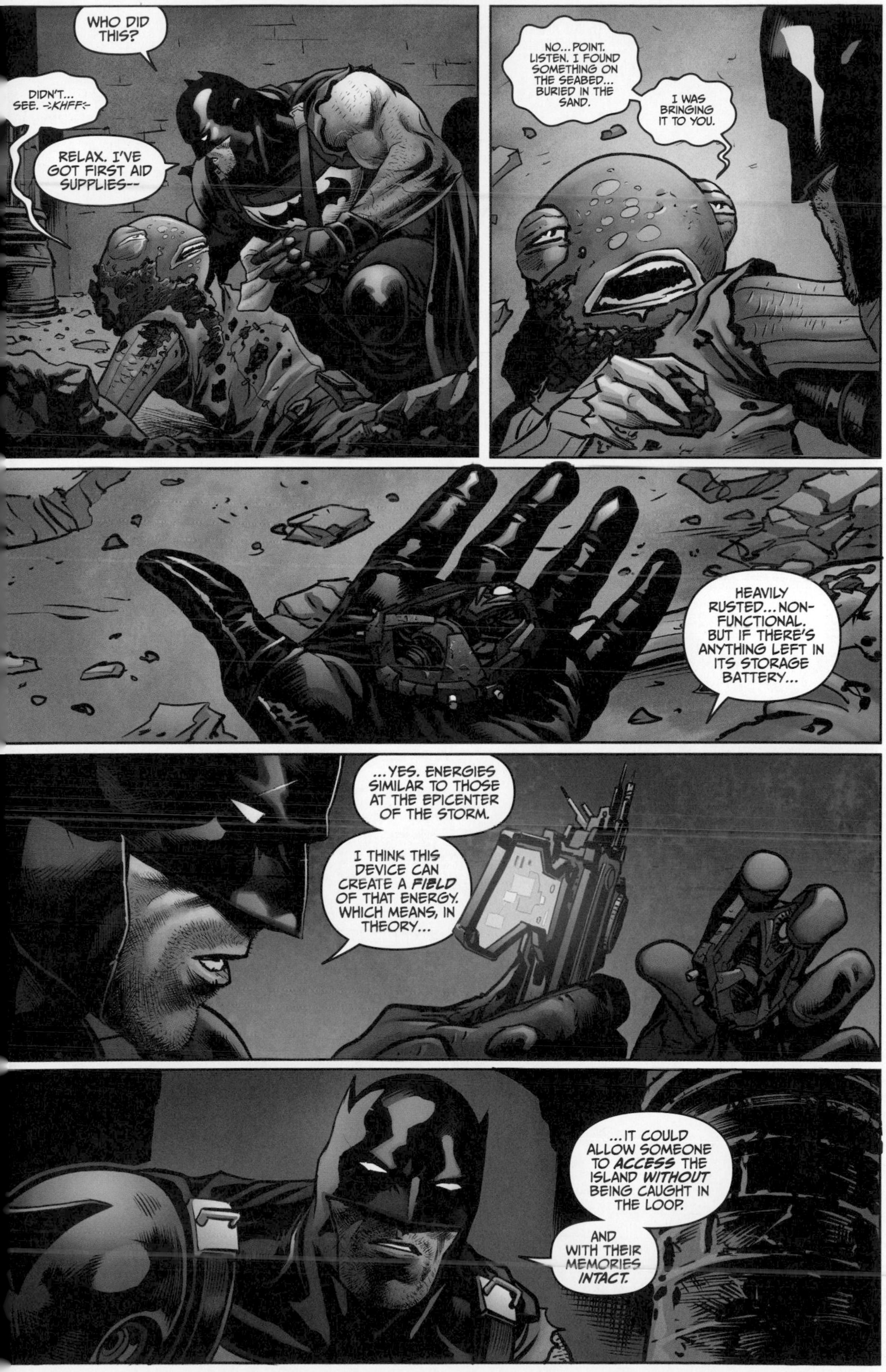
WHO DID THIS?
DIDN'T... SEE. -KHFF-
RELAX. I'VE GOT FIRST AID SUPPLIES--
NO... POINT. LISTEN. I FOUND SOMETHING ON THE SEABED... BURIED IN THE SAND.
I WAS BRINGING IT TO YOU.
HEAVILY RUSTED... NON-FUNCTIONAL. BUT IF THERE'S ANYTHING LEFT IN ITS STORAGE BATTERY...
...YES. ENERGIES SIMILAR TO THOSE AT THE EPICENTER OF THE STORM.
I THINK THIS DEVICE CAN CREATE A FIELD OF THAT ENERGY. WHICH MEANS, IN THEORY...
...IT COULD ALLOW SOMEONE TO ACCESS THE ISLAND WITHOUT BEING CAUGHT IN THE LOOP.
AND WITH THEIR MEMORIES INTACT.

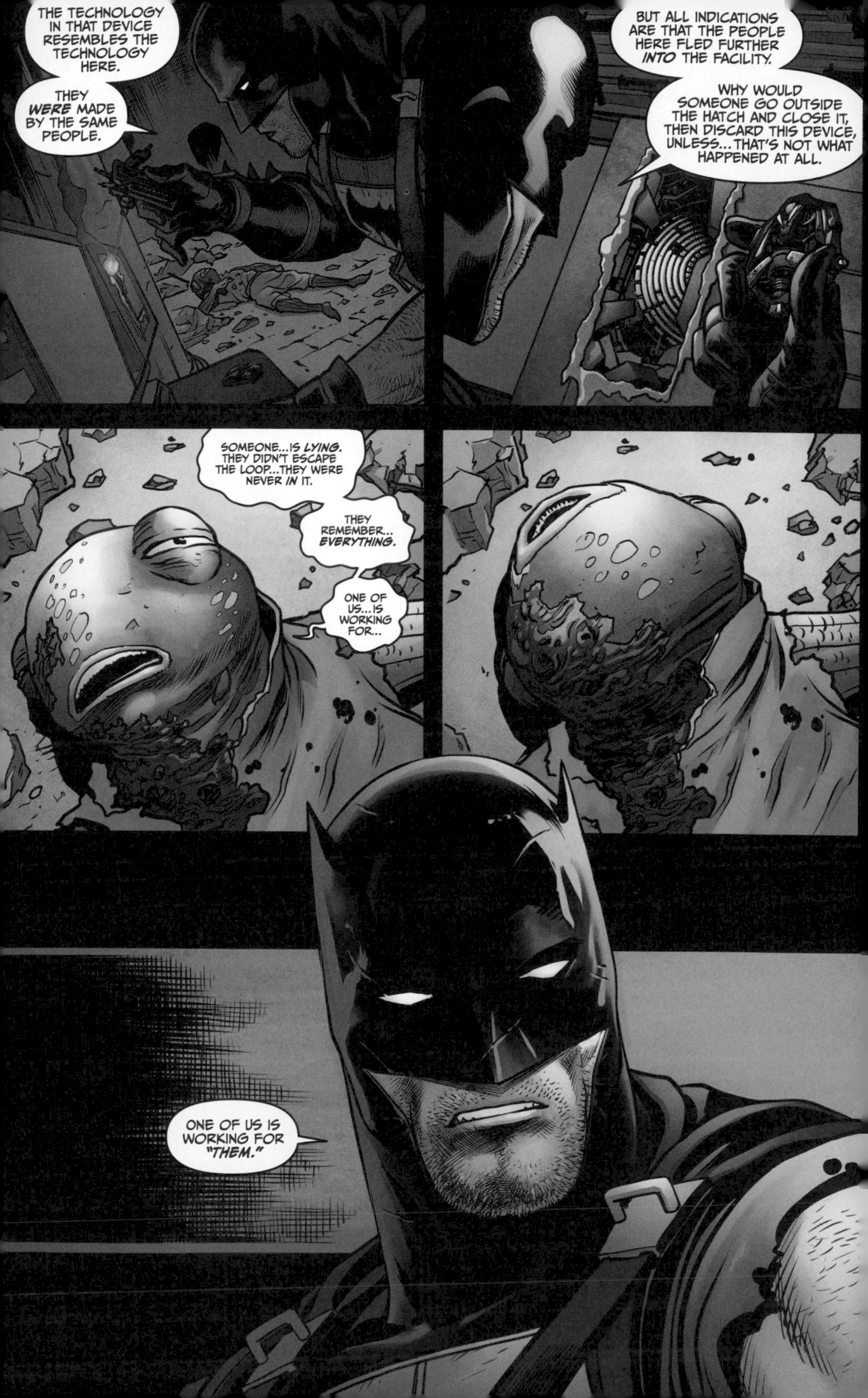
THE TECHNOLOGY IN THAT DEVICE RESEMBLES THE TECHNOLOGY HERE.
THEY *WERE* MADE BY THE SAME PEOPLE.
BUT ALL INDICATIONS ARE THAT THE PEOPLE HERE FLED FURTHER *INTO* THE FACILITY.
WHY WOULD SOMEONE GO OUTSIDE THE HATCH AND CLOSE IT, THEN DISCARD THIS DEVICE, UNLESS... THAT'S NOT WHAT HAPPENED AT ALL.
SOMEONE...IS *LYING*. THEY DIDN'T ESCAPE THE LOOP...THEY WERE NEVER *IN* IT.
THEY REMEMBER... *EVERYTHING*.
ONE OF US...IS WORKING FOR...
ONE OF US IS WORKING FOR *"THEM."*

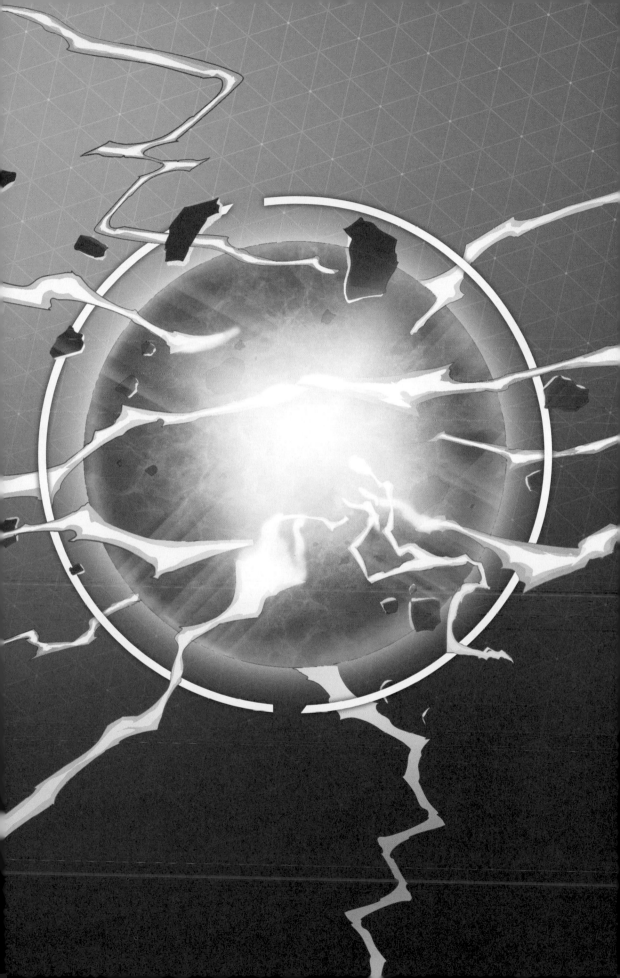

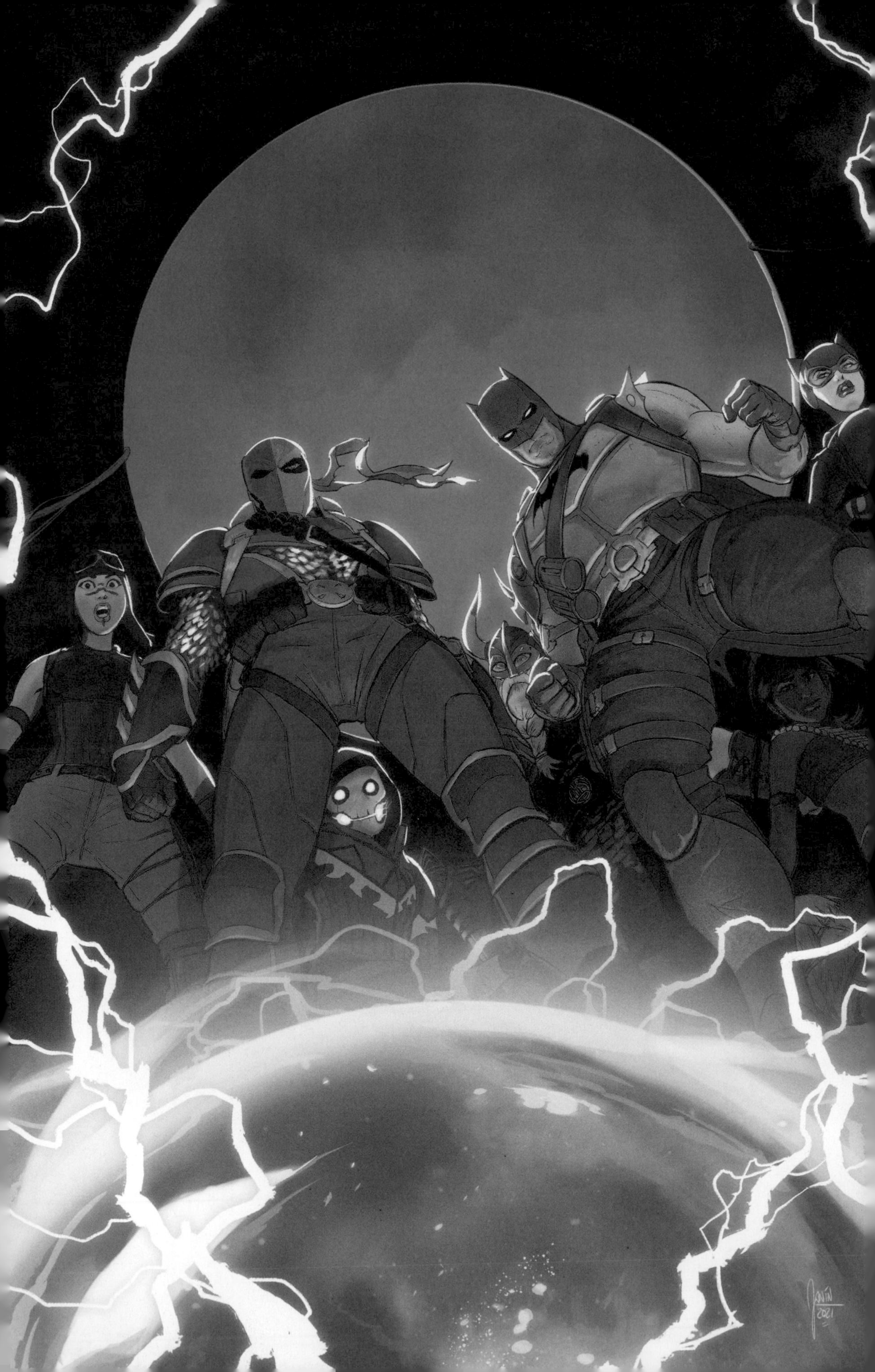

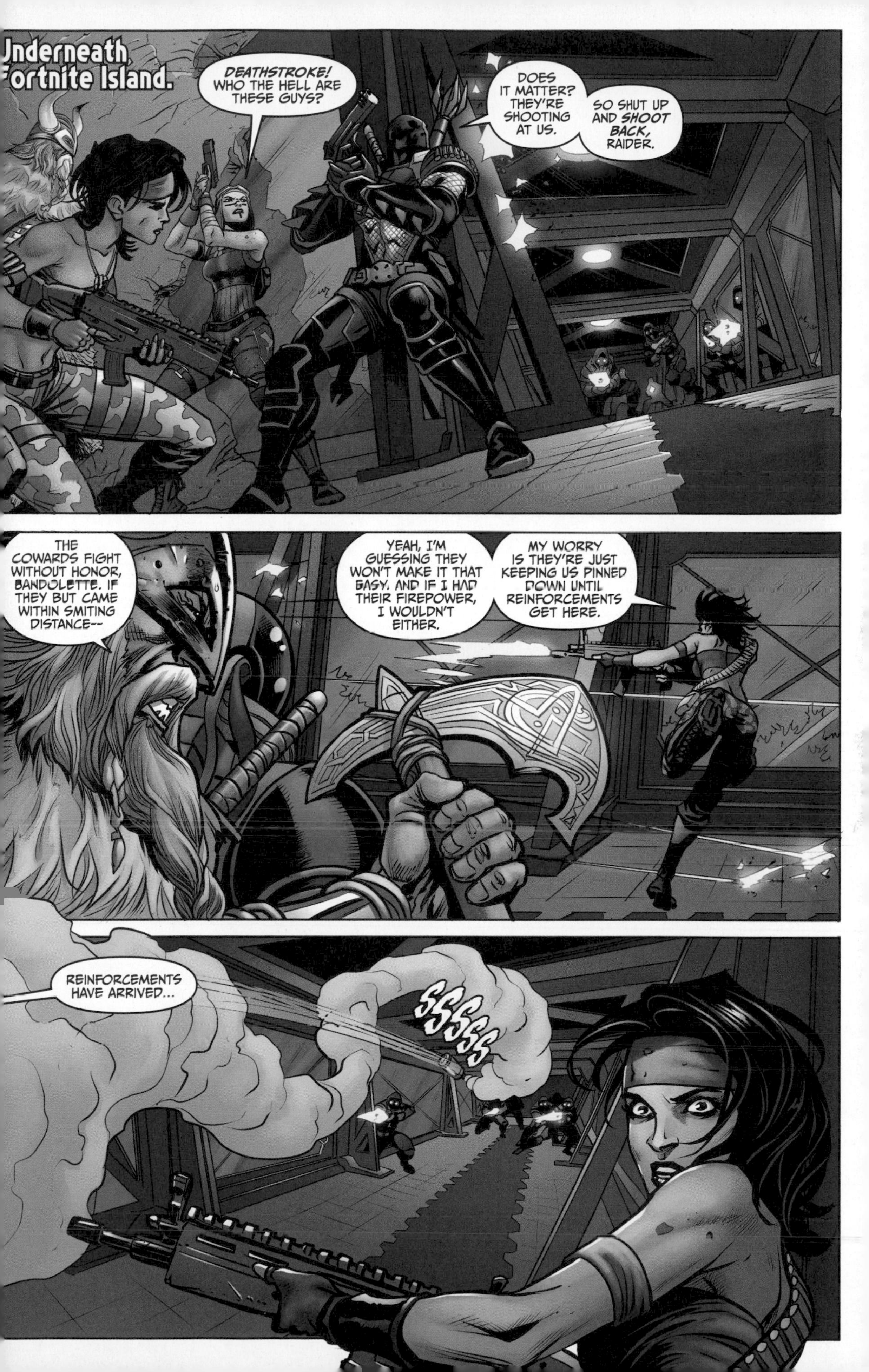
Underneath Fortnite Island.
DEATHSTROKE! WHO THE HELL ARE THESE GUYS?
DOES IT MATTER? THEY'RE SHOOTING AT US.
SO SHUT UP AND SHOOT BACK, RAIDER.
THE COWARDS FIGHT WITHOUT HONOR, BANDOLETTE. IF THEY BUT CAME WITHIN SMITING DISTANCE--
YEAH, I'M GUESSING THEY WON'T MAKE IT THAT EASY. AND IF I HAD THEIR FIREPOWER, I WOULDN'T EITHER.
MY WORRY IS THEY'RE JUST KEEPING US PINNED DOWN UNTIL REINFORCEMENTS GET HERE.
REINFORCEMENTS HAVE ARRIVED...
SSSSS

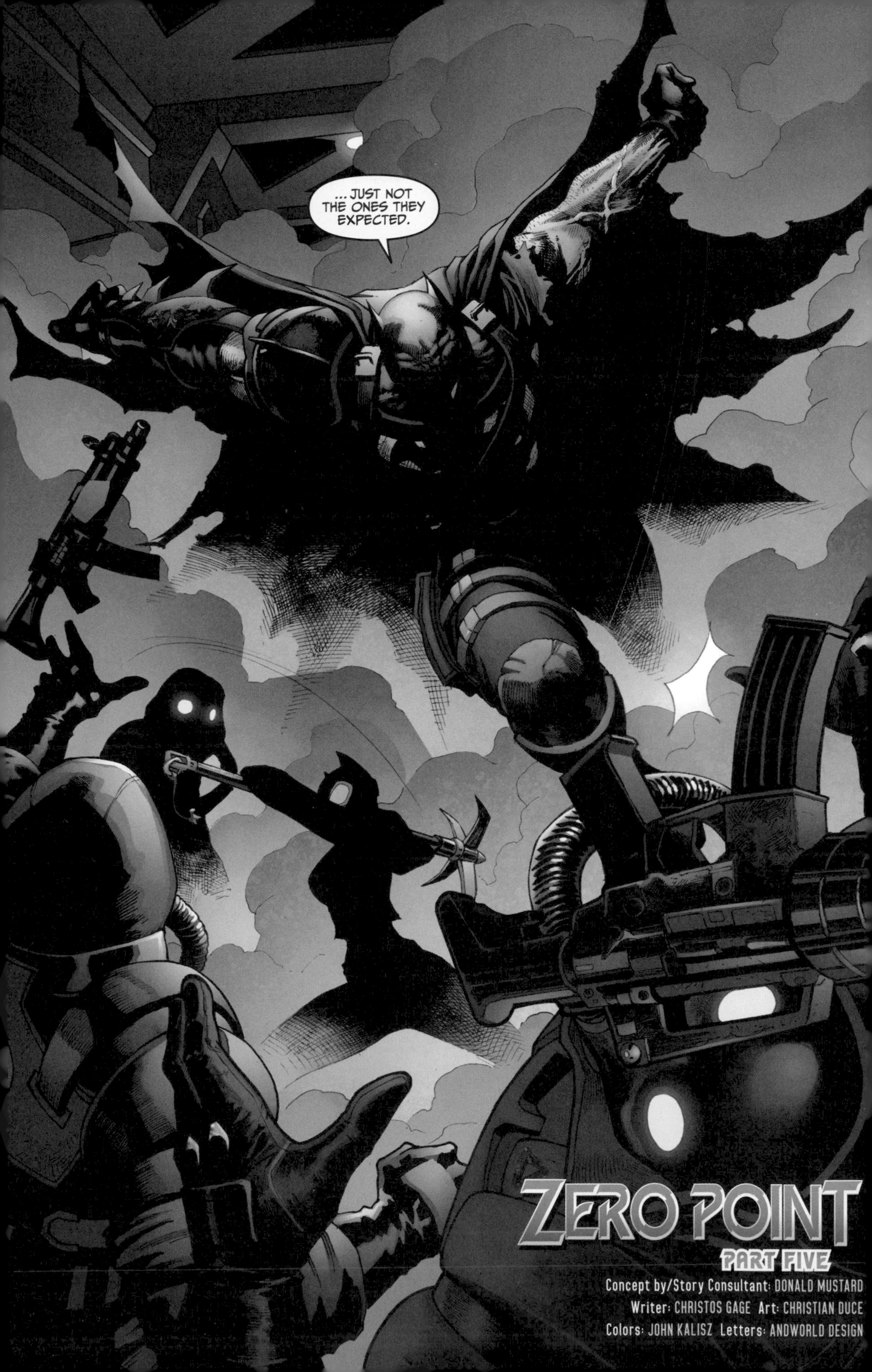
... JUST NOT THE ONES THEY EXPECTED.
ZERO POINT
PART FIVE
Concept by/Story Consultant: DONALD MUSTARD
Writer: CHRISTOS GAGE Art: CHRISTIAN DUCE
Colors: JOHN KALISZ Letters: ANDWORLD DESIGN

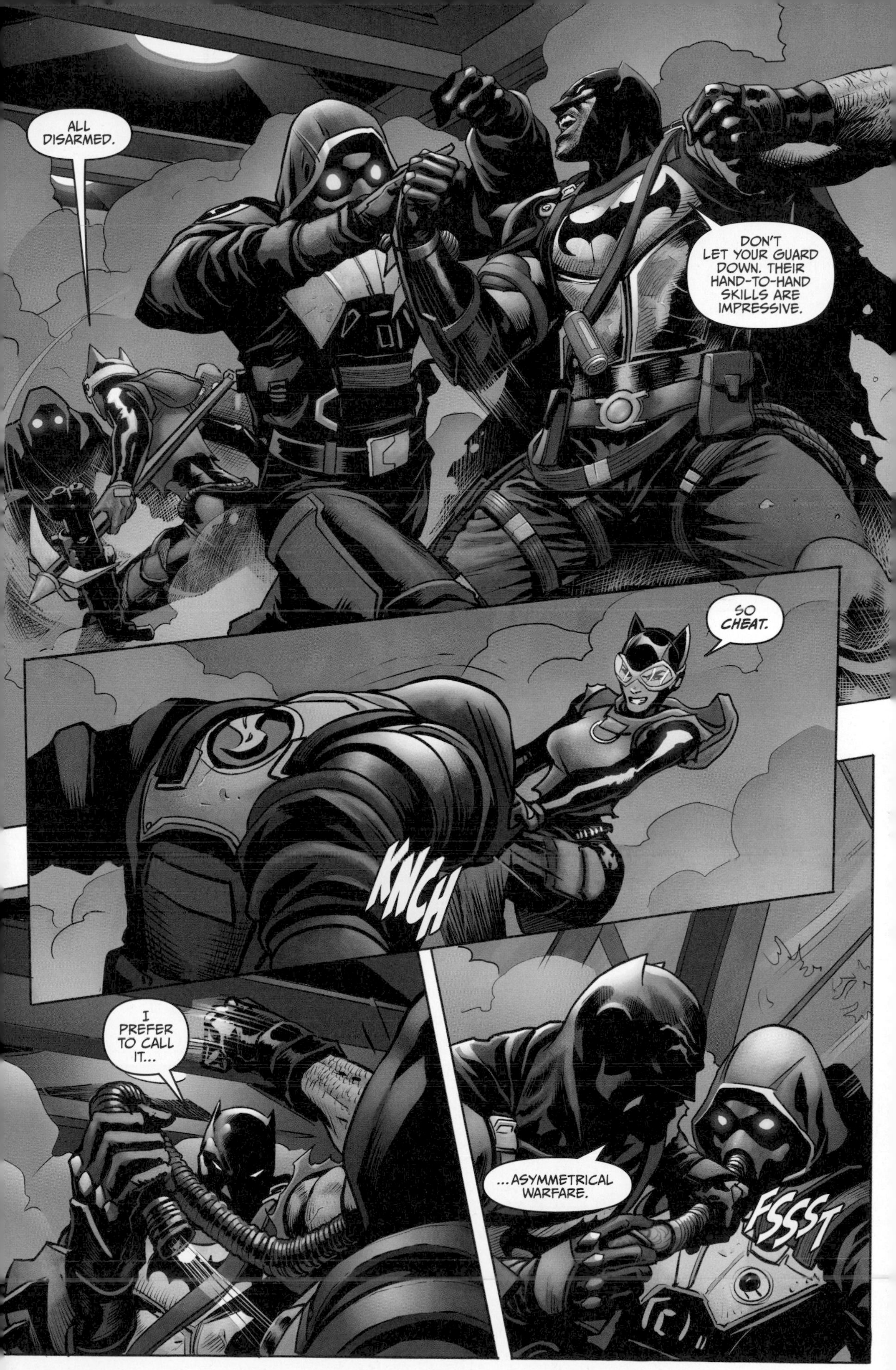
ALL DISARMED.
DON'T LET YOUR GUARD DOWN. THEIR HAND-TO-HAND SKILLS ARE IMPRESSIVE.
SO CHEAT.
KNCH
I PREFER TO CALL IT...
...ASYMMETRICAL WARFARE.
FSSST

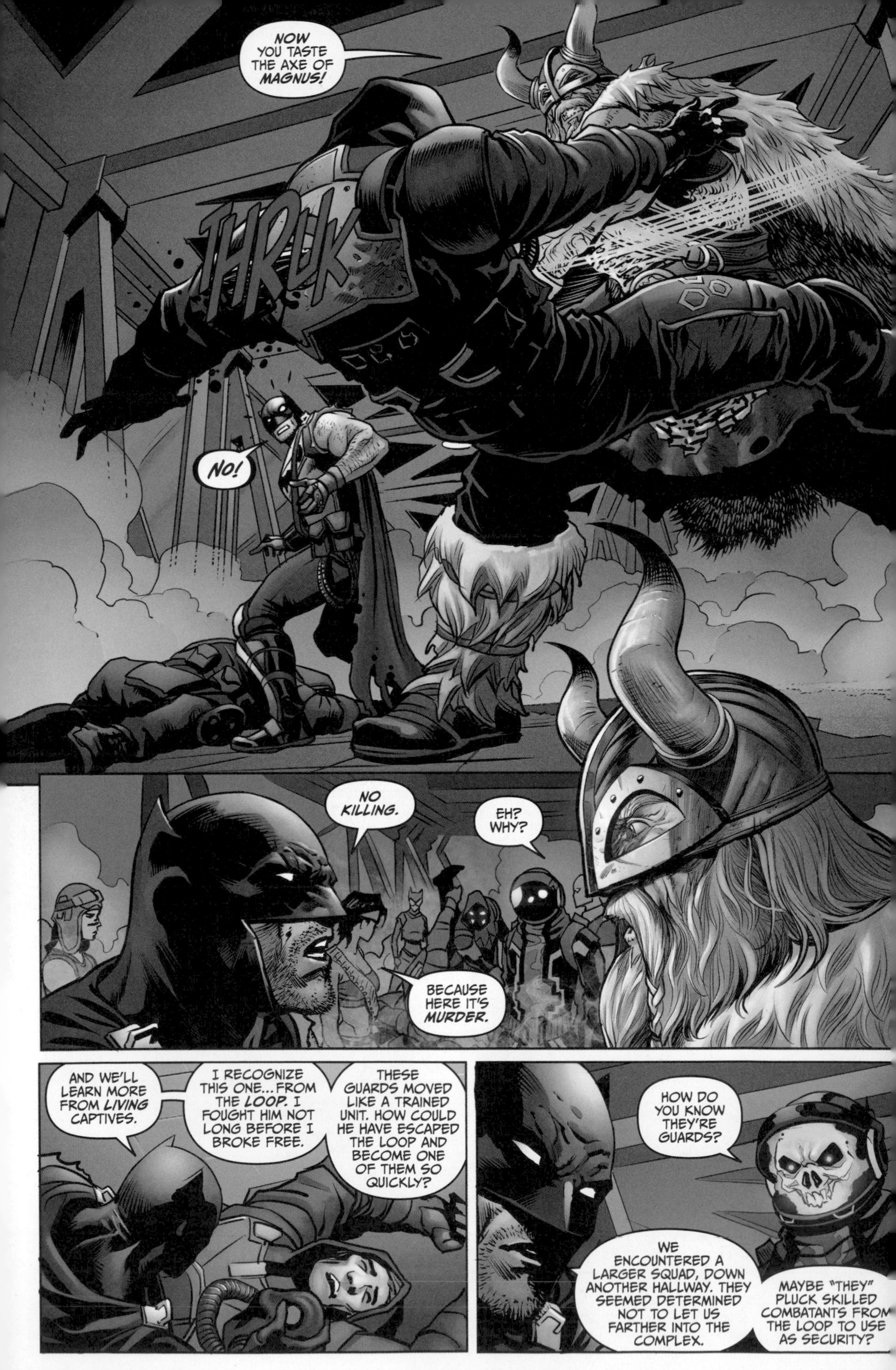
NOW YOU TASTE THE AXE OF MAGNUS!
THRUK
NO!
NO KILLING.
EH? WHY?
BECAUSE HERE IT'S MURDER.
AND WE'LL LEARN MORE FROM LIVING CAPTIVES.
I RECOGNIZE THIS ONE... FROM THE LOOP. I FOUGHT HIM NOT LONG BEFORE I BROKE FREE.
THESE GUARDS MOVED LIKE A TRAINED UNIT. HOW COULD HE HAVE ESCAPED THE LOOP AND BECOME ONE OF THEM SO QUICKLY?
HOW DO YOU KNOW THEY'RE GUARDS?
WE ENCOUNTERED A LARGER SQUAD, DOWN ANOTHER HALLWAY. THEY SEEMED DETERMINED NOT TO LET US FARTHER INTO THE COMPLEX.
MAYBE "THEY" PLUCK SKILLED COMBATANTS FROM THE LOOP TO USE AS SECURITY?

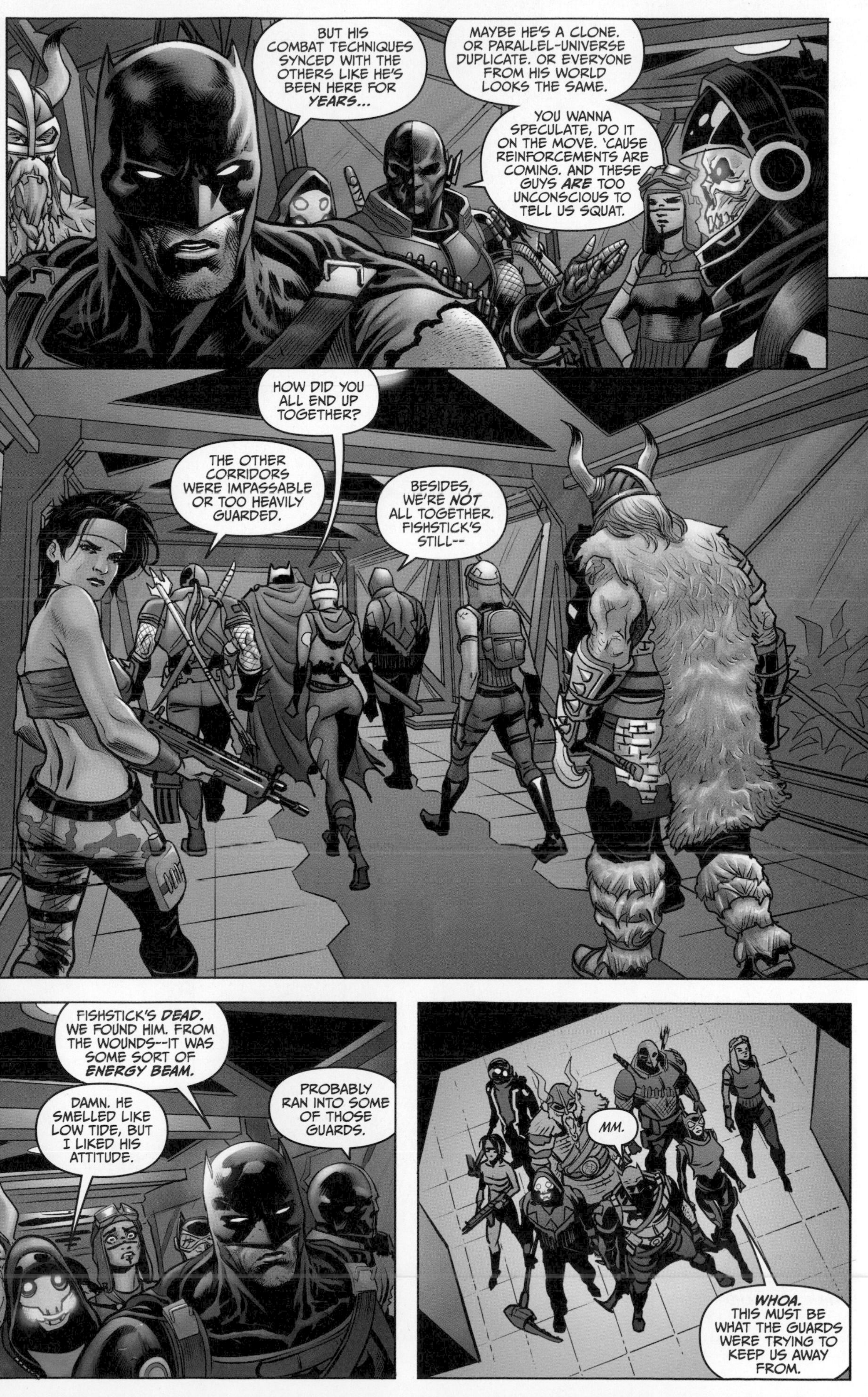

BUT HIS COMBAT TECHNIQUES SYNCED WITH THE OTHERS LIKE HE'S BEEN HERE FOR YEARS...
MAYBE HE'S A CLONE. OR PARALLEL-UNIVERSE DUPLICATE. OR EVERYONE FROM HIS WORLD LOOKS THE SAME.
YOU WANNA SPECULATE, DO IT ON THE MOVE. 'CAUSE REINFORCEMENTS ARE COMING. AND THESE GUYS ARE TOO UNCONSCIOUS TO TELL US SQUAT.
HOW DID YOU ALL END UP TOGETHER?
THE OTHER CORRIDORS WERE IMPASSABLE OR TOO HEAVILY GUARDED.
BESIDES, WE'RE NOT ALL TOGETHER. FISHSTICK'S STILL--
FISHSTICK'S DEAD. WE FOUND HIM. FROM THE WOUNDS--IT WAS SOME SORT OF ENERGY BEAM.
DAMN. HE SMELLED LIKE LOW TIDE, BUT I LIKED HIS ATTITUDE.
PROBABLY RAN INTO SOME OF THOSE GUARDS.
MM.
WHOA. THIS MUST BE WHAT THE GUARDS WERE TRYING TO KEEP US AWAY FROM.

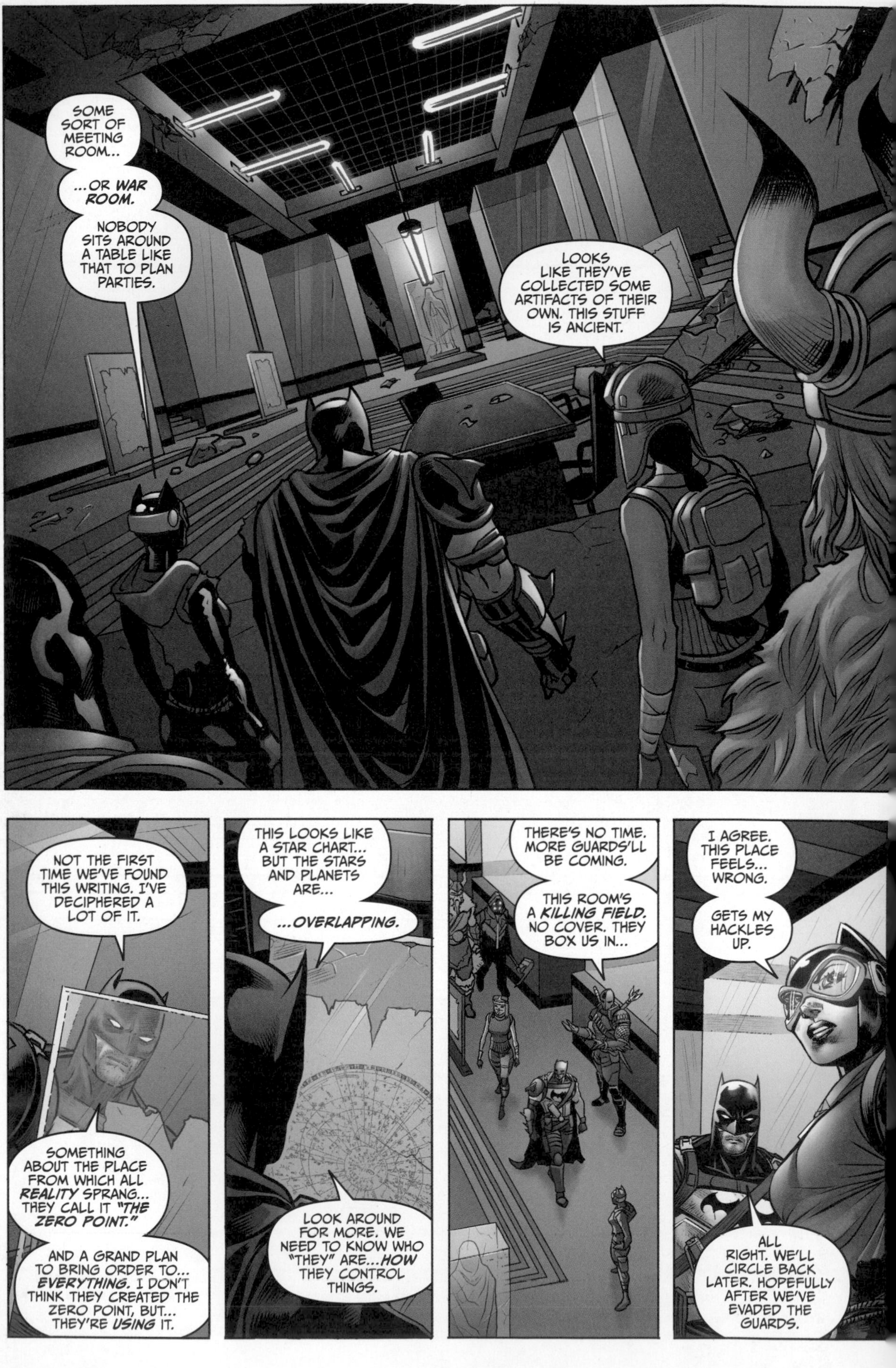
SOME SORT OF MEETING ROOM...
...OR WAR ROOM.
NOBODY SITS AROUND A TABLE LIKE THAT TO PLAN PARTIES.
LOOKS LIKE THEY'VE COLLECTED SOME ARTIFACTS OF THEIR OWN. THIS STUFF IS ANCIENT.
NOT THE FIRST TIME WE'VE FOUND THIS WRITING. I'VE DECIPHERED A LOT OF IT.
SOMETHING ABOUT THE PLACE FROM WHICH ALL REALITY SPRANG... THEY CALL IT "THE ZERO POINT."
AND A GRAND PLAN TO BRING ORDER TO... EVERYTHING. I DON'T THINK THEY CREATED THE ZERO POINT, BUT... THEY'RE USING IT.
THIS LOOKS LIKE A STAR CHART... BUT THE STARS AND PLANETS ARE...
...OVERLAPPING.
LOOK AROUND FOR MORE. WE NEED TO KNOW WHO "THEY" ARE...HOW THEY CONTROL THINGS.
THERE'S NO TIME. MORE GUARDS'LL BE COMING.
THIS ROOM'S A KILLING FIELD. NO COVER. THEY BOX US IN...
I AGREE. THIS PLACE FEELS... WRONG.
GETS MY HACKLES UP.
ALL RIGHT. WE'LL CIRCLE BACK LATER. HOPEFULLY AFTER WE'VE EVADED THE GUARDS.

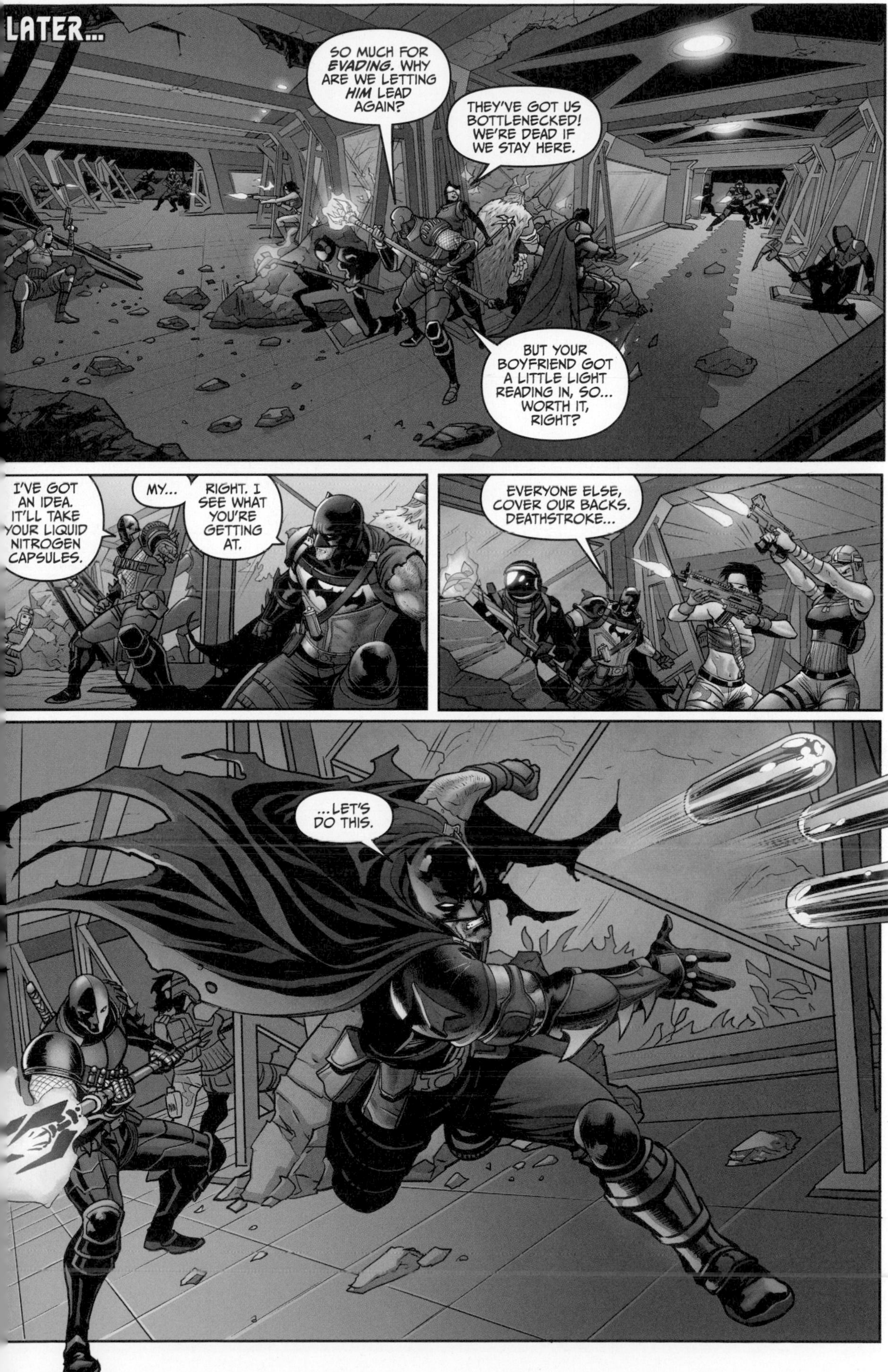
LATER...
SO MUCH FOR *EVADING.* WHY ARE WE LETTING *HIM* LEAD AGAIN?
THEY'VE GOT US BOTTLENECKED! WE'RE DEAD IF WE STAY HERE.
BUT YOUR BOYFRIEND GOT A LITTLE LIGHT READING IN, SO... WORTH IT, RIGHT?
I'VE GOT AN IDEA. IT'LL TAKE YOUR LIQUID NITROGEN CAPSULES.
MY...
RIGHT. I SEE WHAT YOU'RE GETTING AT.
EVERYONE ELSE, COVER OUR BACKS. DEATHSTROKE...
...LET'S DO THIS.

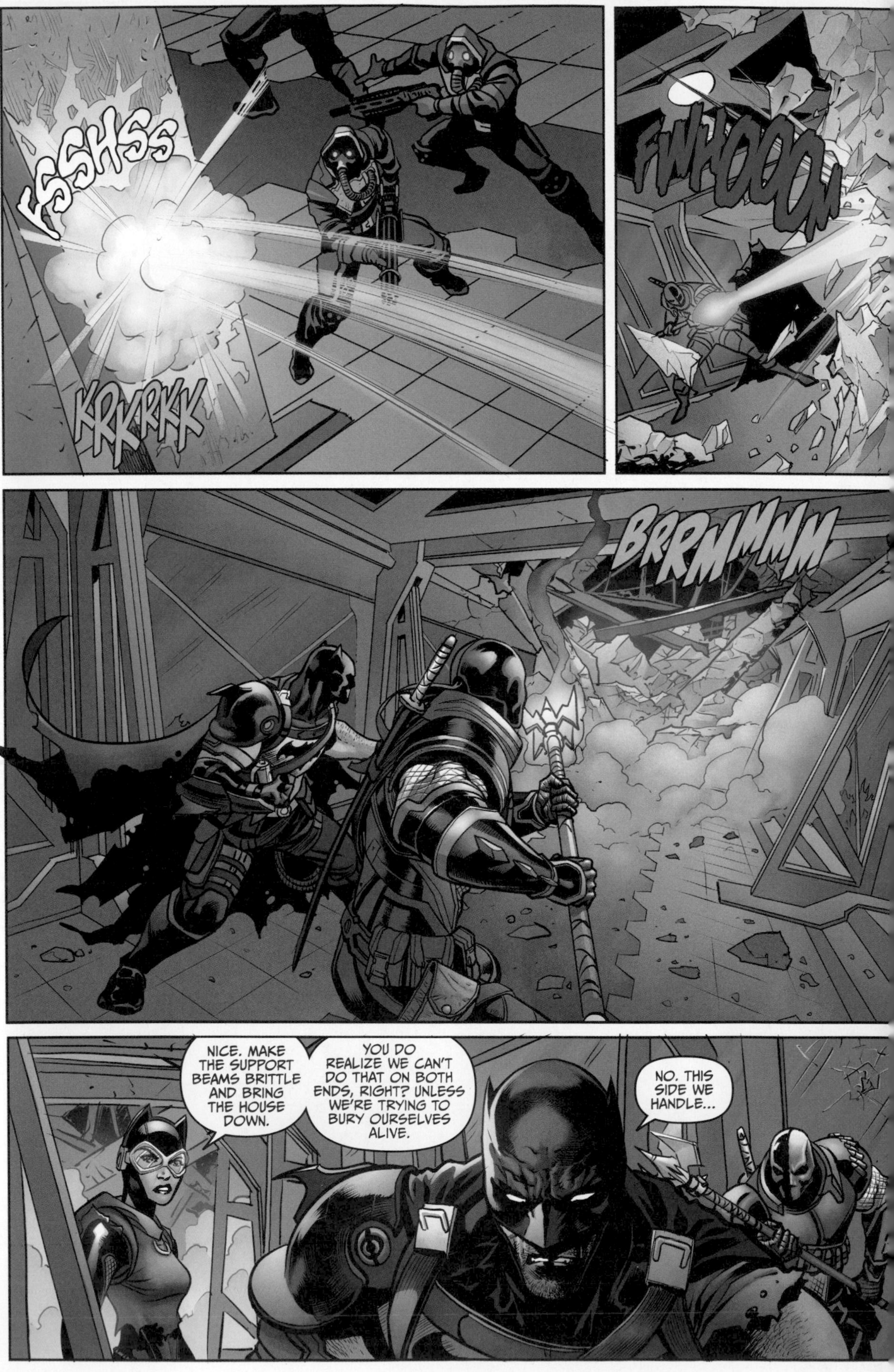
FSSHSS
KRKRKK
FWHOOOM
BRRMMMM
NICE. MAKE THE SUPPORT BEAMS BRITTLE AND BRING THE HOUSE DOWN.
YOU DO REALIZE WE CAN'T DO THAT ON BOTH ENDS, RIGHT? UNLESS WE'RE TRYING TO BURY OURSELVES ALIVE.
NO. THIS SIDE WE HANDLE...

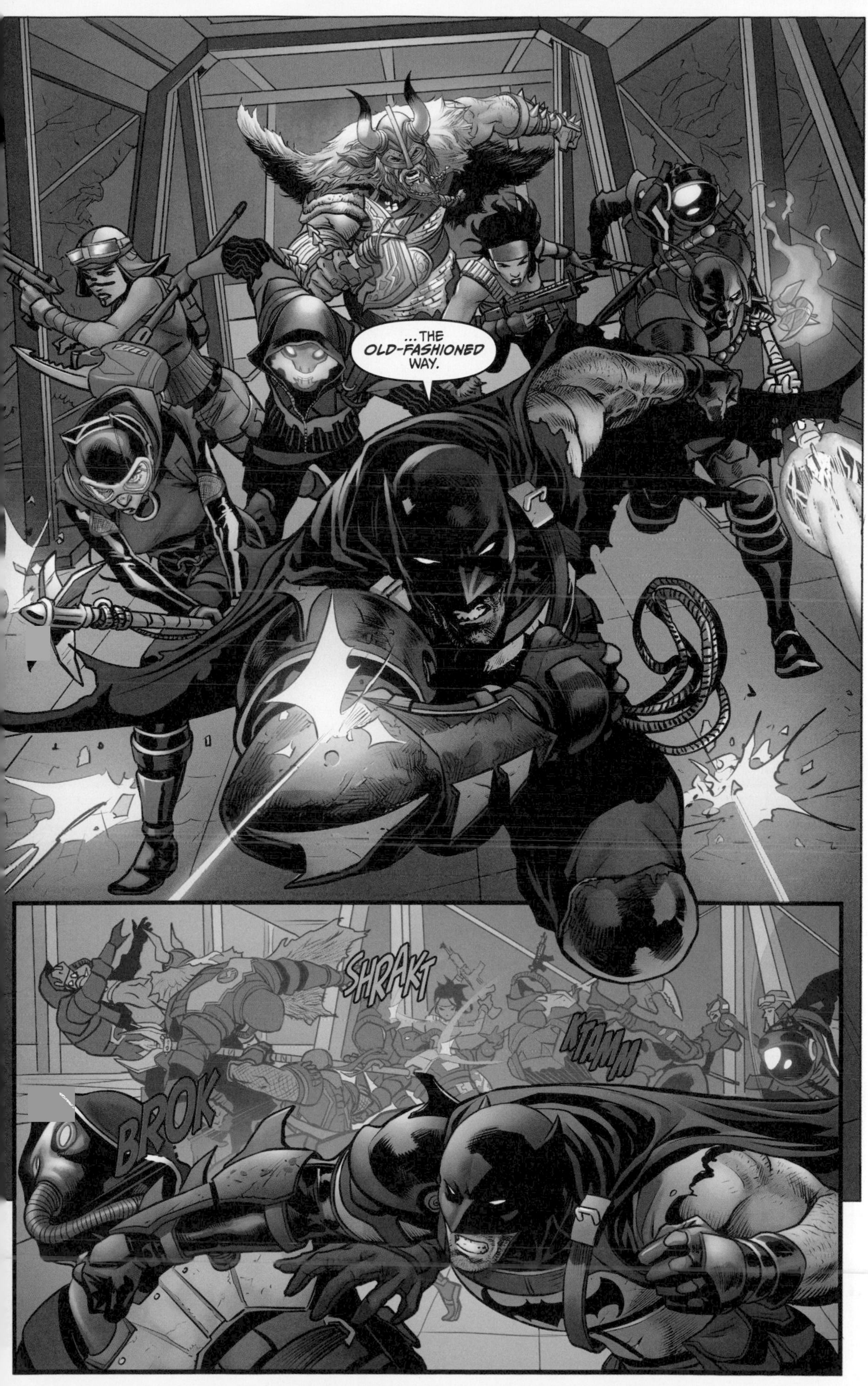
...THE OLD-FASHIONED WAY.
SHRAKT
KTAMM
BROK

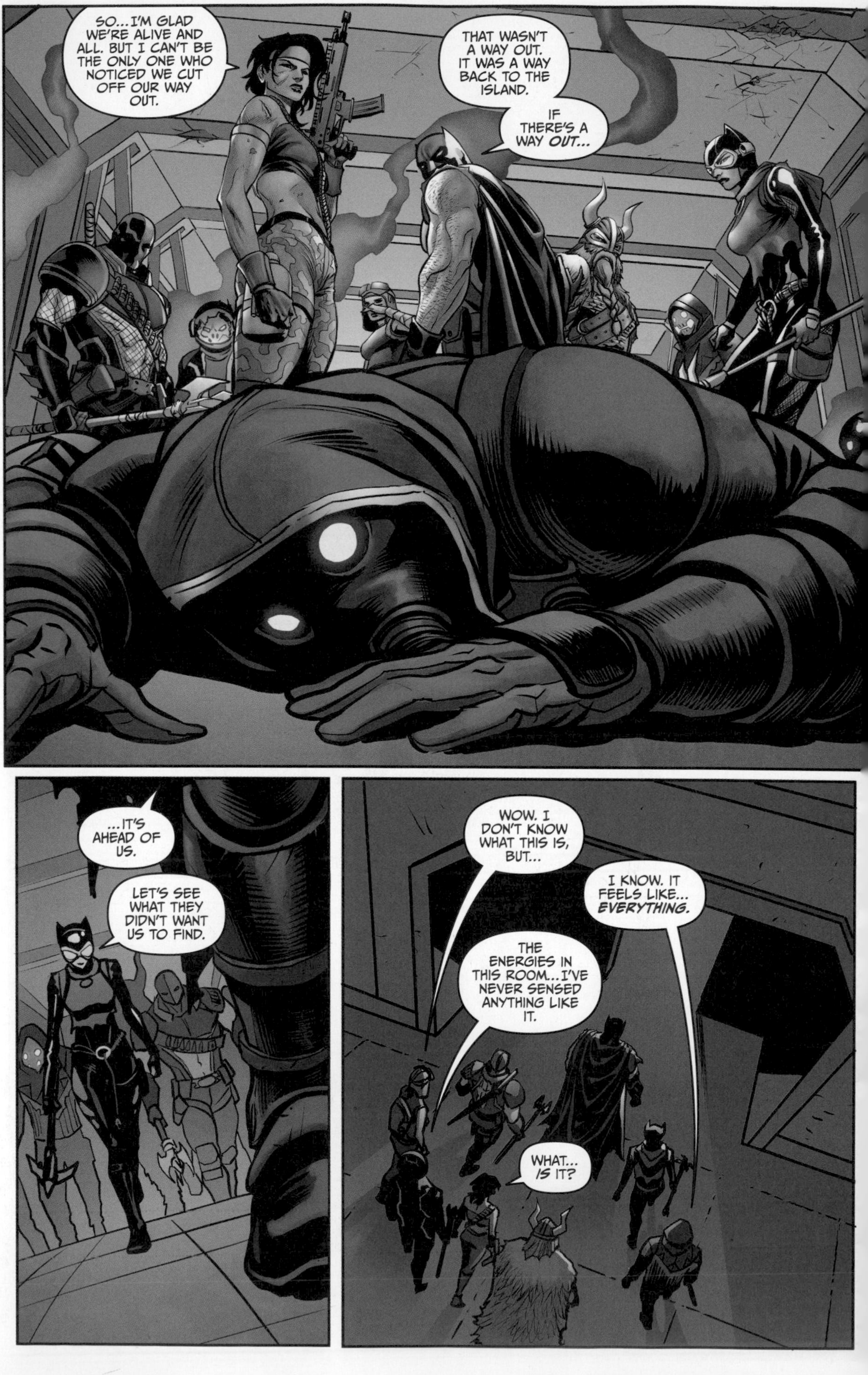
SO... I'M GLAD WE'RE ALIVE AND ALL. BUT I CAN'T BE THE ONLY ONE WHO NOTICED WE CUT OFF OUR WAY OUT.
THAT WASN'T A WAY OUT. IT WAS A WAY BACK TO THE ISLAND.
IF THERE'S A WAY OUT...
...IT'S AHEAD OF US.
LET'S SEE WHAT THEY DIDN'T WANT US TO FIND.
WOW. I DON'T KNOW WHAT THIS IS, BUT...
I KNOW. IT FEELS LIKE... EVERYTHING.
THE ENERGIES IN THIS ROOM... I'VE NEVER SENSED ANYTHING LIKE IT.
WHAT... IS IT?

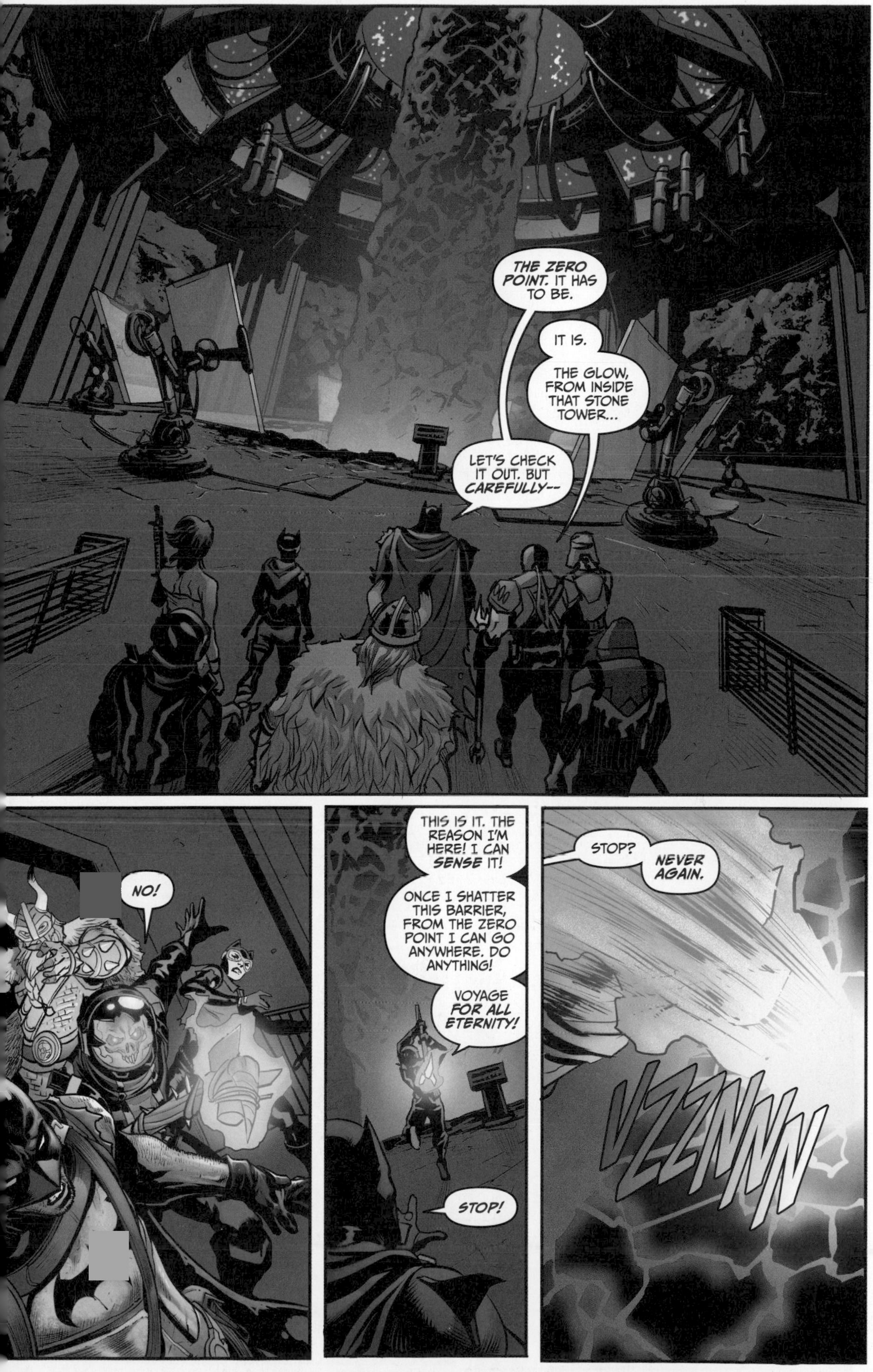
THE ZERO POINT. IT HAS TO BE.
IT IS.
THE GLOW, FROM INSIDE THAT STONE TOWER...
LET'S CHECK IT OUT. BUT CAREFULLY--
NO!
THIS IS IT. THE REASON I'M HERE! I CAN SENSE IT!
ONCE I SHATTER THIS BARRIER, FROM THE ZERO POINT I CAN GO ANYWHERE. DO ANYTHING!
VOYAGE FOR ALL ETERNITY!
STOP!
STOP?
NEVER AGAIN.
VZZNNNN

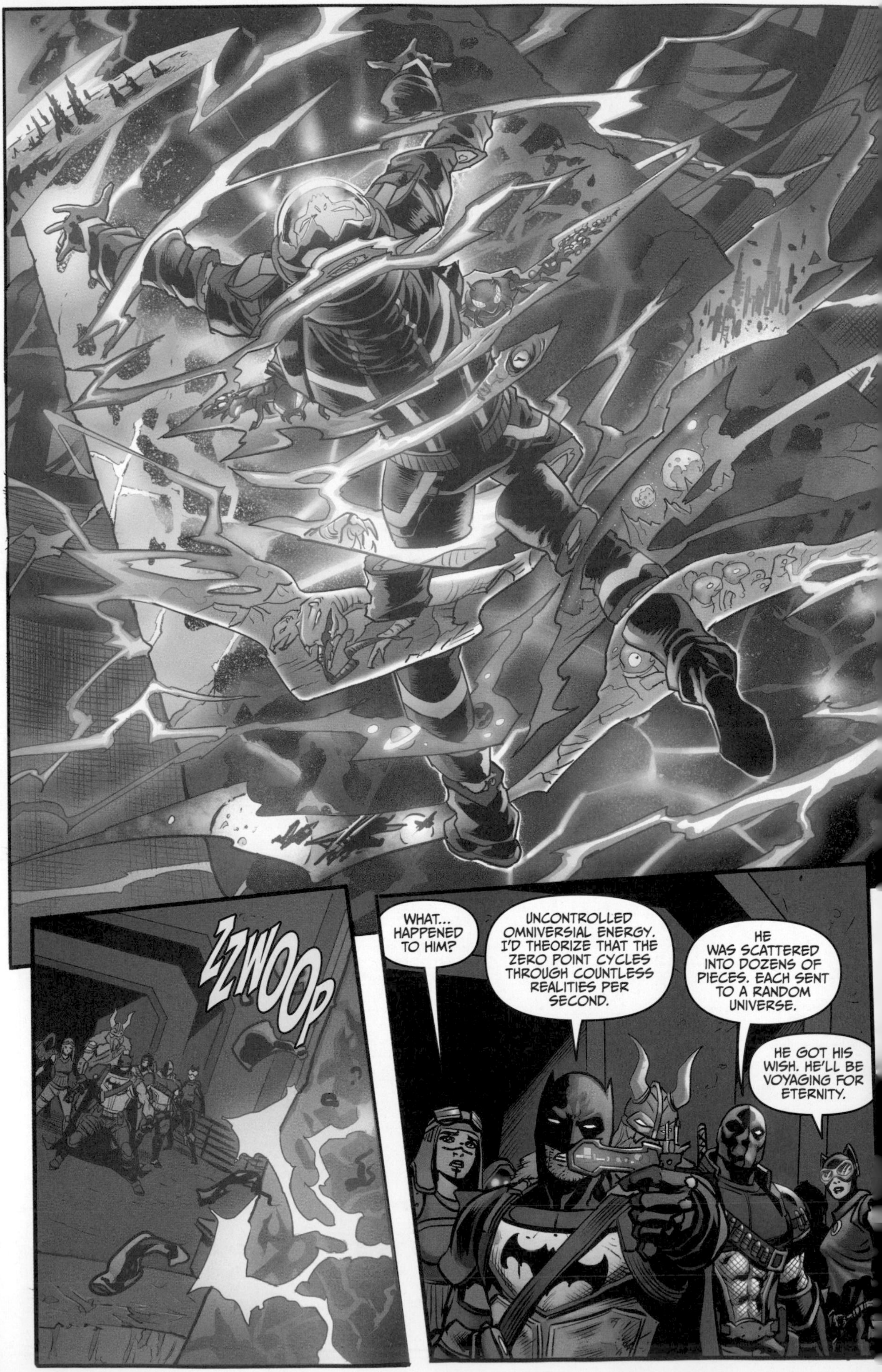

ZZWOOP
WHAT... HAPPENED TO HIM?
UNCONTROLLED OMNIVERSIAL ENERGY. I'D THEORIZE THAT THE ZERO POINT CYCLES THROUGH COUNTLESS REALITIES PER SECOND.
HE WAS SCATTERED INTO DOZENS OF PIECES. EACH SENT TO A RANDOM UNIVERSE.
HE GOT HIS WISH. HE'LL BE VOYAGING FOR ETERNITY.

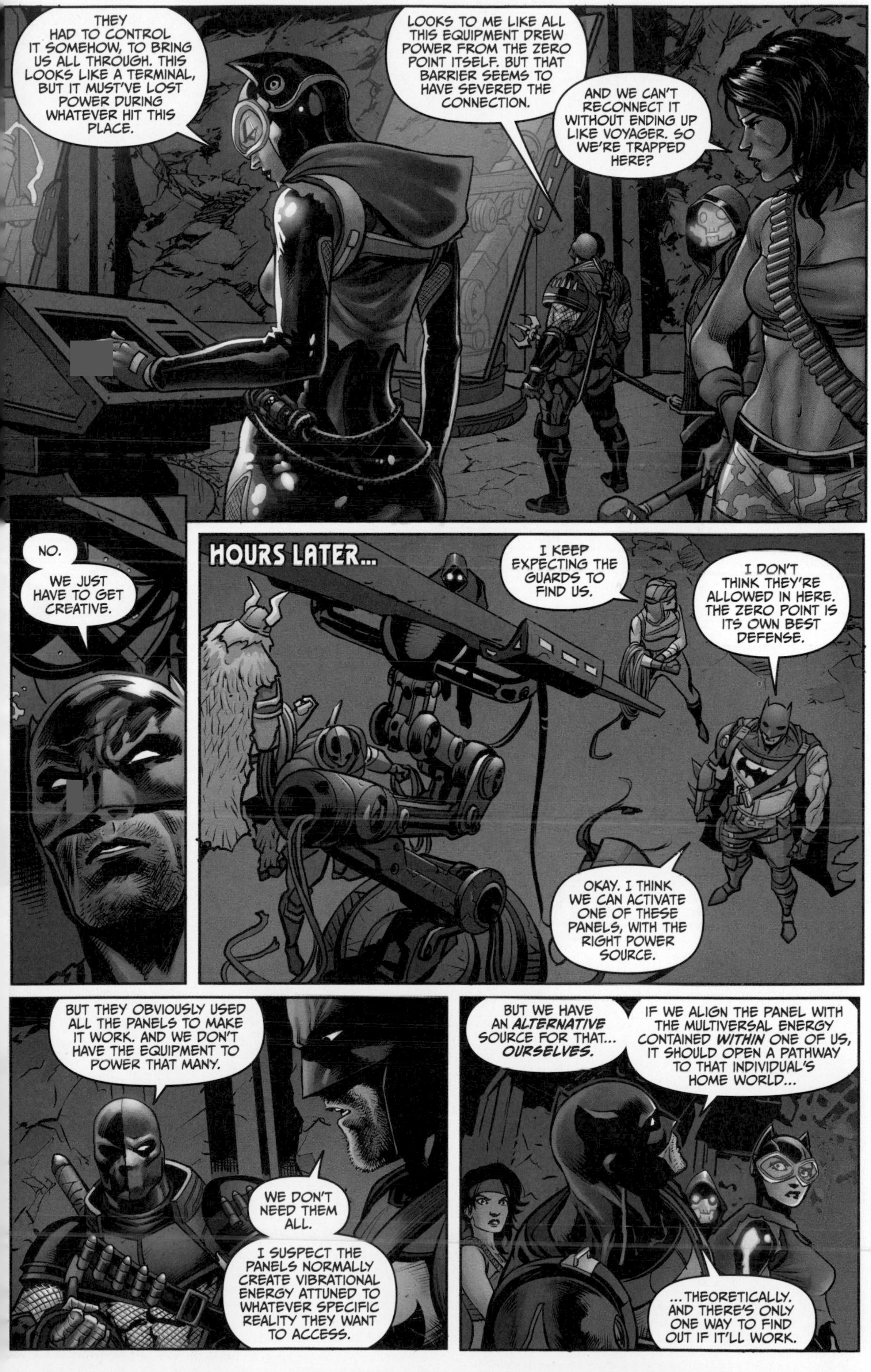
THEY HAD TO CONTROL IT SOMEHOW, TO BRING US ALL THROUGH. THIS LOOKS LIKE A TERMINAL, BUT IT MUST'VE LOST POWER DURING WHATEVER HIT THIS PLACE.
LOOKS TO ME LIKE ALL THIS EQUIPMENT DREW POWER FROM THE ZERO POINT ITSELF. BUT THAT BARRIER SEEMS TO HAVE SEVERED THE CONNECTION.
AND WE CAN'T RECONNECT IT WITHOUT ENDING UP LIKE VOYAGER. SO WE'RE TRAPPED HERE?
NO.
WE JUST HAVE TO GET CREATIVE.
HOURS LATER...
I KEEP EXPECTING THE GUARDS TO FIND US.
I DON'T THINK THEY'RE ALLOWED IN HERE. THE ZERO POINT IS ITS OWN BEST DEFENSE.
OKAY. I THINK WE CAN ACTIVATE ONE OF THESE PANELS, WITH THE RIGHT POWER SOURCE.
BUT THEY OBVIOUSLY USED ALL THE PANELS TO MAKE IT WORK. AND WE DON'T HAVE THE EQUIPMENT TO POWER THAT MANY.
WE DON'T NEED THEM ALL.
I SUSPECT THE PANELS NORMALLY CREATE VIBRATIONAL ENERGY ATTUNED TO WHATEVER SPECIFIC REALITY THEY WANT TO ACCESS.
BUT WE HAVE AN *ALTERNATIVE* SOURCE FOR THAT... ***OURSELVES.***
IF WE ALIGN THE PANEL WITH THE MULTIVERSAL ENERGY CONTAINED *WITHIN* ONE OF US, IT SHOULD OPEN A PATHWAY TO THAT INDIVIDUAL'S HOME WORLD...
...THEORETICALLY. AND THERE'S ONLY ONE WAY TO FIND OUT IF IT'LL WORK.

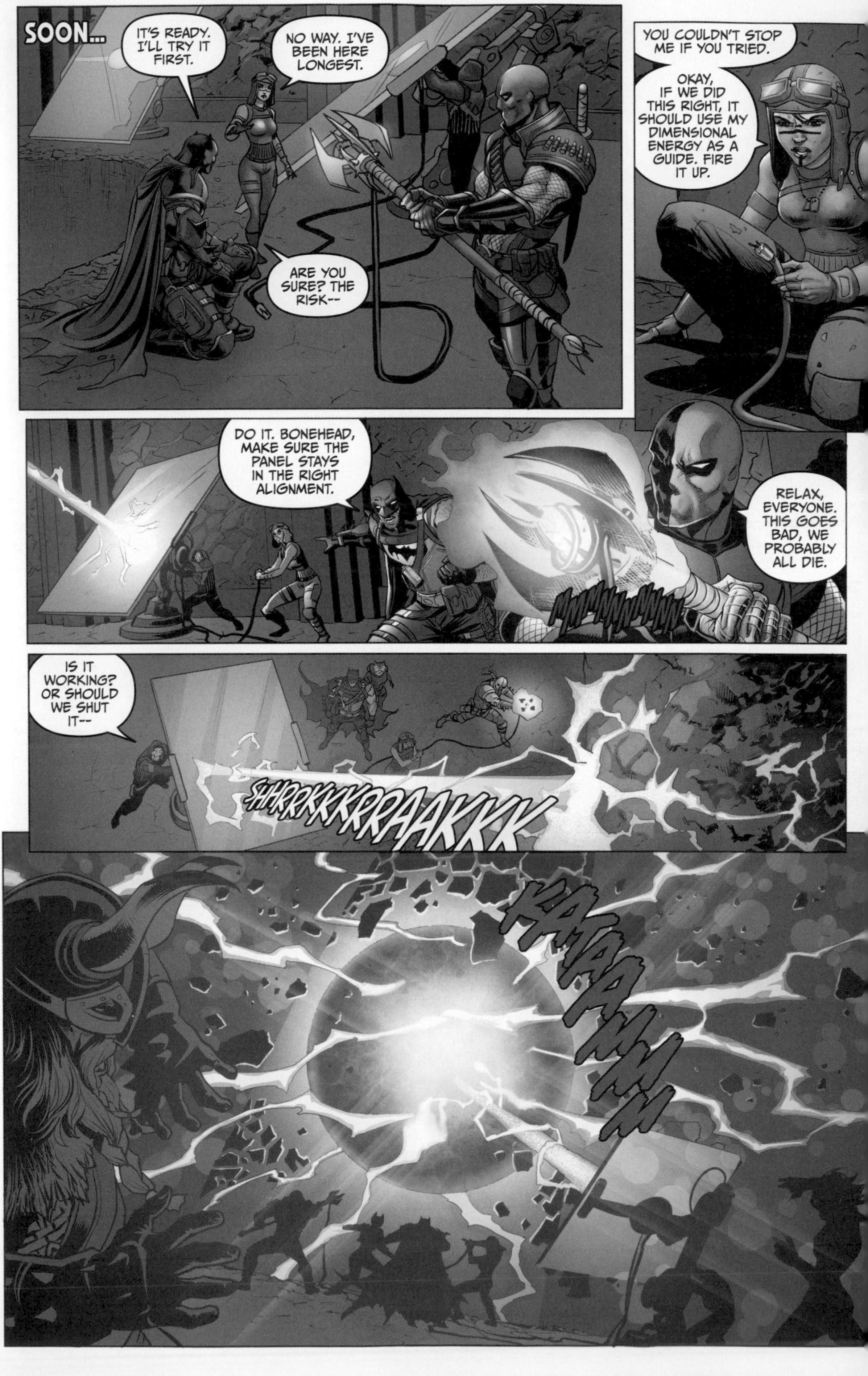
SOON...
IT'S READY. I'LL TRY IT FIRST.
NO WAY. I'VE BEEN HERE LONGEST.
ARE YOU SURE? THE RISK--
YOU COULDN'T STOP ME IF YOU TRIED.
OKAY, IF WE DID THIS RIGHT, IT SHOULD USE MY DIMENSIONAL ENERGY AS A GUIDE. FIRE IT UP.
DO IT. BONEHEAD, MAKE SURE THE PANEL STAYS IN THE RIGHT ALIGNMENT.
RELAX, EVERYONE. THIS GOES BAD, WE PROBABLY ALL DIE.
MMMNNNNNN
IS IT WORKING? OR SHOULD WE SHUT IT--
SHHRRKKKRRAAKKK
KAAAAMMM

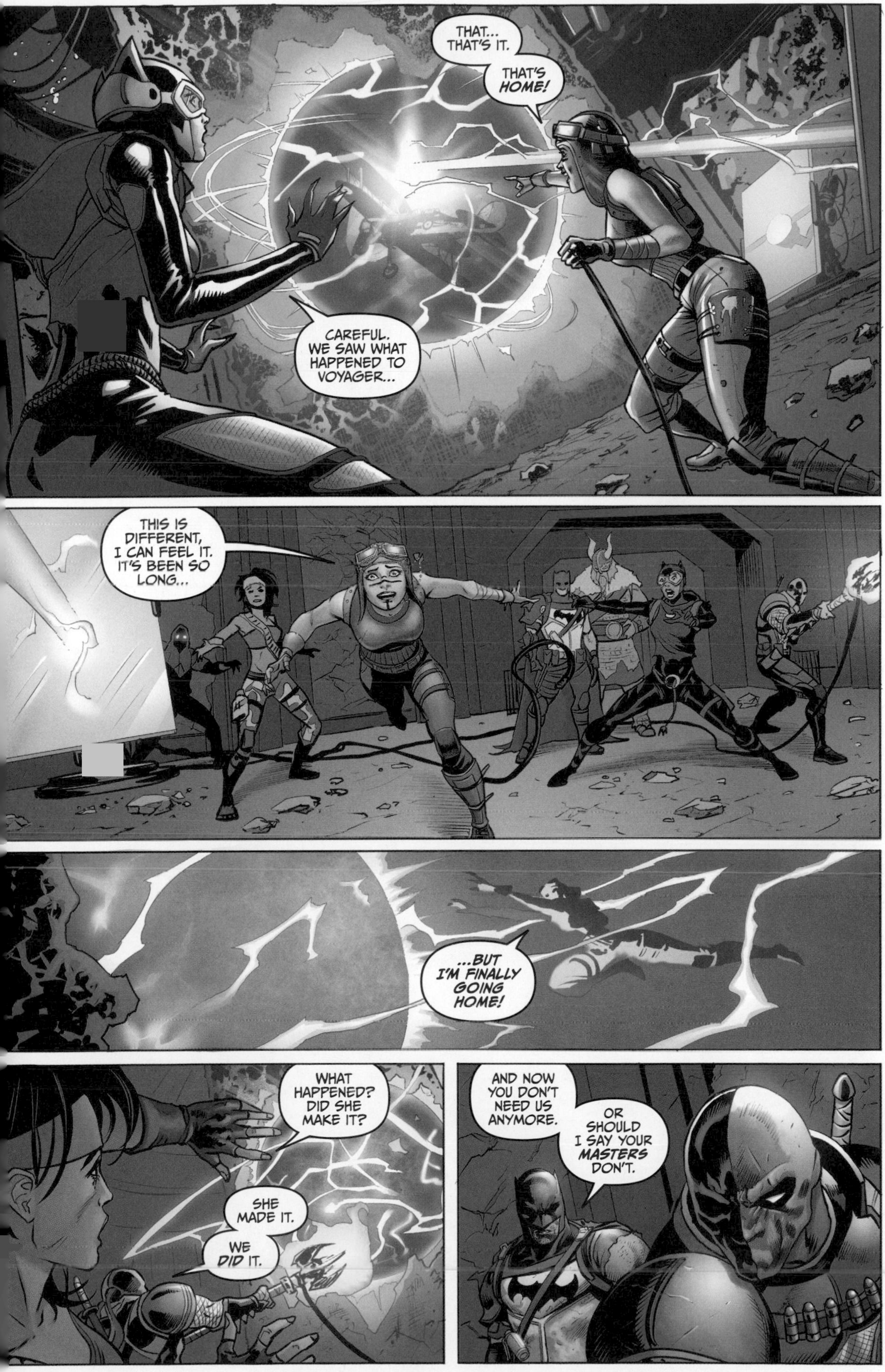
THAT... THAT'S IT.
THAT'S *HOME!*
CAREFUL. WE SAW WHAT HAPPENED TO VOYAGER...
THIS IS DIFFERENT, I CAN FEEL IT. IT'S BEEN SO LONG...
...BUT *I'M FINALLY GOING HOME!*
WHAT HAPPENED? DID SHE MAKE IT?
SHE MADE IT.
WE *DID* IT.
AND NOW YOU DON'T NEED US ANYMORE.
OR SHOULD I SAY YOUR *MASTERS* DON'T.

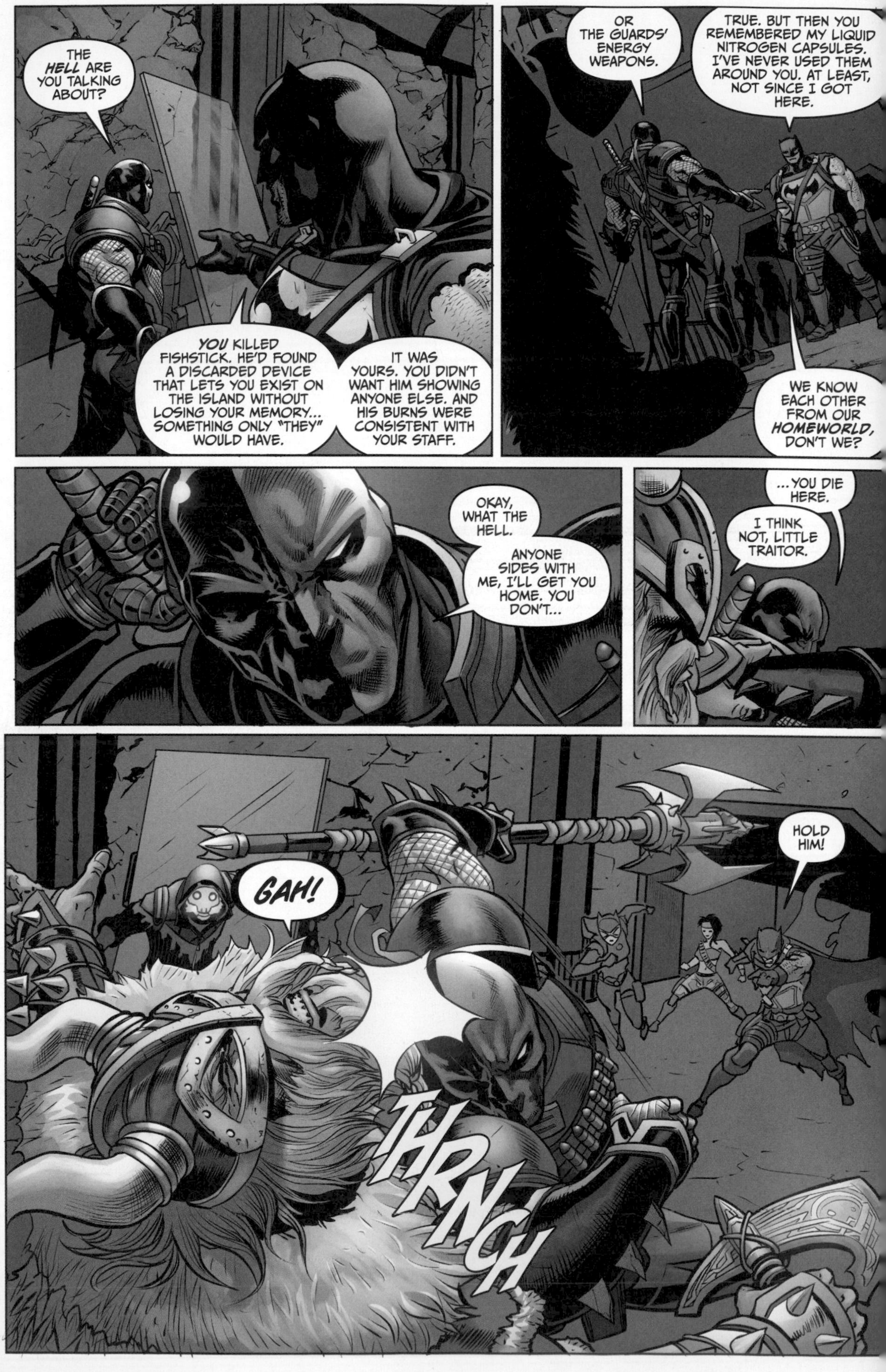
THE HELL ARE YOU TALKING ABOUT?
YOU KILLED FISHSTICK. HE'D FOUND A DISCARDED DEVICE THAT LETS YOU EXIST ON THE ISLAND WITHOUT LOSING YOUR MEMORY... SOMETHING ONLY "THEY" WOULD HAVE.
IT WAS YOURS. YOU DIDN'T WANT HIM SHOWING ANYONE ELSE. AND HIS BURNS WERE CONSISTENT WITH YOUR STAFF.
OR THE GUARDS' ENERGY WEAPONS.
TRUE. BUT THEN YOU REMEMBERED MY LIQUID NITROGEN CAPSULES. I'VE NEVER USED THEM AROUND YOU. AT LEAST, NOT SINCE I GOT HERE.
WE KNOW EACH OTHER FROM OUR HOMEWORLD, DON'T WE?
OKAY, WHAT THE HELL.
ANYONE SIDES WITH ME, I'LL GET YOU HOME. YOU DON'T...
...YOU DIE HERE.
I THINK NOT, LITTLE TRAITOR.
GAH!
HOLD HIM!
THRNCH

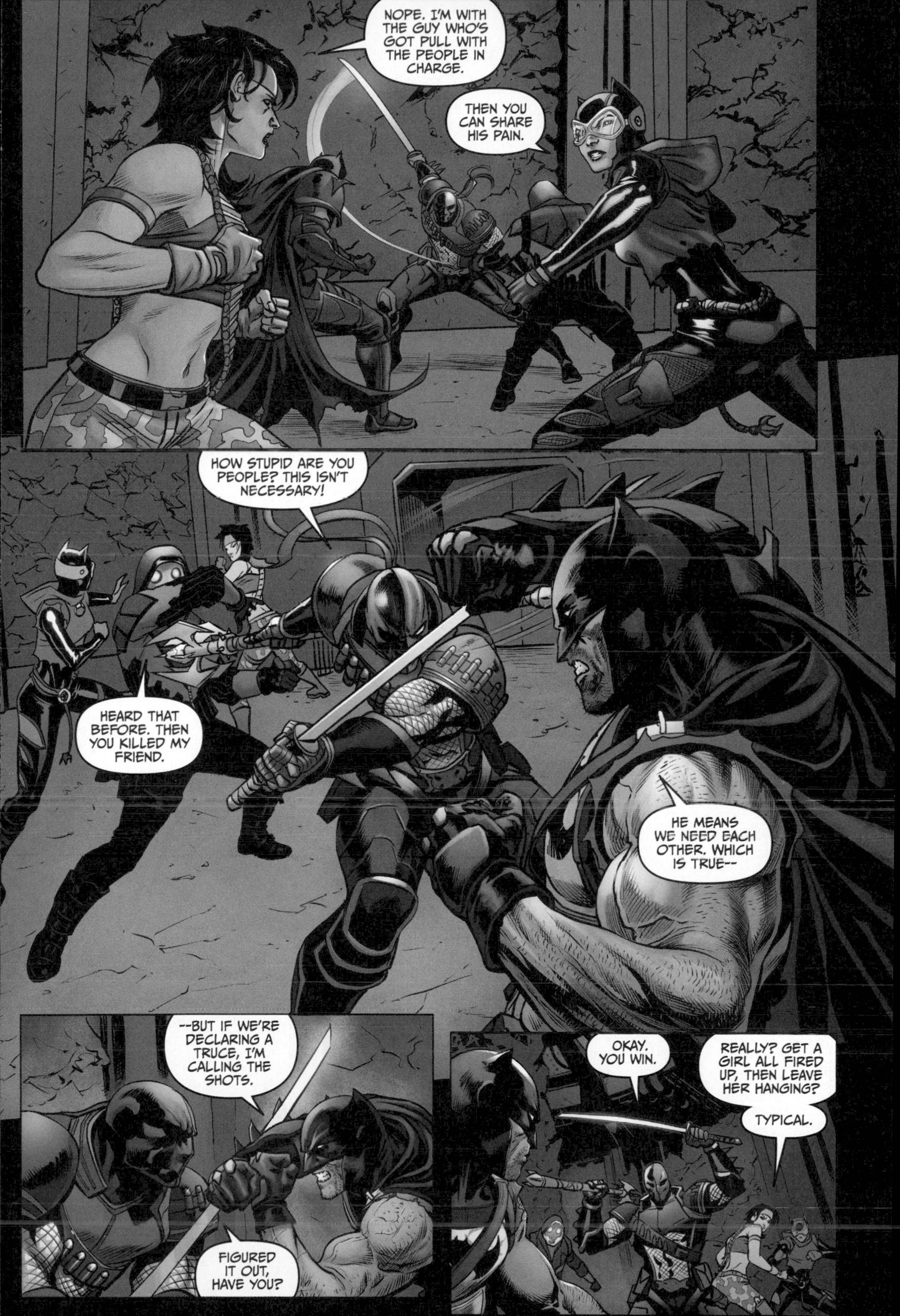
NOPE. I'M WITH THE GUY WHO'S GOT PULL WITH THE PEOPLE IN CHARGE.
THEN YOU CAN SHARE HIS PAIN.
HOW STUPID ARE YOU PEOPLE? THIS ISN'T NECESSARY!
HEARD THAT BEFORE. THEN YOU KILLED MY FRIEND.
HE MEANS WE NEED EACH OTHER. WHICH IS TRUE--
--BUT IF WE'RE DECLARING A TRUCE, I'M CALLING THE SHOTS.
FIGURED IT OUT, HAVE YOU?
OKAY. YOU WIN.
REALLY? GET A GIRL ALL FIRED UP, THEN LEAVE HER HANGING?
TYPICAL.

FIGURED OUT WHAT? I ALWAYS FEEL THREE STEPS BEHIND YOU PEOPLE.

THAT WE NEED EACH OTHER TO GET HOME. BANDOLETTE, YOU FIRST.

UH, SURE. SORRY FOR THE, Y'KNOW, TURNING-ON-YOU THING.

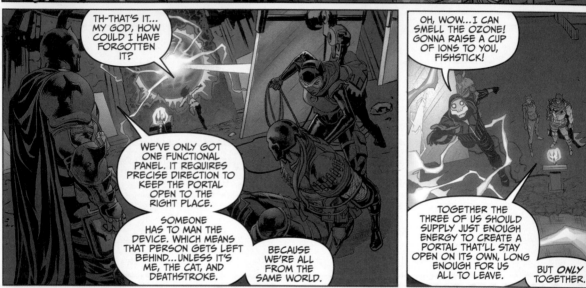

TH-THAT'S IT... MY GOD, HOW COULD I HAVE FORGOTTEN IT?

WE'VE ONLY GOT ONE FUNCTIONAL PANEL. IT REQUIRES PRECISE DIRECTION TO KEEP THE PORTAL OPEN TO THE RIGHT PLACE.

SOMEONE HAS TO MAN THE DEVICE. WHICH MEANS THAT PERSON GETS LEFT BEHIND...UNLESS IT'S ME, THE CAT, AND DEATHSTROKE.

BECAUSE WE'RE ALL FROM THE SAME WORLD.

OH, WOW...I CAN SMELL THE OZONE! GONNA RAISE A CUP OF IONS TO YOU, FISHSTICK!

TOGETHER THE THREE OF US SHOULD SUPPLY JUST ENOUGH ENERGY TO CREATE A PORTAL THAT'LL STAY OPEN ON ITS OWN, LONG ENOUGH FOR US ALL TO LEAVE.

BUT *ONLY* TOGETHER.

WE'LL BE LINKING TO A CRACK IN THE SKY THAT'S ALREADY THERE. BUT YOU'VE GOT THE BASICS RIGHT.

THEN I WISH YOU WELL, MY FRIEND. WE WILL SING SONGS OF YOU IN THE MEAD HALLS OF MY WORLD.

I ALMOST WANT TO GO WITH HIM JUST TO HEAR THOSE.

JUST US LEFT. I'VE TURNED THE STAFF TO FULL POWER. CAT, LET'S GET DEATHSTROKE IN POSITION...ADD HIS OMNIVERSIAL ENERGY TO OURS.

OR--AND HEAR ME OUT HERE--

--HELL NO.

SLIKT

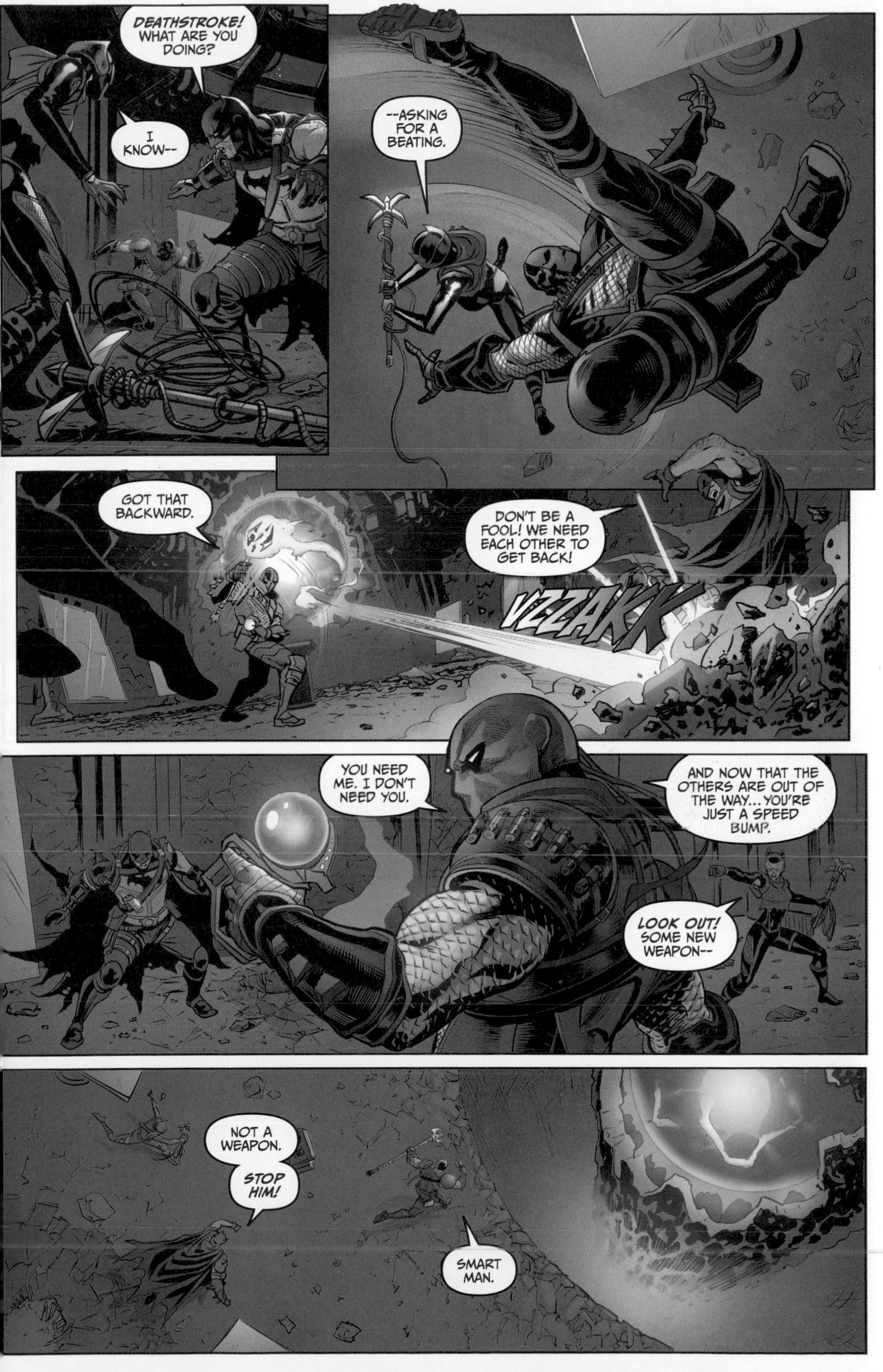
DEATHSTROKE! WHAT ARE YOU DOING?
I KNOW--
--ASKING FOR A BEATING.
GOT THAT BACKWARD.
DON'T BE A FOOL! WE NEED EACH OTHER TO GET BACK!
VZZAKK
YOU NEED ME. I DON'T NEED YOU.
AND NOW THAT THE OTHERS ARE OUT OF THE WAY... YOU'RE JUST A SPEED BUMP.
LOOK OUT! SOME NEW WEAPON--
NOT A WEAPON.
STOP HIM!
SMART MAN.

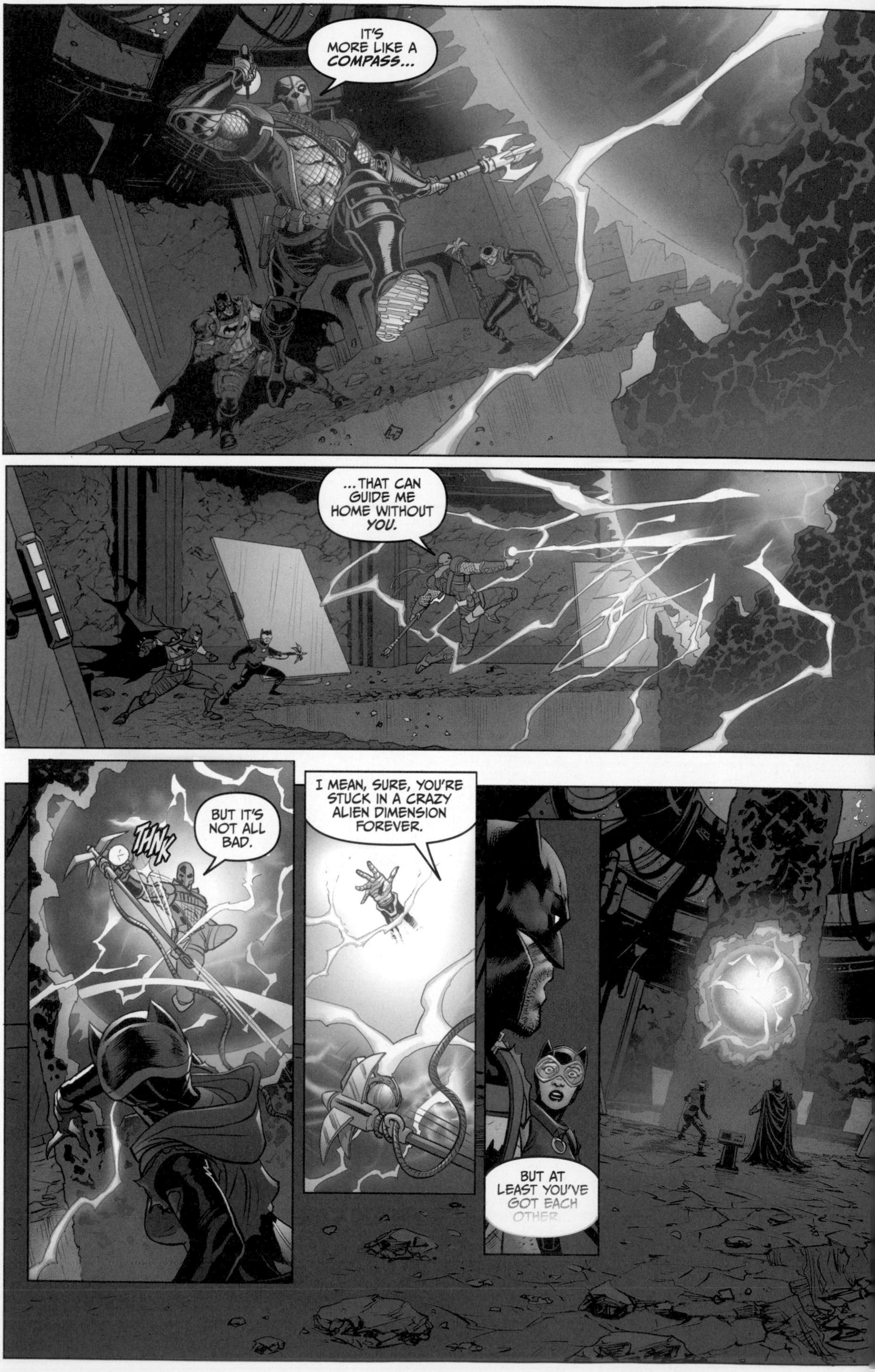
IT'S MORE LIKE A COMPASS...
...THAT CAN GUIDE ME HOME WITHOUT YOU.
BUT IT'S NOT ALL BAD.
THNK
I MEAN, SURE, YOU'RE STUCK IN A CRAZY ALIEN DIMENSION FOREVER.
BUT AT LEAST YOU'VE GOT EACH OTHER

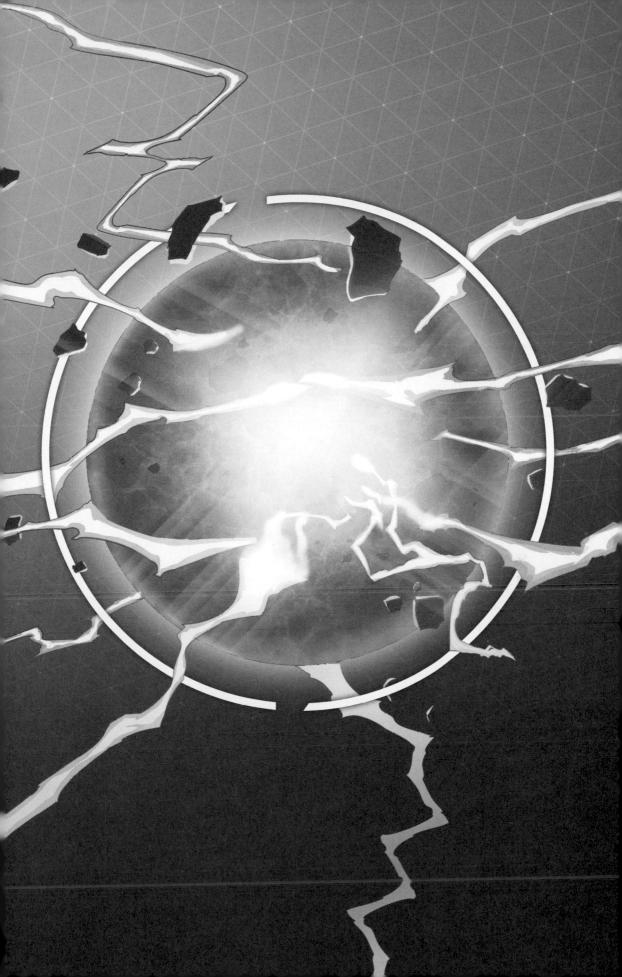

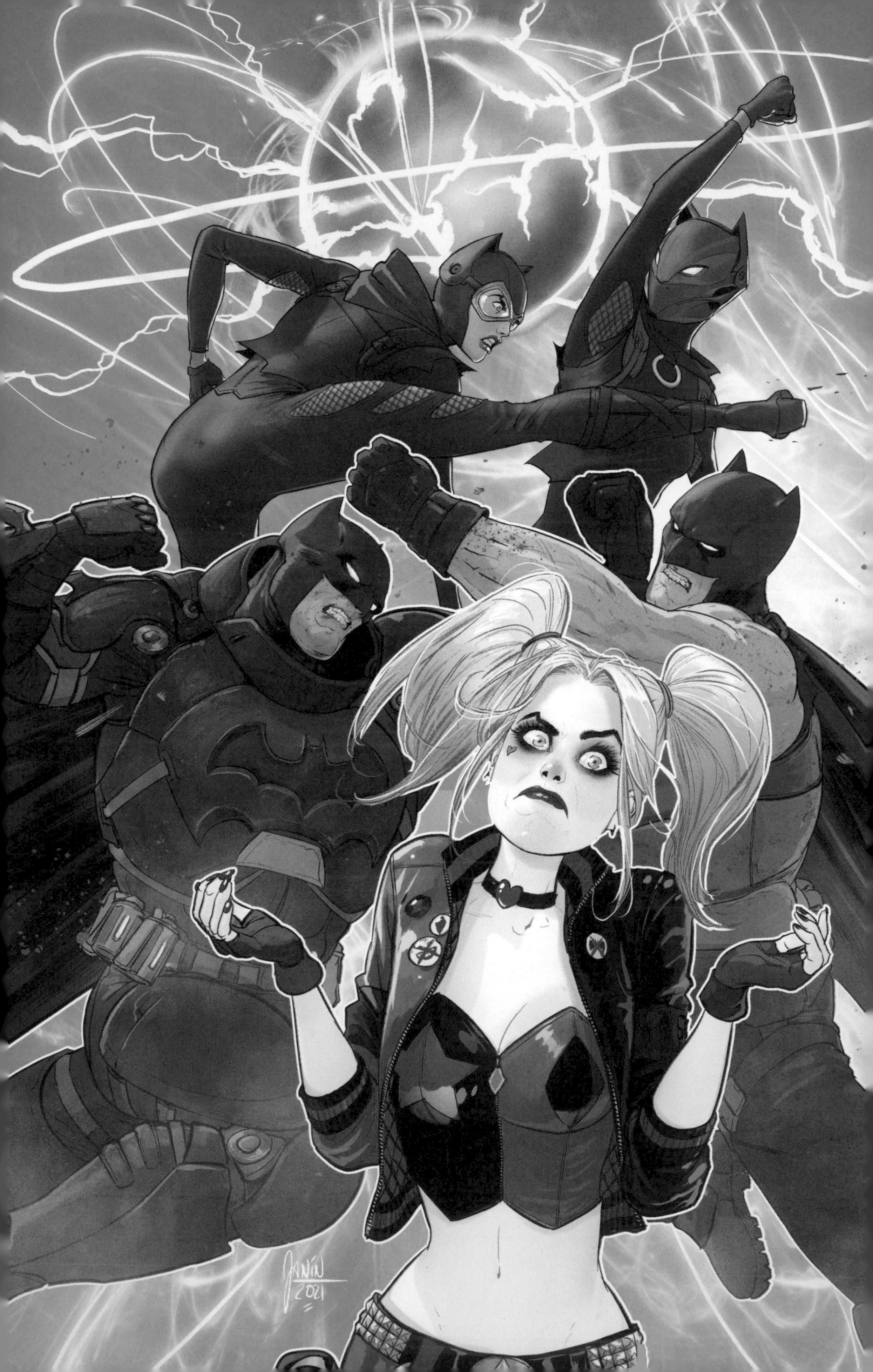
JANÍN
2021

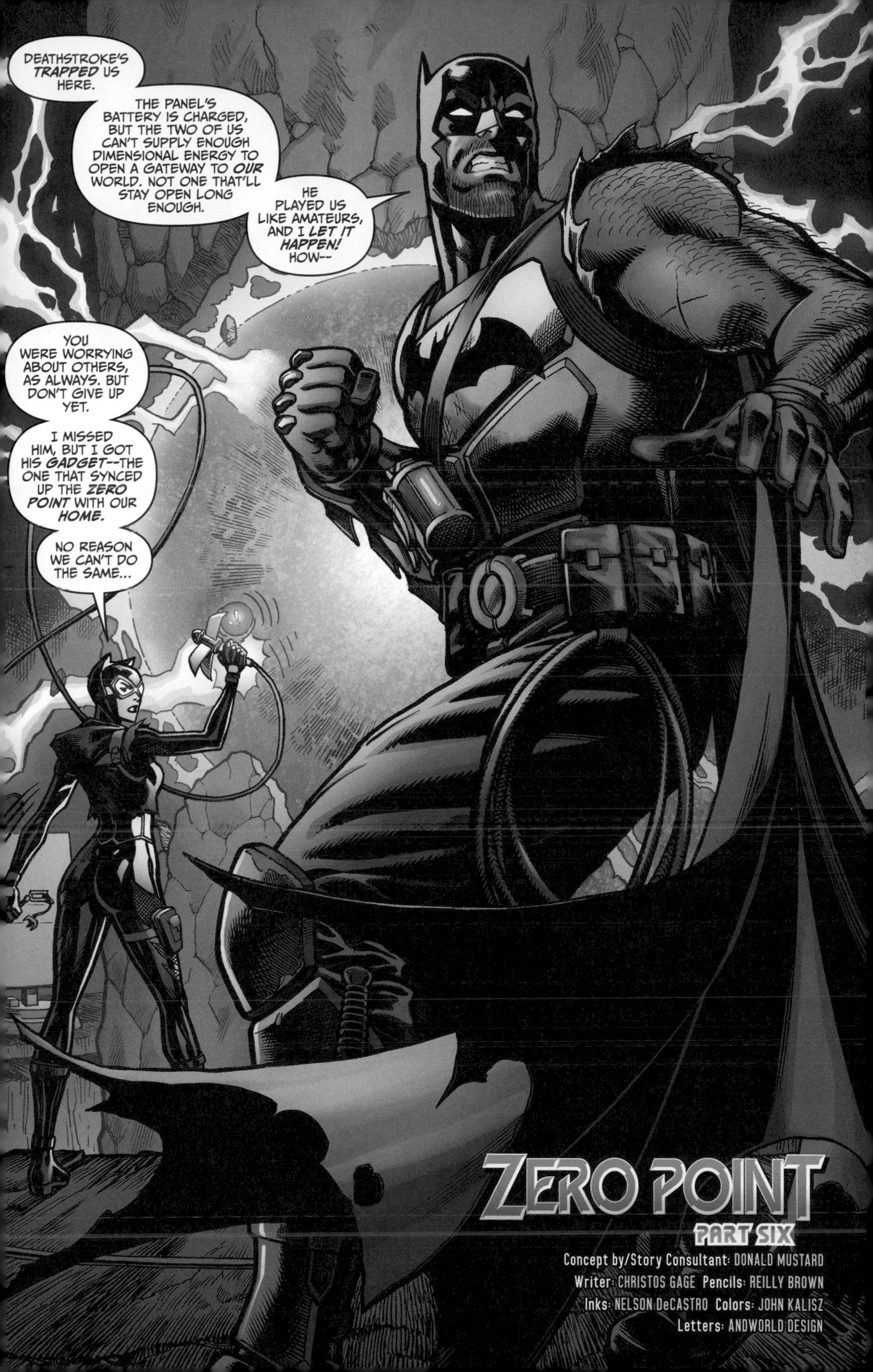
DEATHSTROKE'S *TRAPPED* US HERE.
THE PANEL'S BATTERY IS CHARGED, BUT THE TWO OF US CAN'T SUPPLY ENOUGH DIMENSIONAL ENERGY TO OPEN A GATEWAY TO *OUR* WORLD. NOT ONE THAT'LL STAY OPEN LONG ENOUGH.
HE PLAYED US LIKE AMATEURS, AND I *LET IT HAPPEN!* HOW--
YOU WERE WORRYING ABOUT OTHERS, AS ALWAYS. BUT DON'T GIVE UP YET.
I MISSED HIM, BUT I GOT HIS *GADGET*--THE ONE THAT SYNCED UP THE *ZERO POINT* WITH OUR *HOME.*
NO REASON WE CAN'T DO THE SAME...
ZERO POINT
PART SIX
Concept by/Story Consultant: DONALD MUSTARD
Writer: CHRISTOS GAGE Pencils: REILLY BROWN
Inks: NELSON DeCASTRO Colors: JOHN KALISZ
Letters: ANDWORLD DESIGN

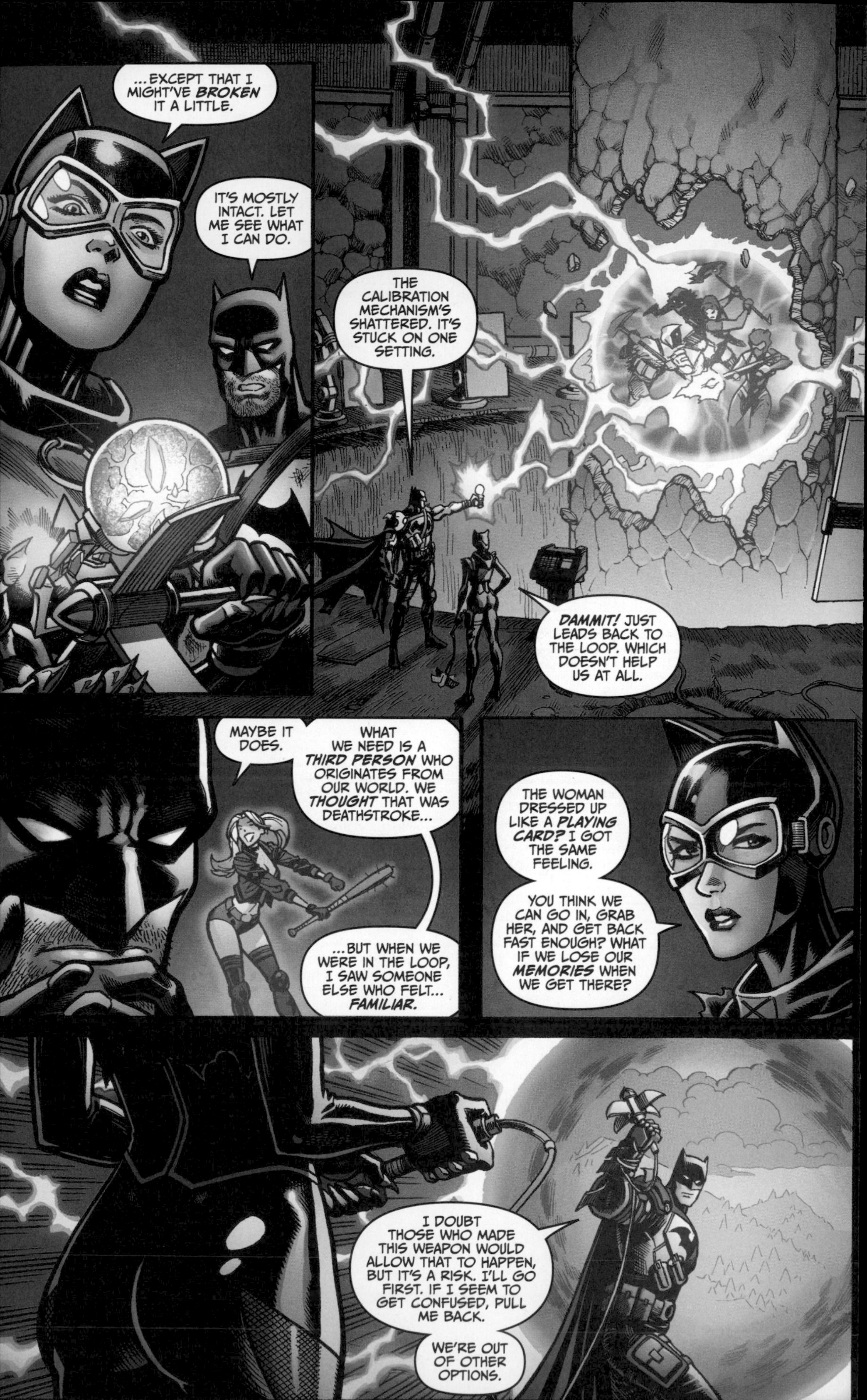
...EXCEPT THAT I MIGHT'VE **BROKEN** IT A LITTLE.
IT'S MOSTLY INTACT. LET ME SEE WHAT I CAN DO.
THE CALIBRATION MECHANISM'S SHATTERED. IT'S STUCK ON ONE SETTING.
DAMMIT! JUST LEADS BACK TO THE LOOP. WHICH DOESN'T HELP US AT ALL.
MAYBE IT DOES.
WHAT WE NEED IS A **THIRD PERSON** WHO ORIGINATES FROM OUR WORLD. WE **THOUGHT** THAT WAS DEATHSTROKE...
...BUT WHEN WE WERE IN THE LOOP, I SAW SOMEONE ELSE WHO FELT... **FAMILIAR.**
THE WOMAN DRESSED UP LIKE A **PLAYING CARD?** I GOT THE SAME FEELING.
YOU THINK WE CAN GO IN, GRAB HER, AND GET BACK FAST ENOUGH? WHAT IF WE LOSE OUR **MEMORIES** WHEN WE GET THERE?
I DOUBT THOSE WHO MADE THIS WEAPON WOULD ALLOW THAT TO HAPPEN, BUT IT'S A RISK. I'LL GO FIRST. IF I SEEM TO GET CONFUSED, PULL ME BACK.
WE'RE OUT OF OTHER OPTIONS.

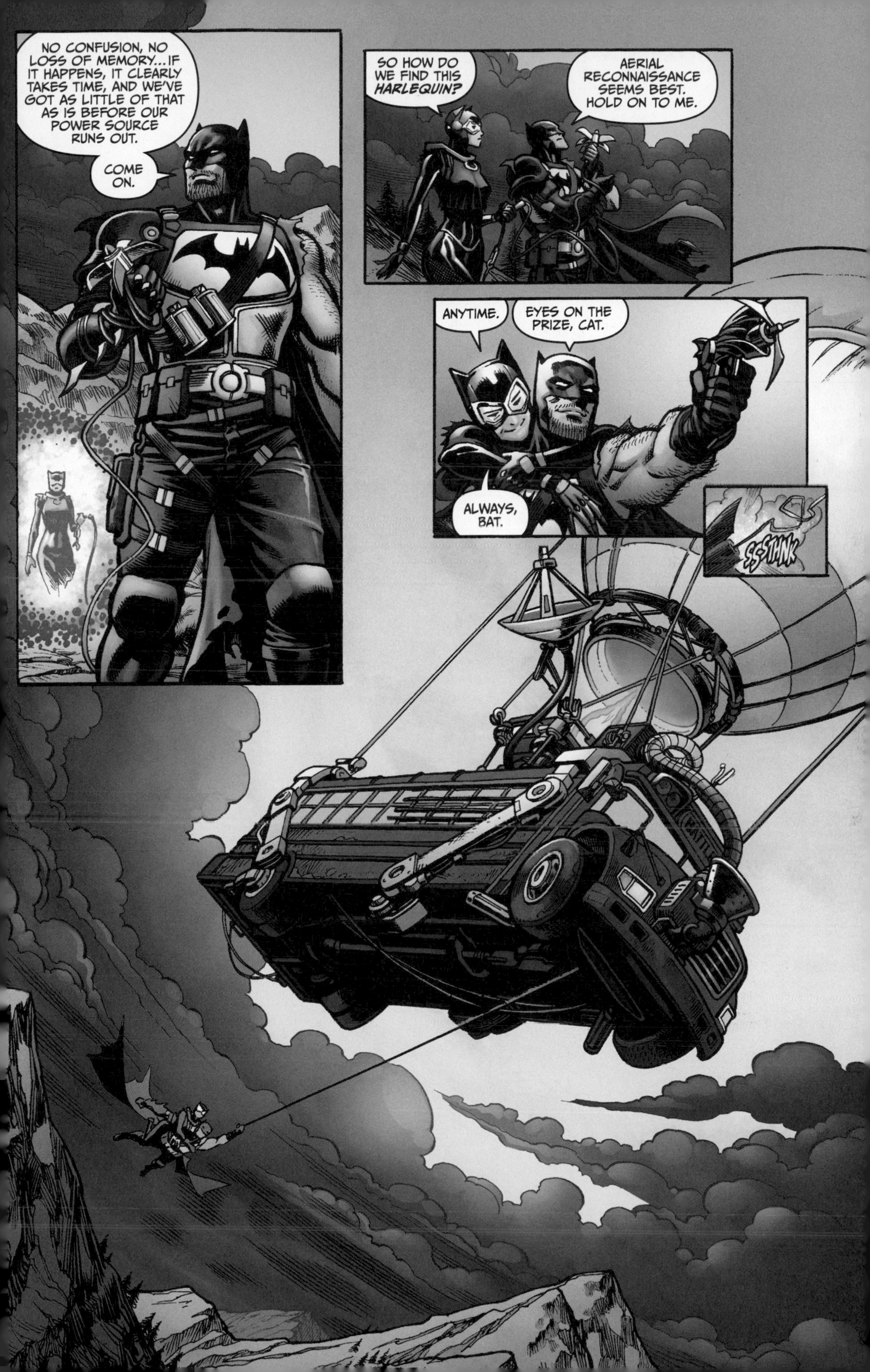
NO CONFUSION, NO LOSS OF MEMORY...IF IT HAPPENS, IT CLEARLY TAKES TIME, AND WE'VE GOT AS LITTLE OF THAT AS IS BEFORE OUR POWER SOURCE RUNS OUT.
COME ON.
SO HOW DO WE FIND THIS HARLEQUIN?
AERIAL RECONNAISSANCE SEEMS BEST. HOLD ON TO ME.
ANYTIME.
EYES ON THE PRIZE, CAT.
ALWAYS, BAT.
SS-STHNK

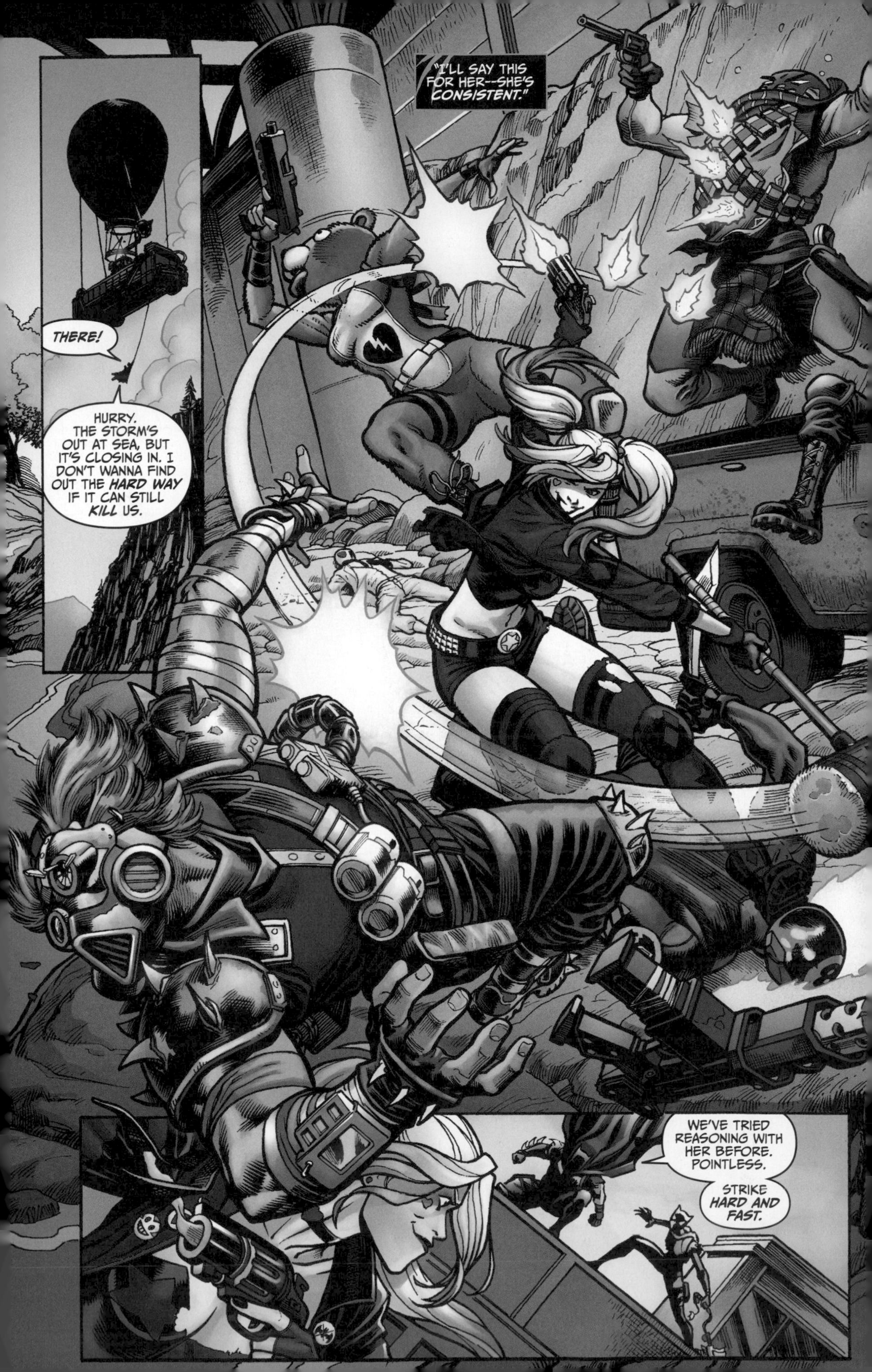
"I'LL SAY THIS FOR HER--SHE'S CONSISTENT."
THERE!
HURRY. THE STORM'S OUT AT SEA, BUT IT'S CLOSING IN. I DON'T WANNA FIND OUT THE HARD WAY IF IT CAN STILL KILL US.
WE'VE TRIED REASONING WITH HER BEFORE. POINTLESS.
STRIKE HARD AND FAST.

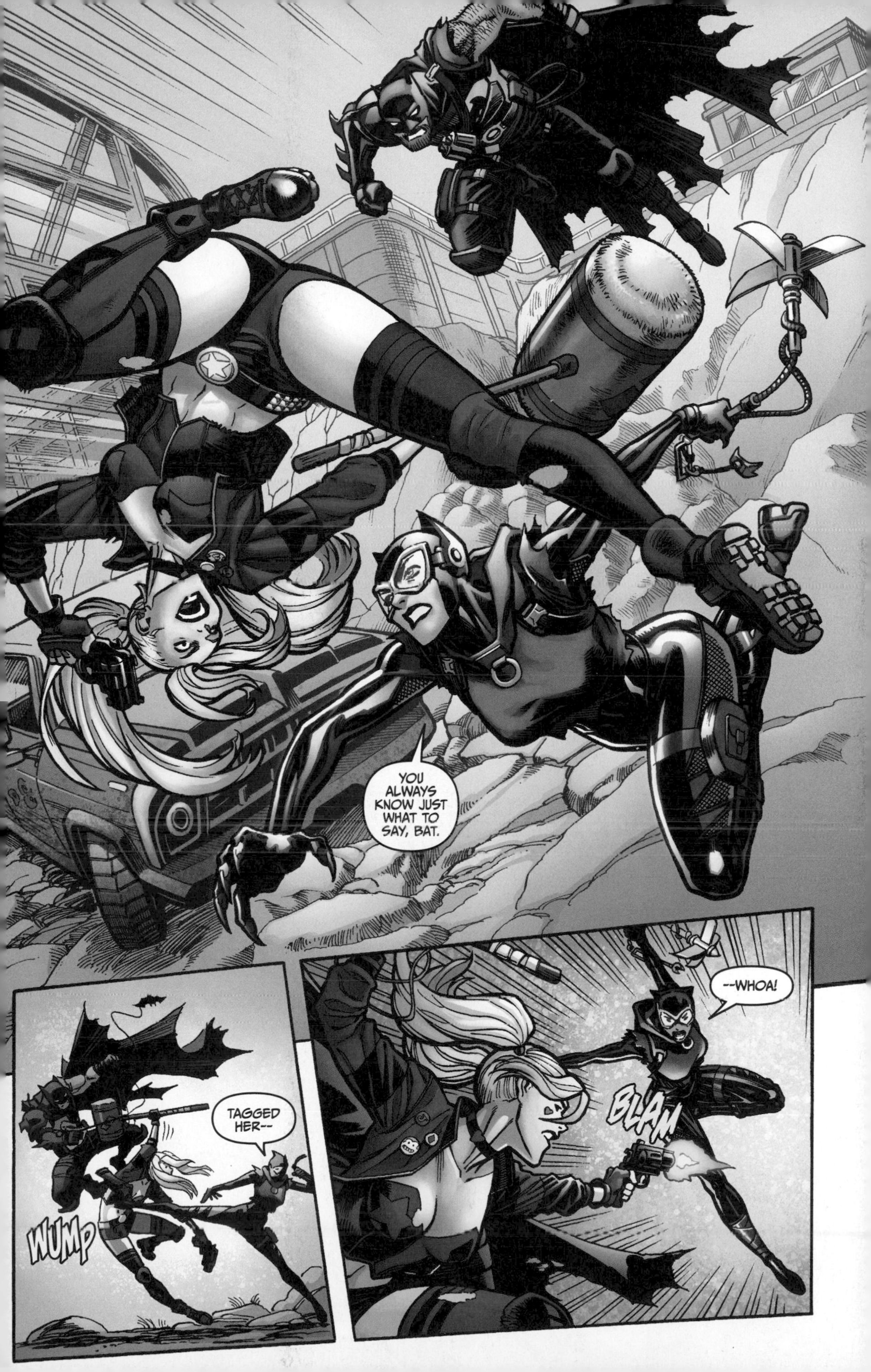
YOU ALWAYS KNOW JUST WHAT TO SAY, BAT.
TAGGED HER--
WUMP
--WHOA!
BLAM

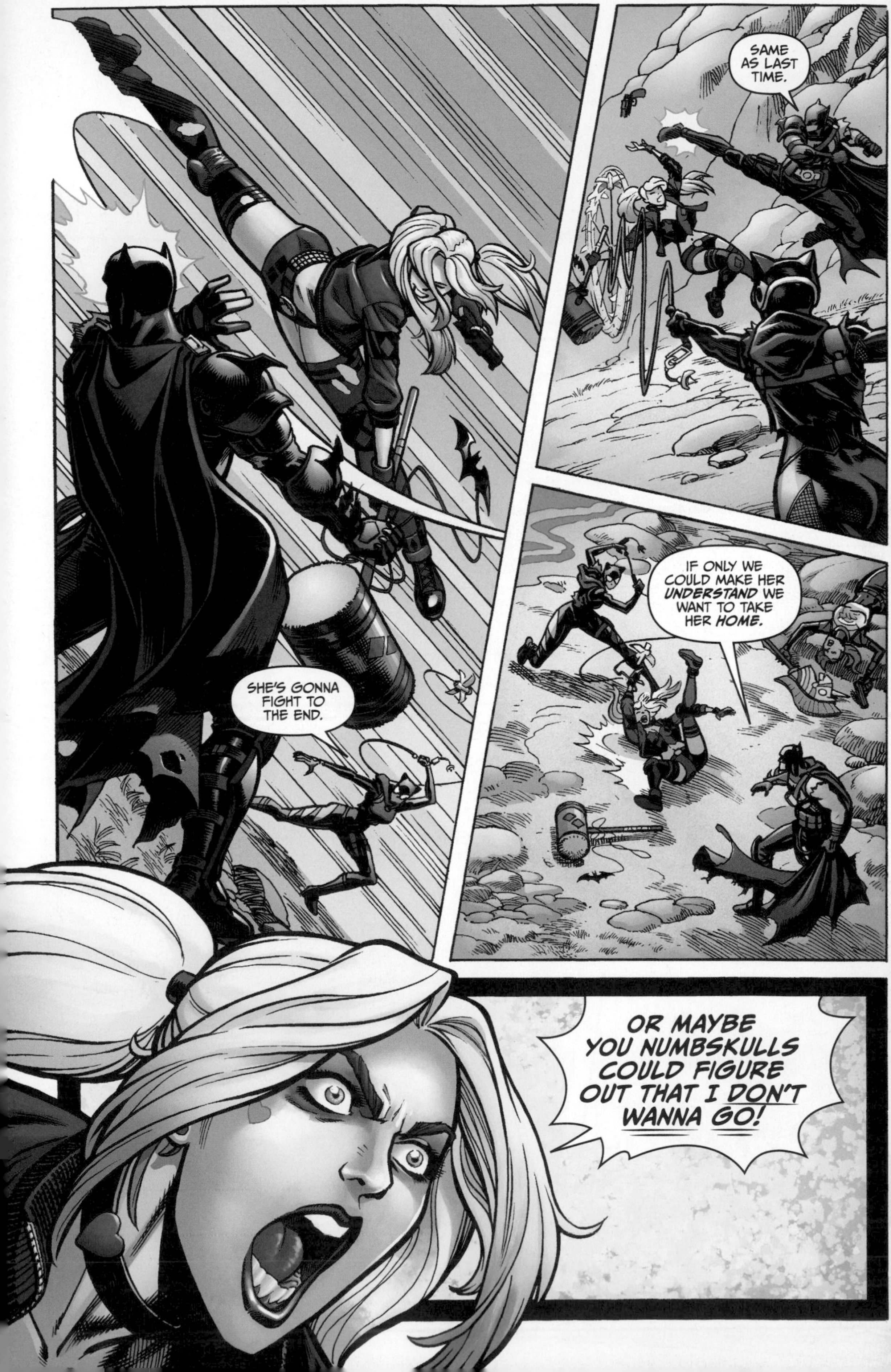
SHE'S GONNA FIGHT TO THE END.
SAME AS LAST TIME.
IF ONLY WE COULD MAKE HER UNDERSTAND WE WANT TO TAKE HER HOME.
OR MAYBE YOU NUMBSKULLS COULD FIGURE OUT THAT I DON'T WANNA GO!

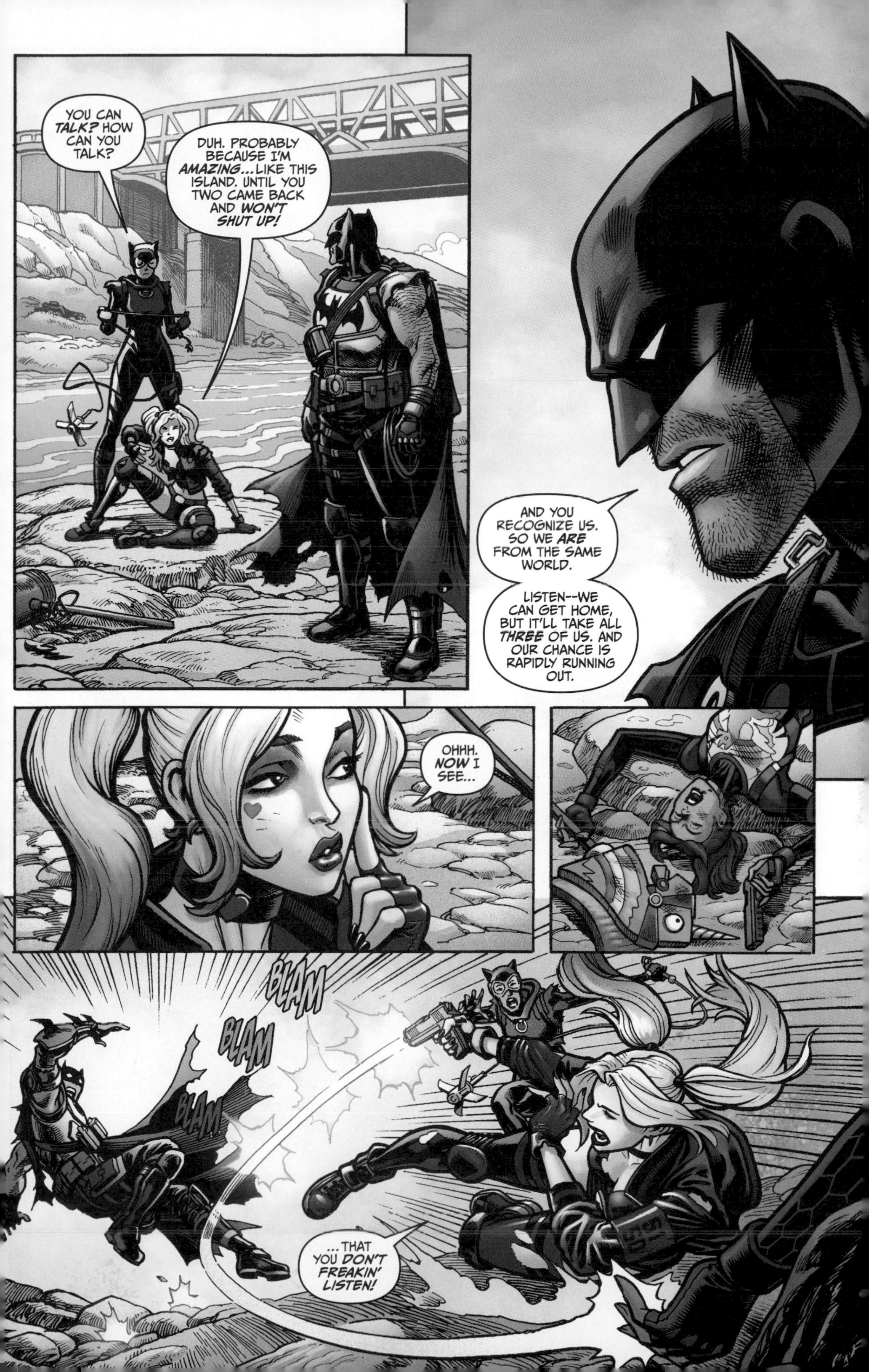
YOU CAN TALK? HOW CAN YOU TALK?
DUH. PROBABLY BECAUSE I'M AMAZING...LIKE THIS ISLAND. UNTIL YOU TWO CAME BACK AND WON'T SHUT UP!
AND YOU RECOGNIZE US. SO WE ARE FROM THE SAME WORLD.
LISTEN--WE CAN GET HOME, BUT IT'LL TAKE ALL THREE OF US. AND OUR CHANCE IS RAPIDLY RUNNING OUT.
OHHH. NOW I SEE...
BLAM
BLAM
BLAM
...THAT YOU DON'T FREAKIN' LISTEN!

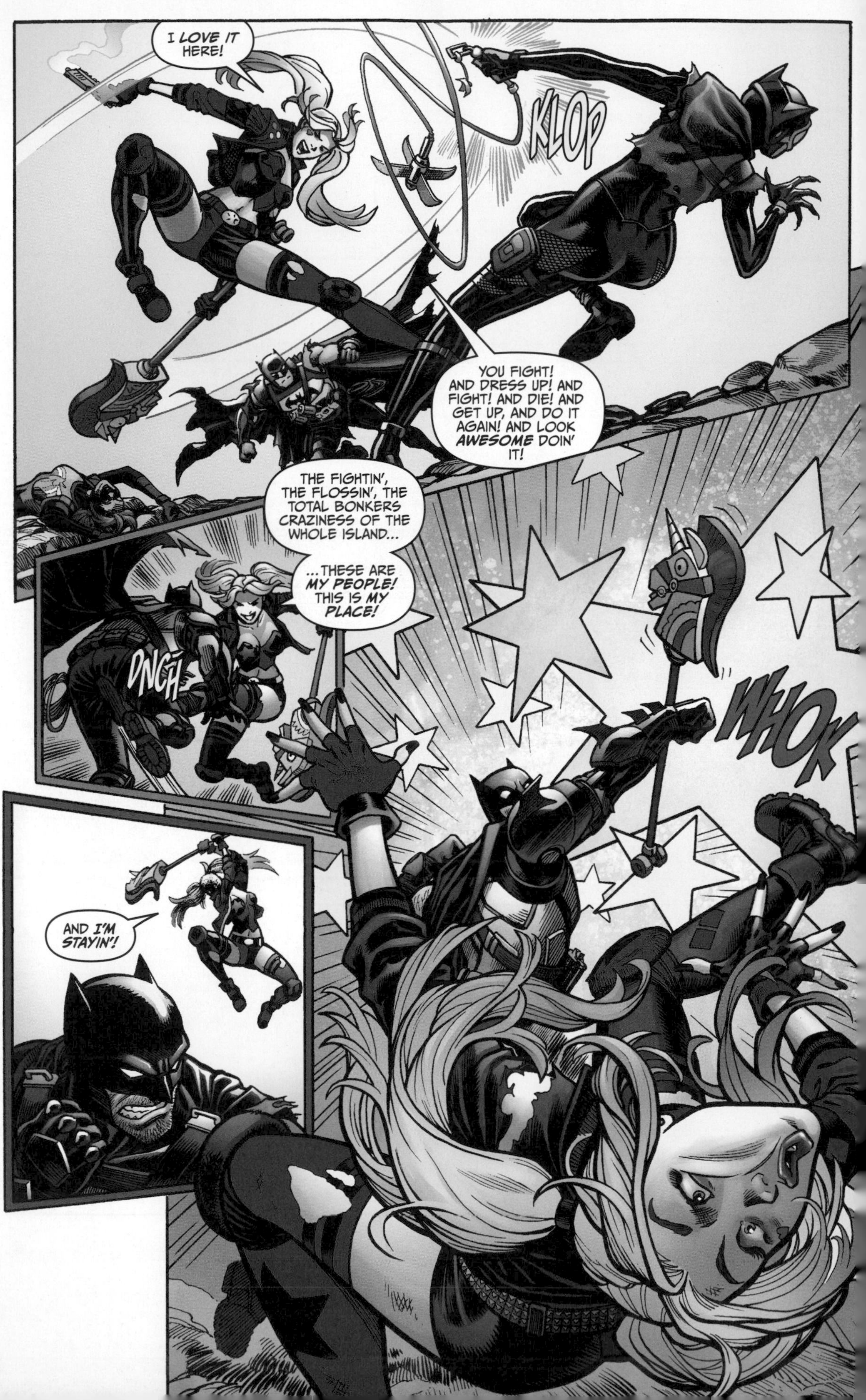
I LOVE IT HERE!
KLOP
YOU FIGHT! AND DRESS UP! AND FIGHT! AND DIE! AND GET UP, AND DO IT AGAIN! AND LOOK AWESOME DOIN' IT!
THE FIGHTIN', THE FLOSSIN', THE TOTAL BONKERS CRAZINESS OF THE WHOLE ISLAND...
...THESE ARE MY PEOPLE! THIS IS MY PLACE!
DNCH
WHOK
AND I'M STAYIN'!

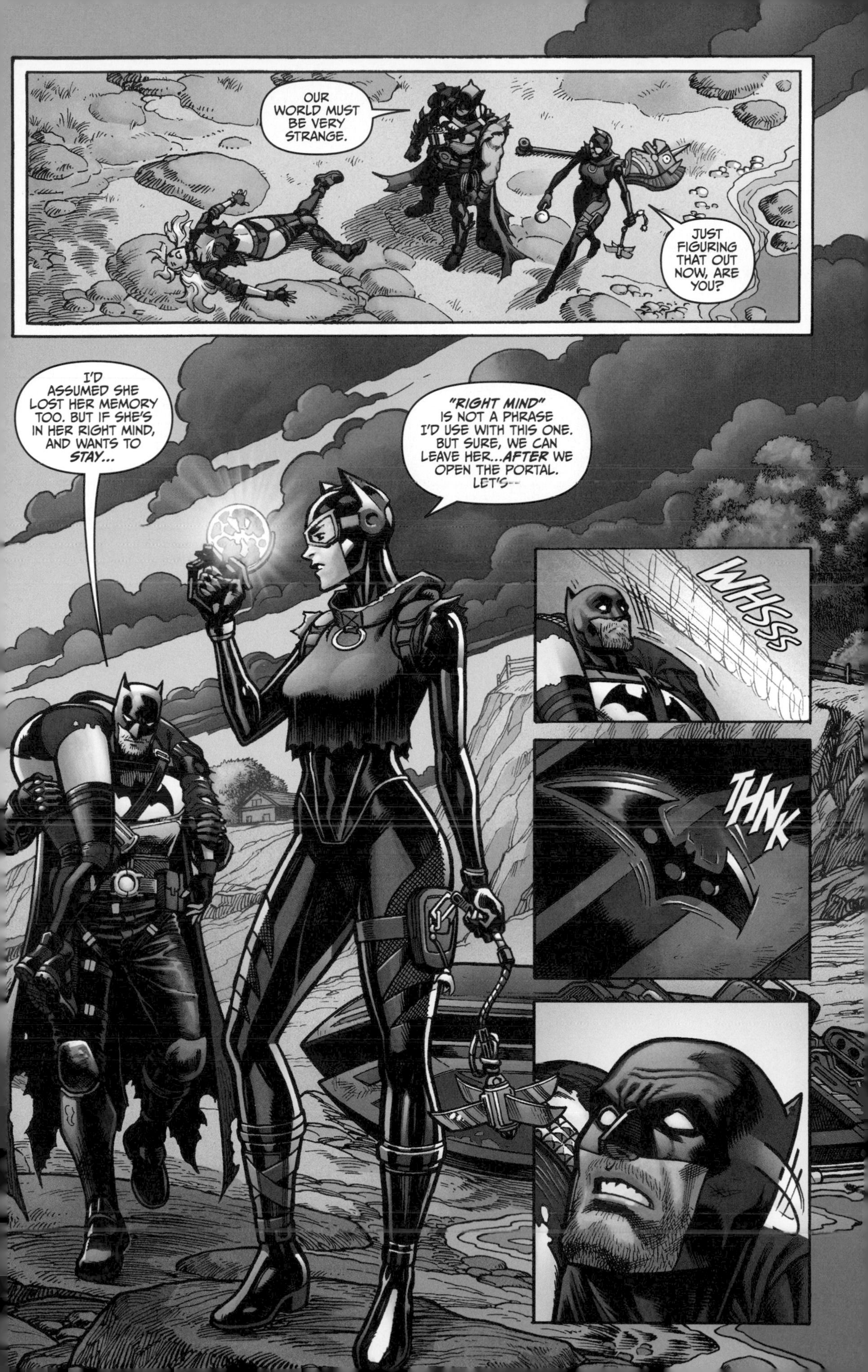
OUR WORLD MUST BE VERY STRANGE.
JUST FIGURING THAT OUT NOW, ARE YOU?
I'D ASSUMED SHE LOST HER MEMORY TOO. BUT IF SHE'S IN HER RIGHT MIND, AND WANTS TO *STAY...*
"RIGHT MIND" IS NOT A PHRASE I'D USE WITH THIS ONE. BUT SURE, WE CAN LEAVE HER...*AFTER* WE OPEN THE PORTAL. LET'S--
WHSSS
THNK

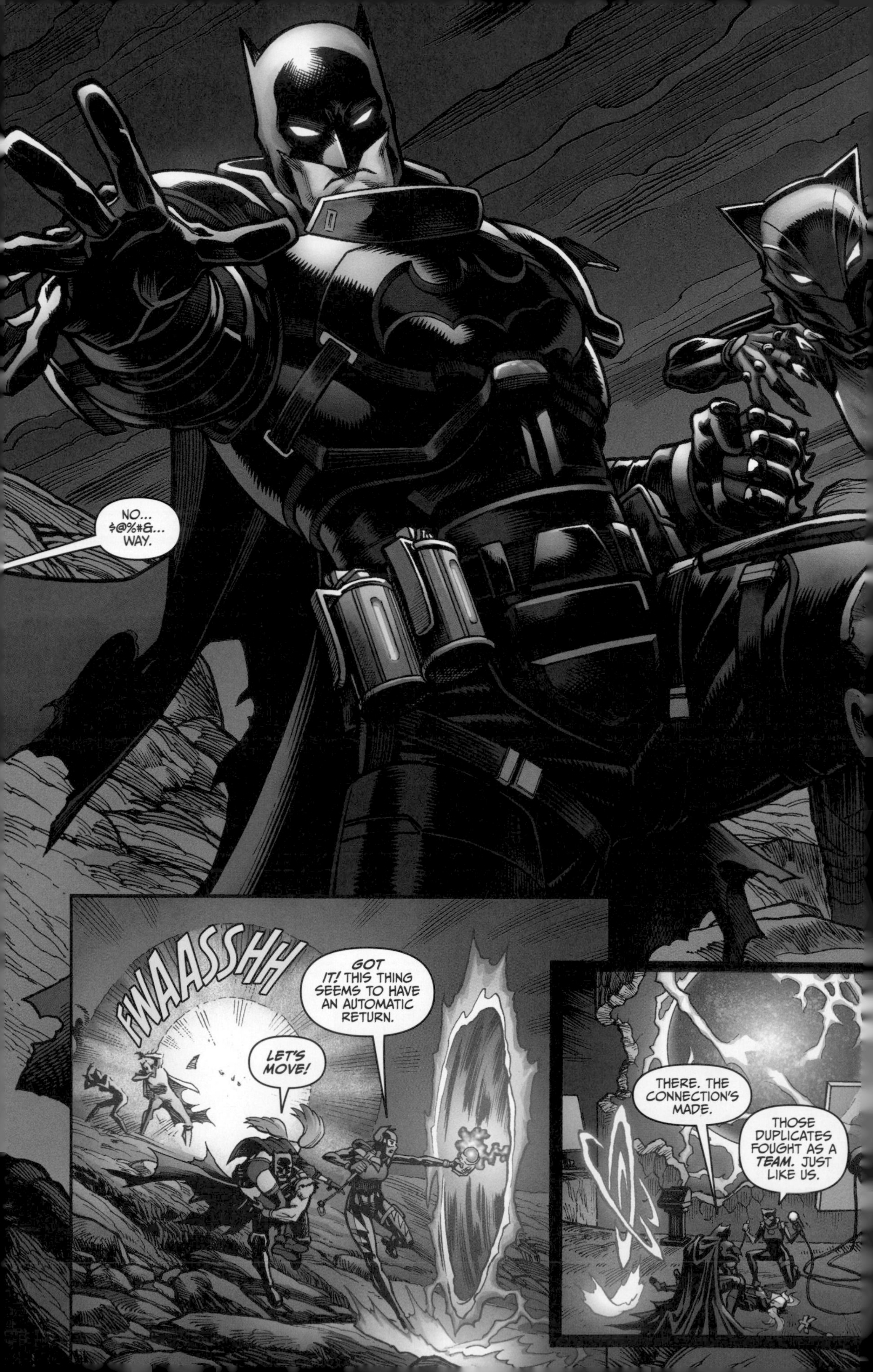
NO... $@%#&... WAY.
FWAASSHH
GOT IT! THIS THING SEEMS TO HAVE AN AUTOMATIC RETURN.
LET'S MOVE!
THERE. THE CONNECTION'S MADE.
THOSE DUPLICATES FOUGHT AS A TEAM. JUST LIKE US.

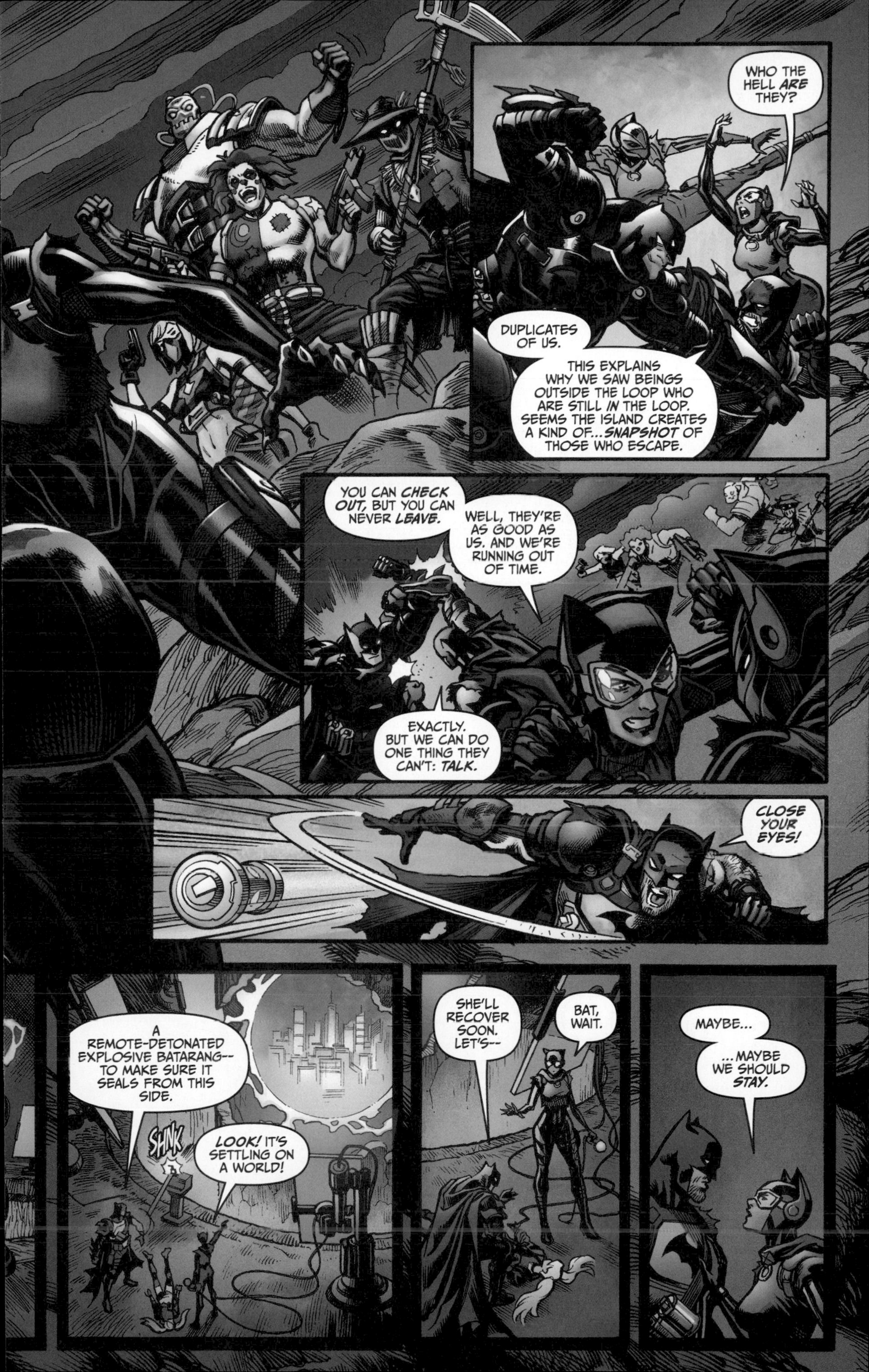
WHO THE HELL ARE THEY?
DUPLICATES OF US.
THIS EXPLAINS WHY WE SAW BEINGS OUTSIDE THE LOOP WHO ARE STILL IN THE LOOP. SEEMS THE ISLAND CREATES A KIND OF...SNAPSHOT OF THOSE WHO ESCAPE.
YOU CAN CHECK OUT, BUT YOU CAN NEVER LEAVE.
WELL, THEY'RE AS GOOD AS US. AND WE'RE RUNNING OUT OF TIME.
EXACTLY. BUT WE CAN DO ONE THING THEY CAN'T: TALK.
CLOSE YOUR EYES!
A REMOTE-DETONATED EXPLOSIVE BATARANG--TO MAKE SURE IT SEALS FROM THIS SIDE.
SHNK
LOOK! IT'S SETTLING ON A WORLD!
SHE'LL RECOVER SOON. LET'S--
BAT, WAIT.
MAYBE...
...MAYBE WE SHOULD STAY.

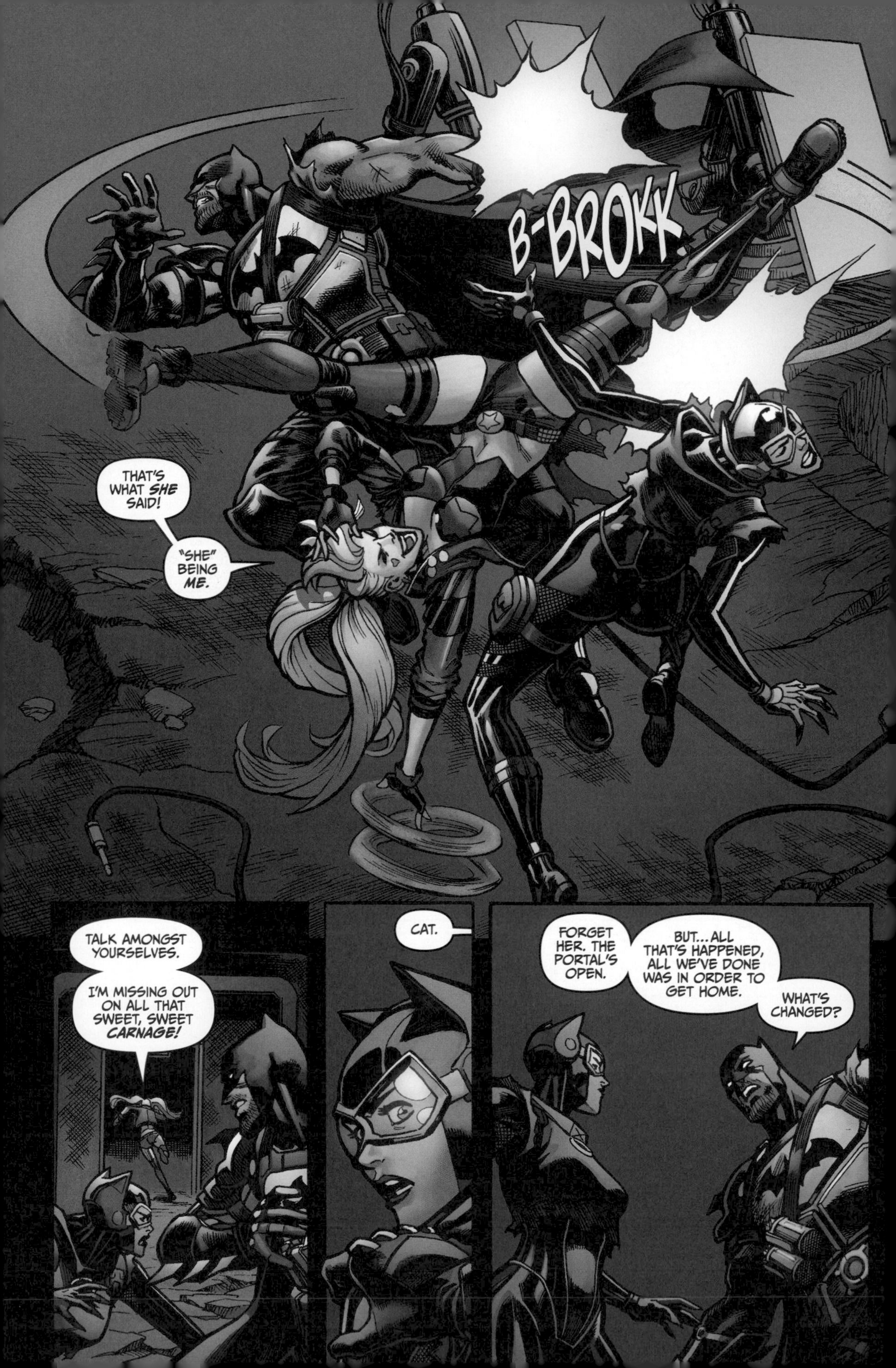

B-BROKK
THAT'S WHAT SHE SAID!
"SHE" BEING ME.
TALK AMONGST YOURSELVES.
I'M MISSING OUT ON ALL THAT SWEET, SWEET CARNAGE!
CAT.
FORGET HER. THE PORTAL'S OPEN.
BUT... ALL THAT'S HAPPENED, ALL WE'VE DONE WAS IN ORDER TO GET HOME.
WHAT'S CHANGED?

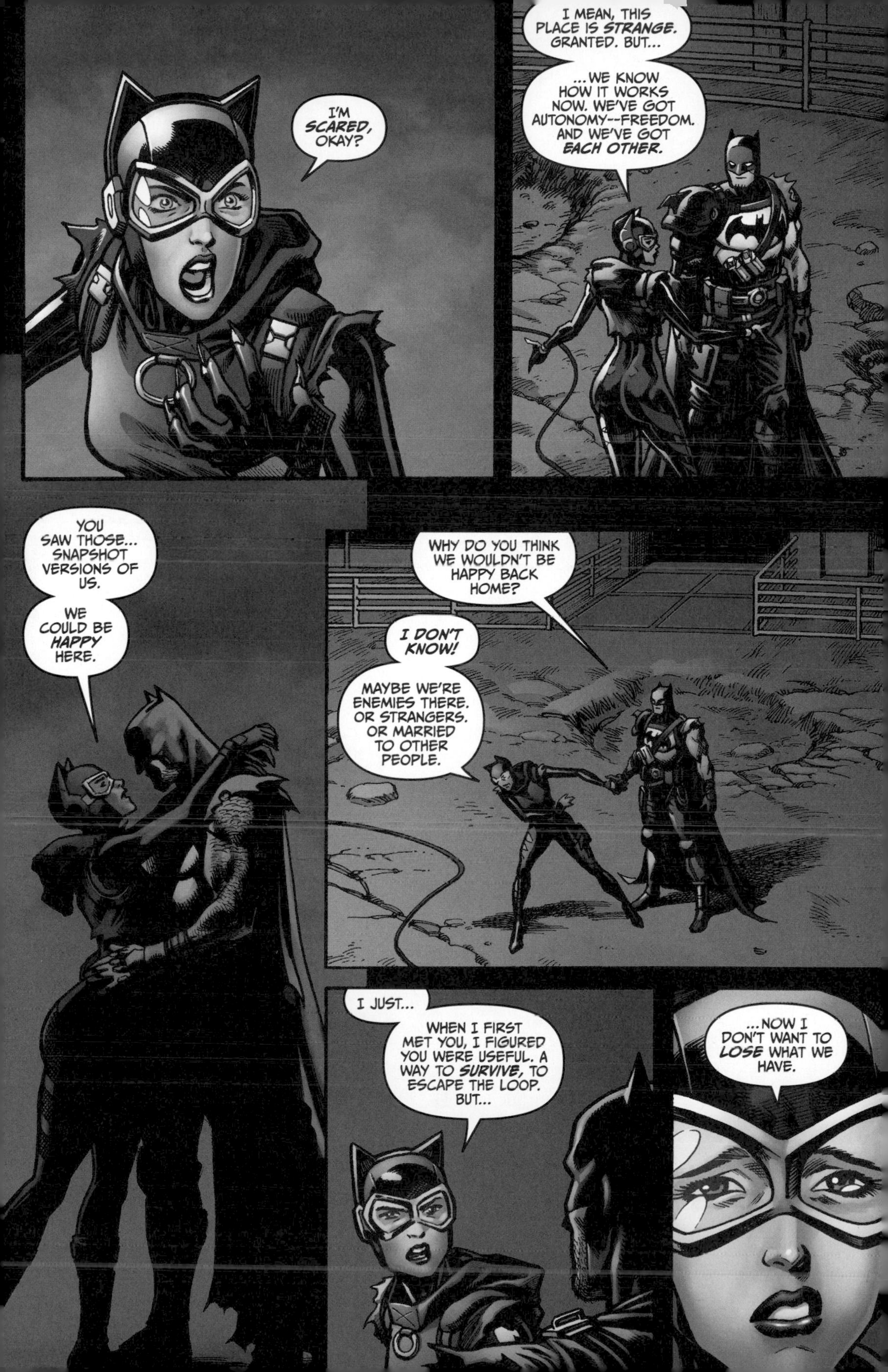

I'M *SCARED*, OKAY?
I MEAN, THIS PLACE IS *STRANGE*. GRANTED. BUT...
...WE KNOW HOW IT WORKS NOW. WE'VE GOT AUTONOMY--FREEDOM. AND WE'VE GOT *EACH OTHER*.
YOU SAW THOSE... SNAPSHOT VERSIONS OF US.
WE COULD BE *HAPPY* HERE.
WHY DO YOU THINK WE WOULDN'T BE HAPPY BACK HOME?
I DON'T KNOW!
MAYBE WE'RE ENEMIES THERE. OR STRANGERS. OR MARRIED TO OTHER PEOPLE.
I JUST...
WHEN I FIRST MET YOU, I FIGURED YOU WERE USEFUL. A WAY TO *SURVIVE*, TO ESCAPE THE LOOP. BUT...
...NOW I DON'T WANT TO *LOSE* WHAT WE HAVE.

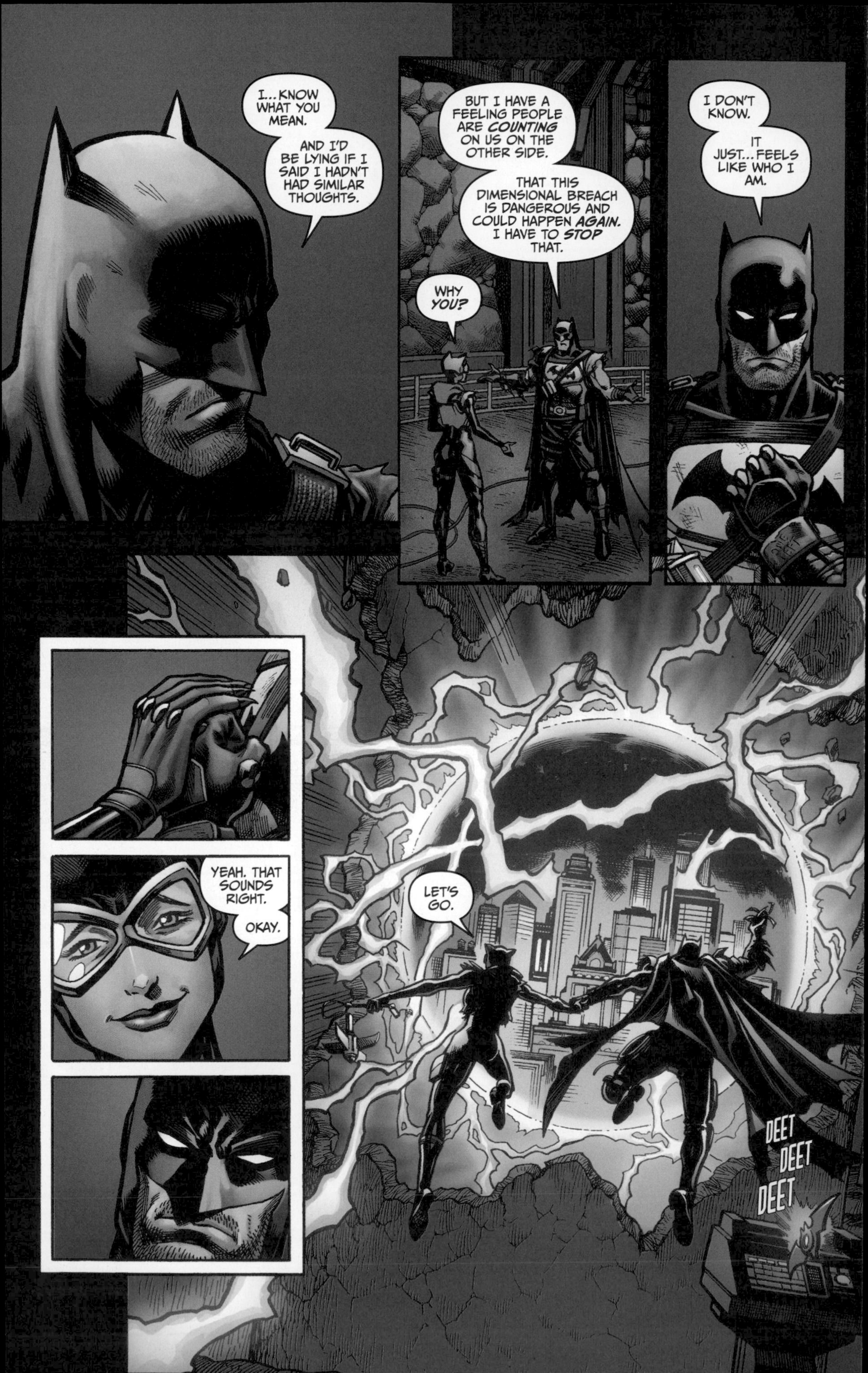
I...KNOW WHAT YOU MEAN.
AND I'D BE LYING IF I SAID I HADN'T HAD SIMILAR THOUGHTS.
BUT I HAVE A FEELING PEOPLE ARE *COUNTING* ON US ON THE OTHER SIDE.
THAT THIS DIMENSIONAL BREACH IS DANGEROUS AND COULD HAPPEN *AGAIN.* I HAVE TO *STOP* THAT.
WHY *YOU?*
I DON'T KNOW.
IT JUST...FEELS LIKE WHO I AM.
YEAH. THAT SOUNDS RIGHT.
OKAY.
LET'S GO.
DEET
DEET
DEET

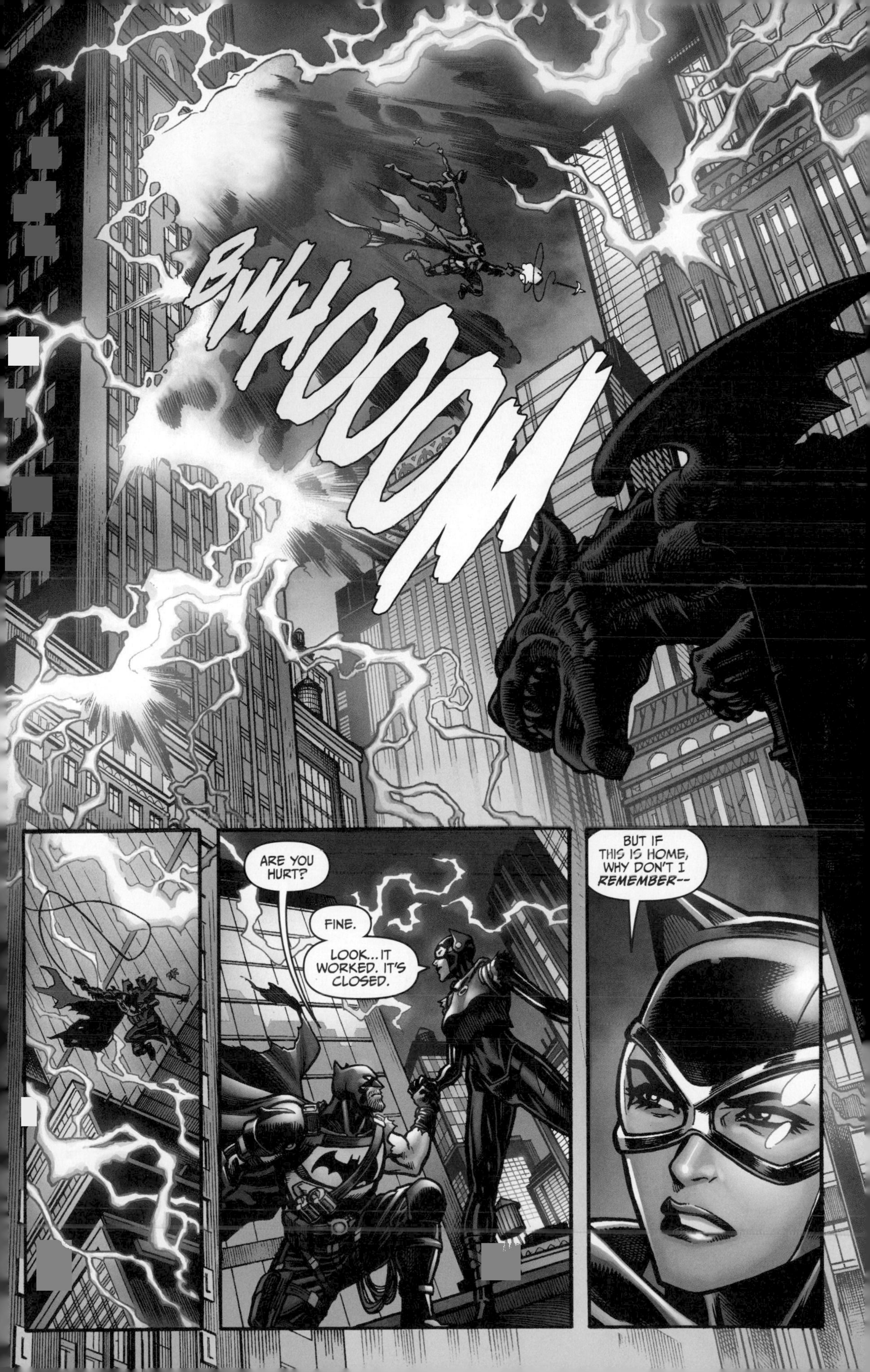
BWHOOOM
ARE YOU HURT?
FINE.
LOOK...IT WORKED. IT'S CLOSED.
BUT IF THIS IS HOME, WHY DON'T I *REMEMBER*--

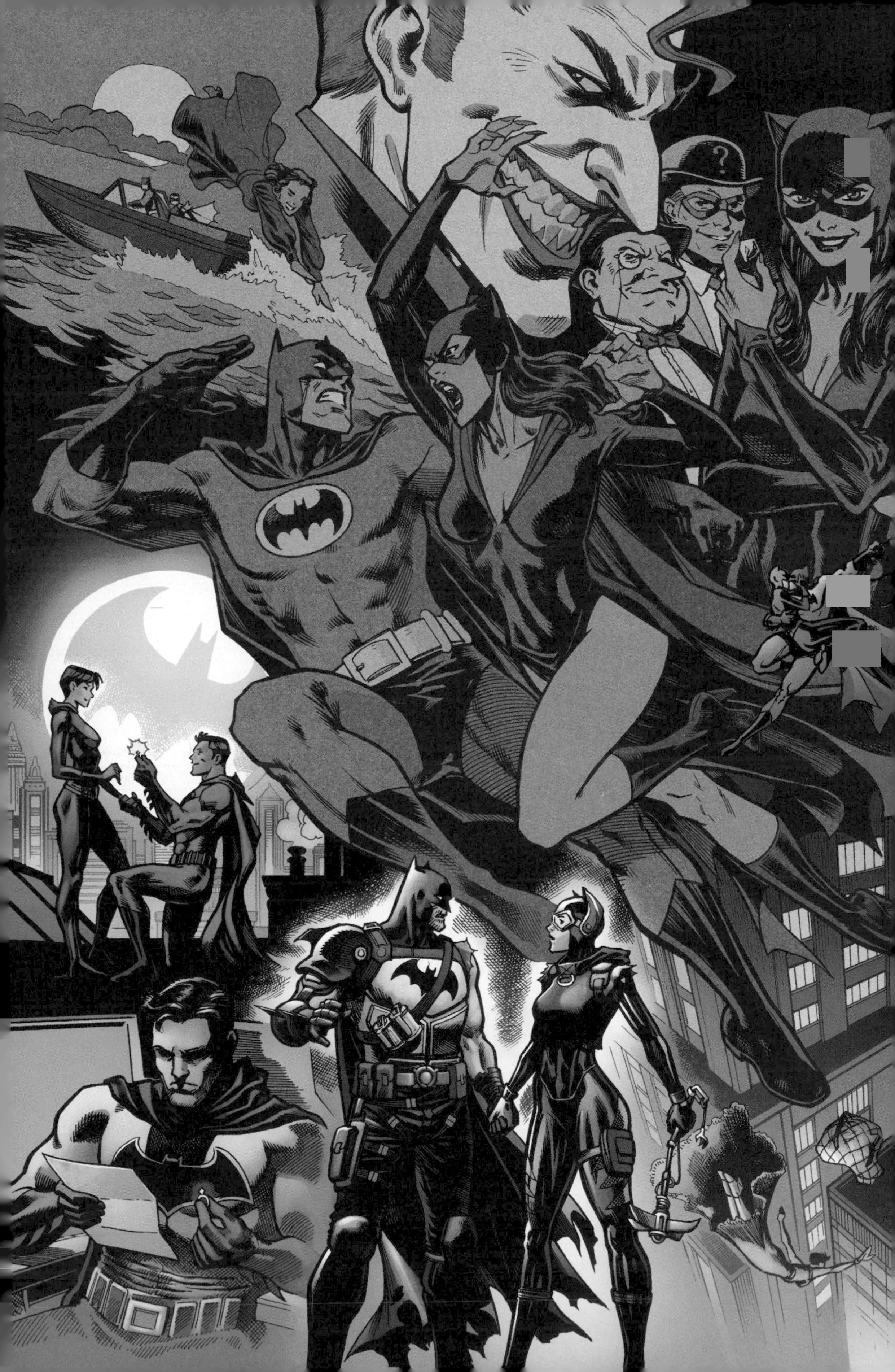

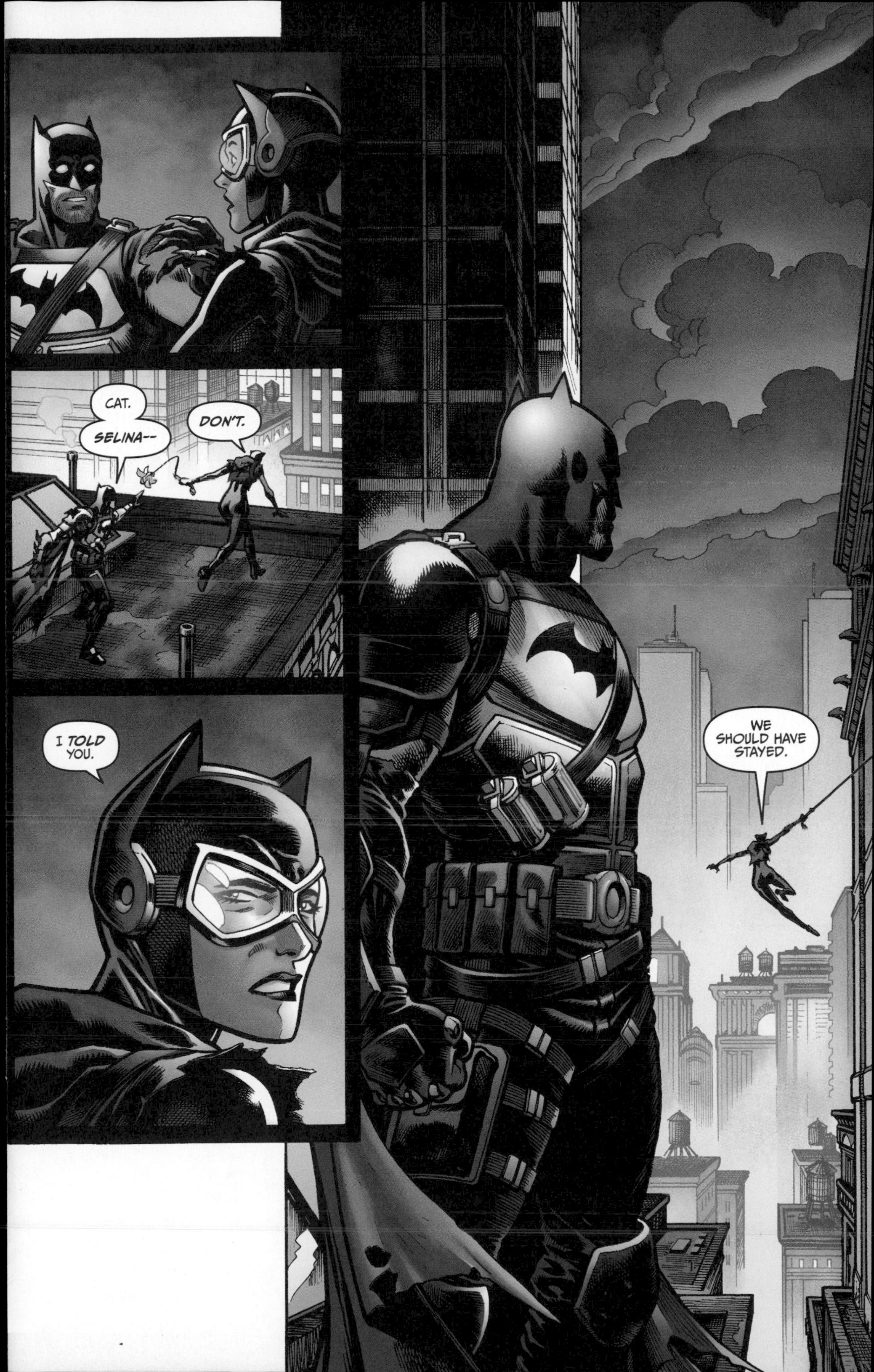
CAT.
SELINA--
DON'T.
I TOLD YOU.
WE SHOULD HAVE STAYED.

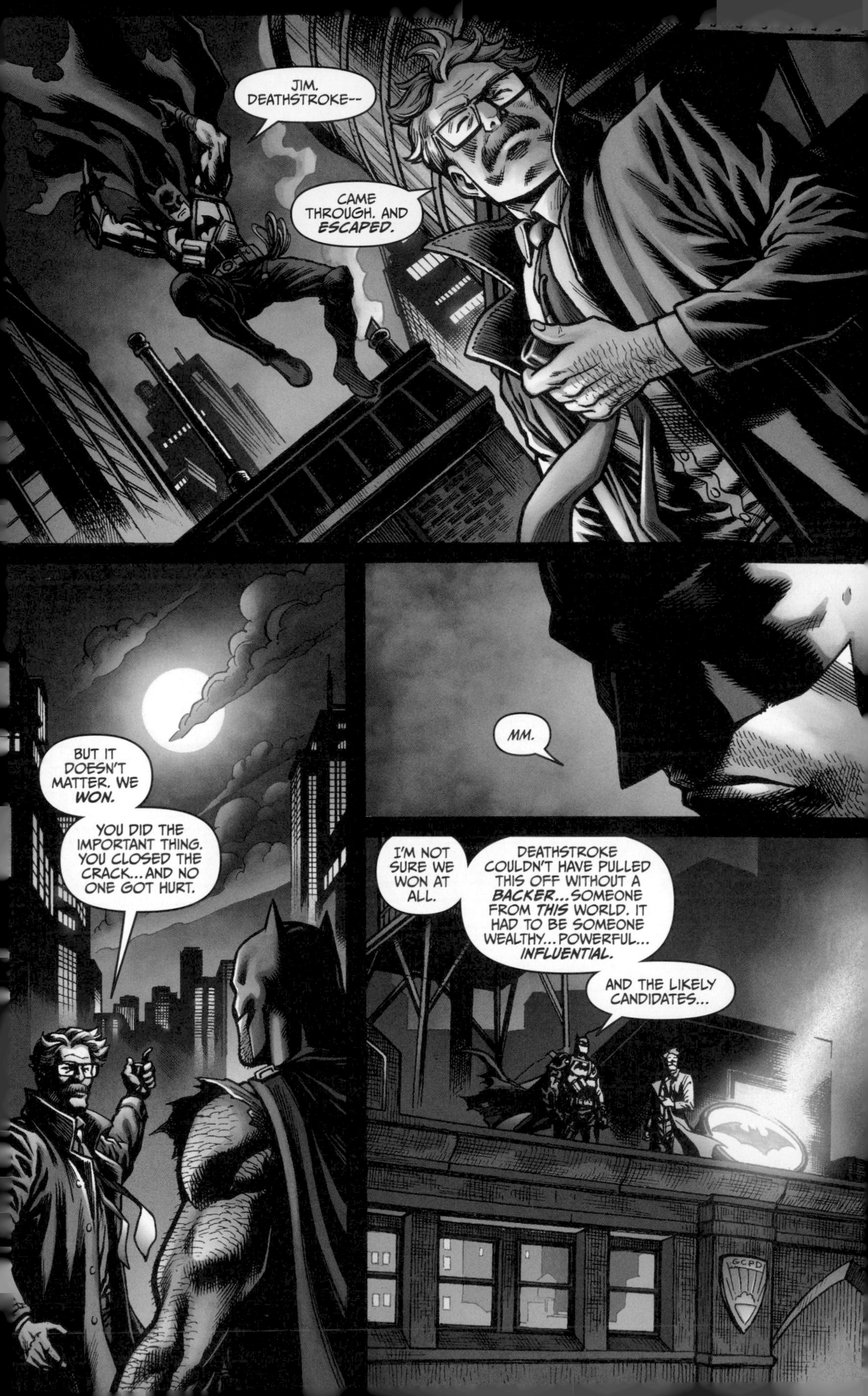
JIM. DEATHSTROKE--
CAME THROUGH. AND *ESCAPED.*
BUT IT DOESN'T MATTER. WE *WON.*
YOU DID THE IMPORTANT THING. YOU CLOSED THE CRACK...AND NO ONE GOT HURT.
MM.
I'M NOT SURE WE WON AT ALL.
DEATHSTROKE COULDN'T HAVE PULLED THIS OFF WITHOUT A *BACKER...*SOMEONE FROM *THIS* WORLD. IT HAD TO BE SOMEONE WEALTHY...POWERFUL... *INFLUENTIAL.*
AND THE LIKELY CANDIDATES...
GCPD

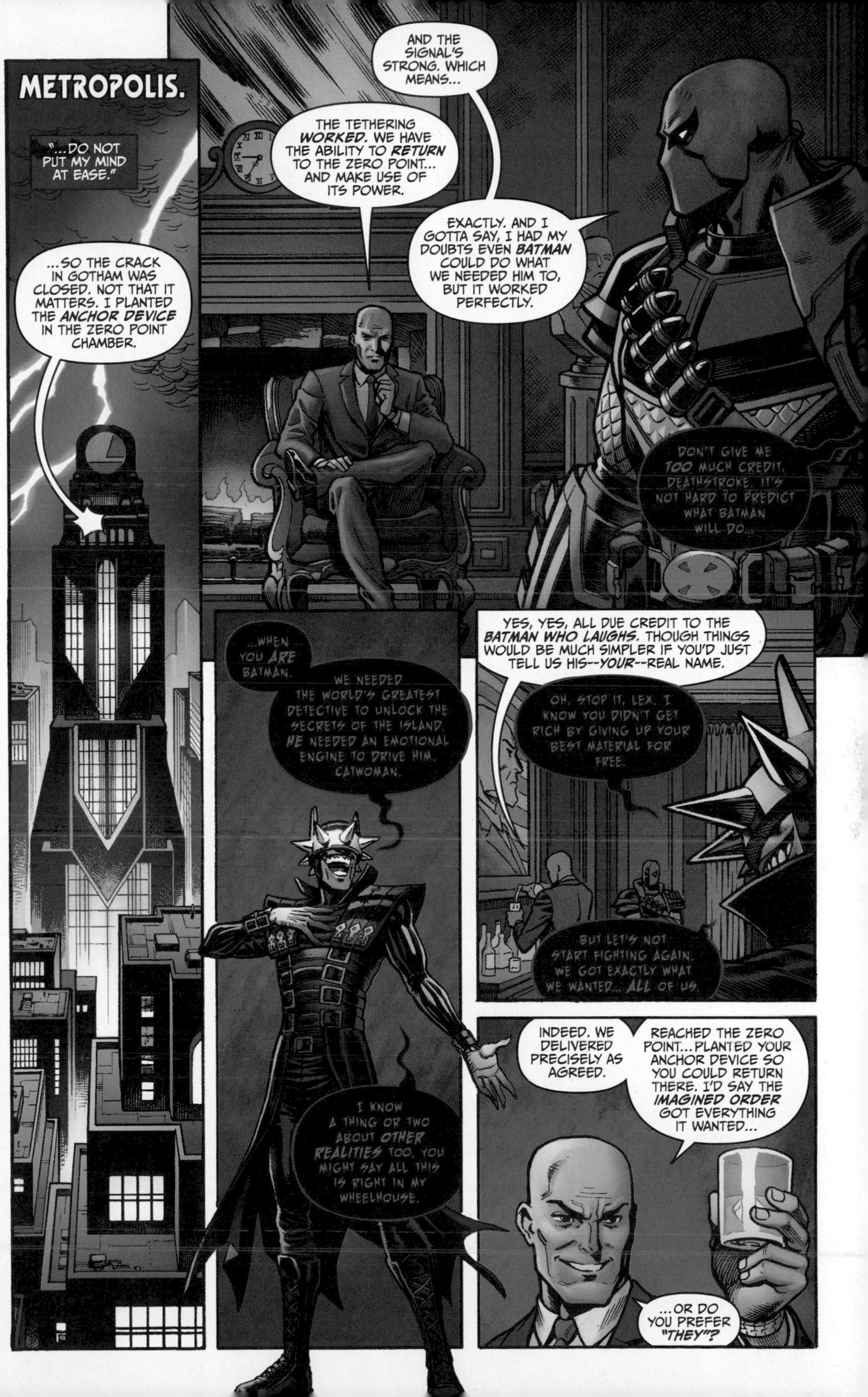

METROPOLIS.
"...DO NOT PUT MY MIND AT EASE."
...SO THE CRACK IN GOTHAM WAS CLOSED. NOT THAT IT MATTERS. I PLANTED THE ANCHOR DEVICE IN THE ZERO POINT CHAMBER.
THE TETHERING WORKED. WE HAVE THE ABILITY TO RETURN TO THE ZERO POINT... AND MAKE USE OF ITS POWER.
AND THE SIGNAL'S STRONG. WHICH MEANS...
EXACTLY. AND I GOTTA SAY, I HAD MY DOUBTS EVEN BATMAN COULD DO WHAT WE NEEDED HIM TO, BUT IT WORKED PERFECTLY.
DON'T GIVE ME TOO MUCH CREDIT, DEATHSTROKE. IT'S NOT HARD TO PREDICT WHAT BATMAN WILL DO...
...WHEN YOU ARE BATMAN.
WE NEEDED THE WORLD'S GREATEST DETECTIVE TO UNLOCK THE SECRETS OF THE ISLAND. HE NEEDED AN EMOTIONAL ENGINE TO DRIVE HIM. CATWOMAN.
I KNOW A THING OR TWO ABOUT OTHER REALITIES TOO. YOU MIGHT SAY ALL THIS IS RIGHT IN MY WHEELHOUSE.
YES, YES, ALL DUE CREDIT TO THE BATMAN WHO LAUGHS. THOUGH THINGS WOULD BE MUCH SIMPLER IF YOU'D JUST TELL US HIS--YOUR--REAL NAME.
OH, STOP IT, LEX. I KNOW YOU DIDN'T GET RICH BY GIVING UP YOUR BEST MATERIAL FOR FREE.
BUT LET'S NOT START FIGHTING AGAIN. WE GOT EXACTLY WHAT WE WANTED... ALL OF US.
INDEED. WE DELIVERED PRECISELY AS AGREED.
REACHED THE ZERO POINT...PLANTED YOUR ANCHOR DEVICE SO YOU COULD RETURN THERE. I'D SAY THE IMAGINED ORDER GOT EVERYTHING IT WANTED...
...OR DO YOU PREFER "THEY"?

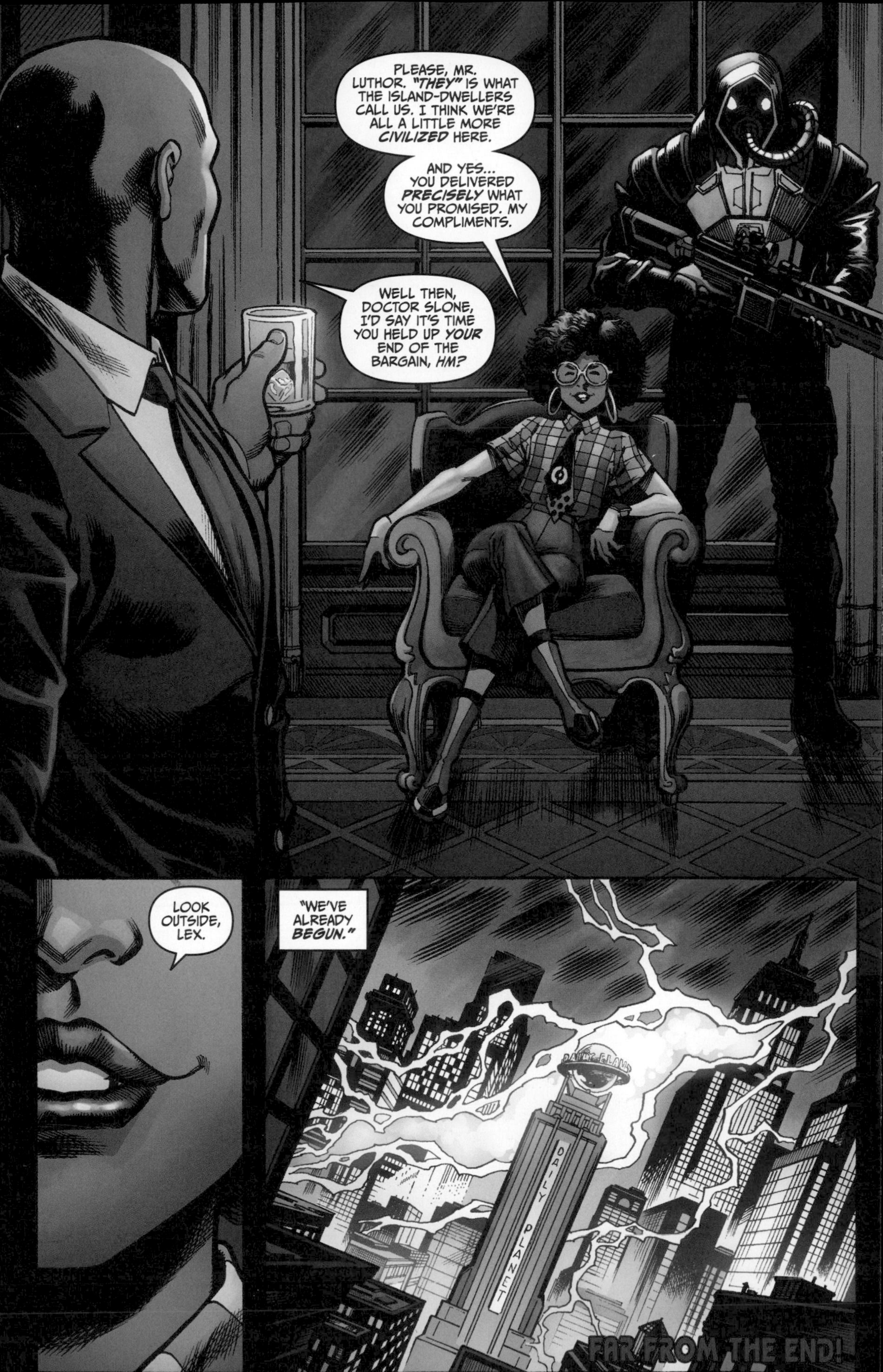

PLEASE, MR. LUTHOR. "THEY" IS WHAT THE ISLAND-DWELLERS CALL US. I THINK WE'RE ALL A LITTLE MORE CIVILIZED HERE.
AND YES... YOU DELIVERED PRECISELY WHAT YOU PROMISED. MY COMPLIMENTS.
WELL THEN, DOCTOR SLONE, I'D SAY IT'S TIME YOU HELD UP YOUR END OF THE BARGAIN, HM?
LOOK OUTSIDE, LEX.
"WE'VE ALREADY BEGUN."
DAILY PLANET
FAR FROM THE END!

VARIANT AND PREMIUM COVERS FOR *BATMAN/FORTNITE: ZERO POINT*

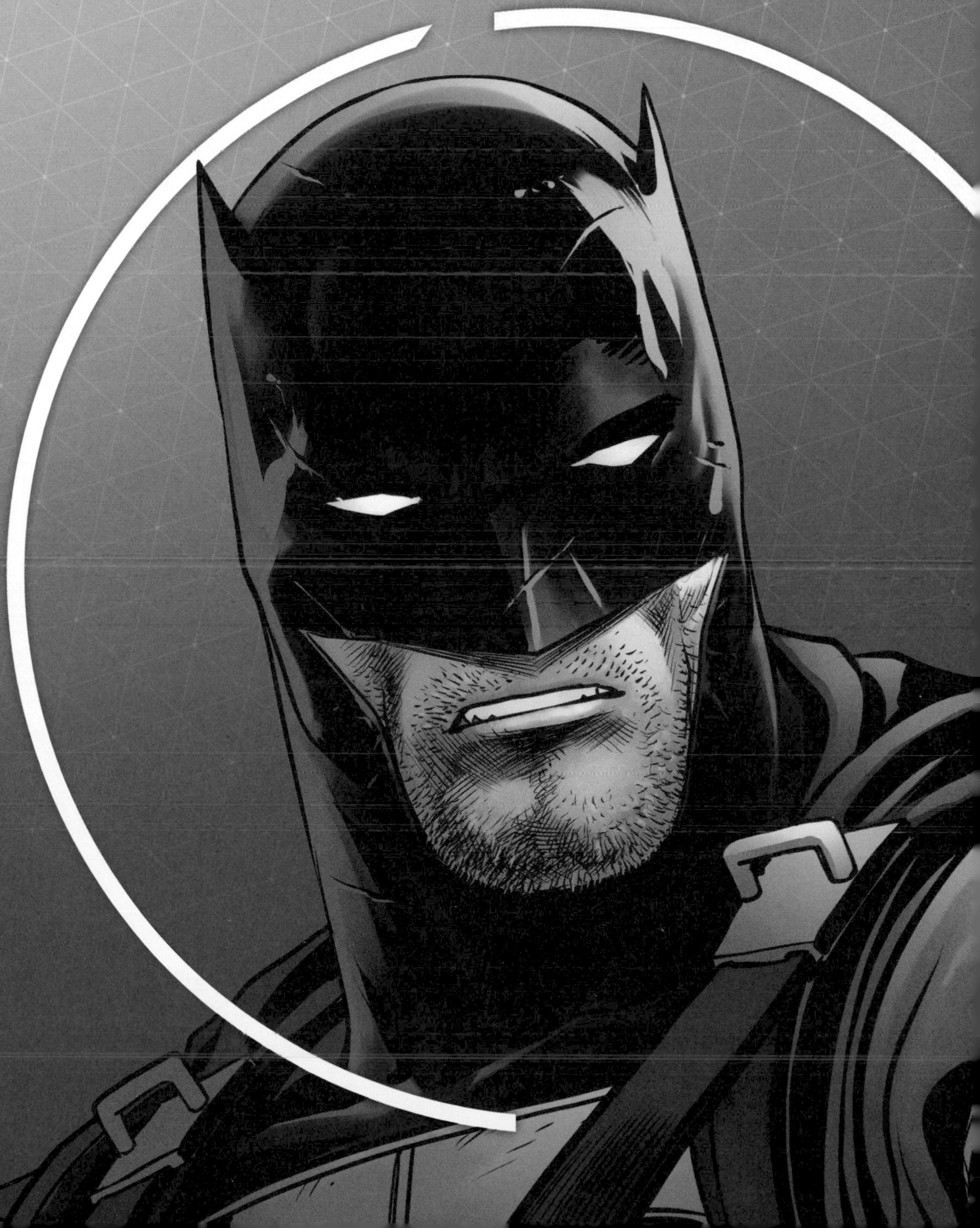

Batman/Fortnite: Zero Point #1
variant cover by KENNETH ROCAFORT

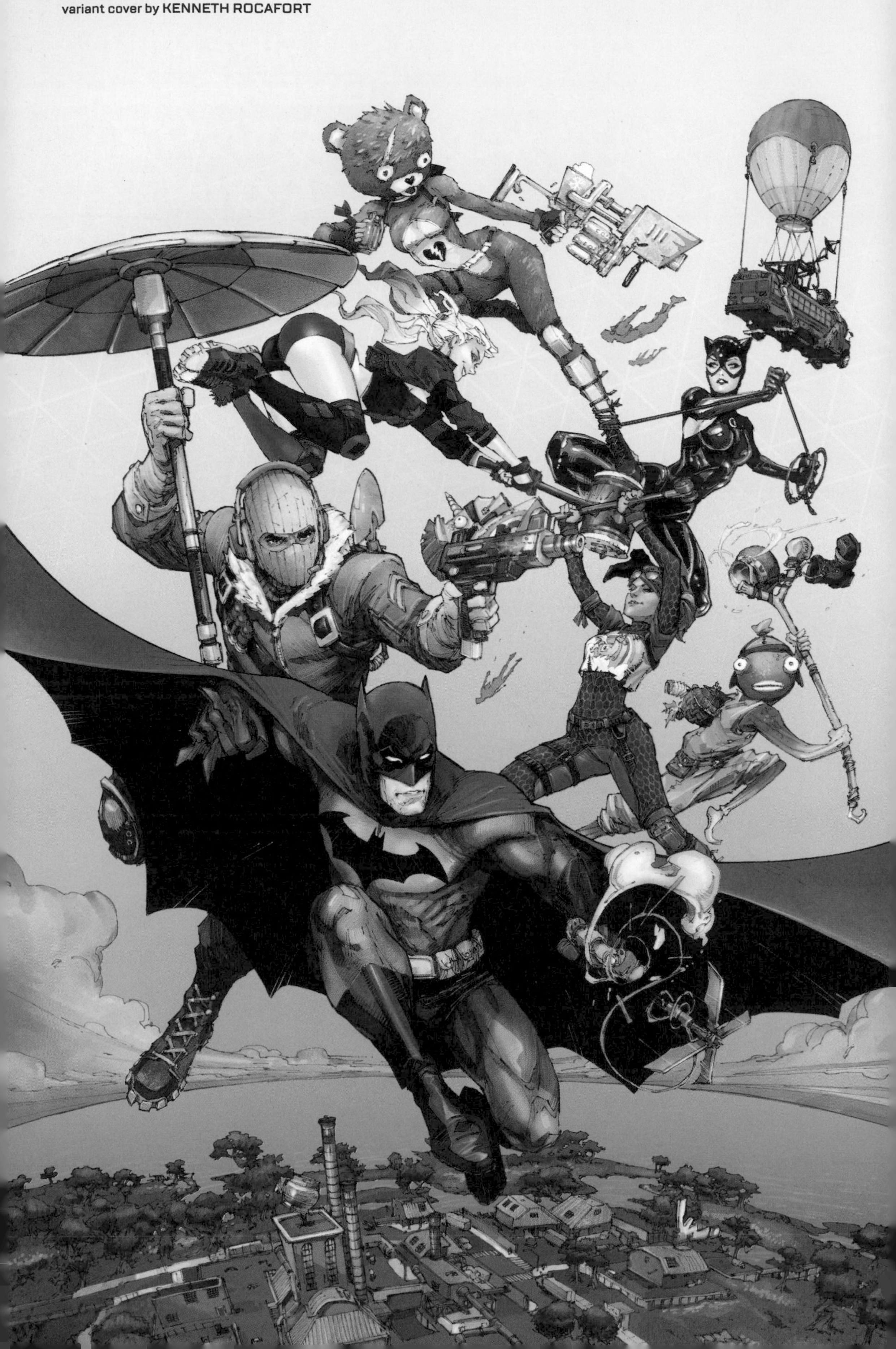

Batman/Fortnite: Zero Point #1
premium variant cover by DONALD MUSTARD

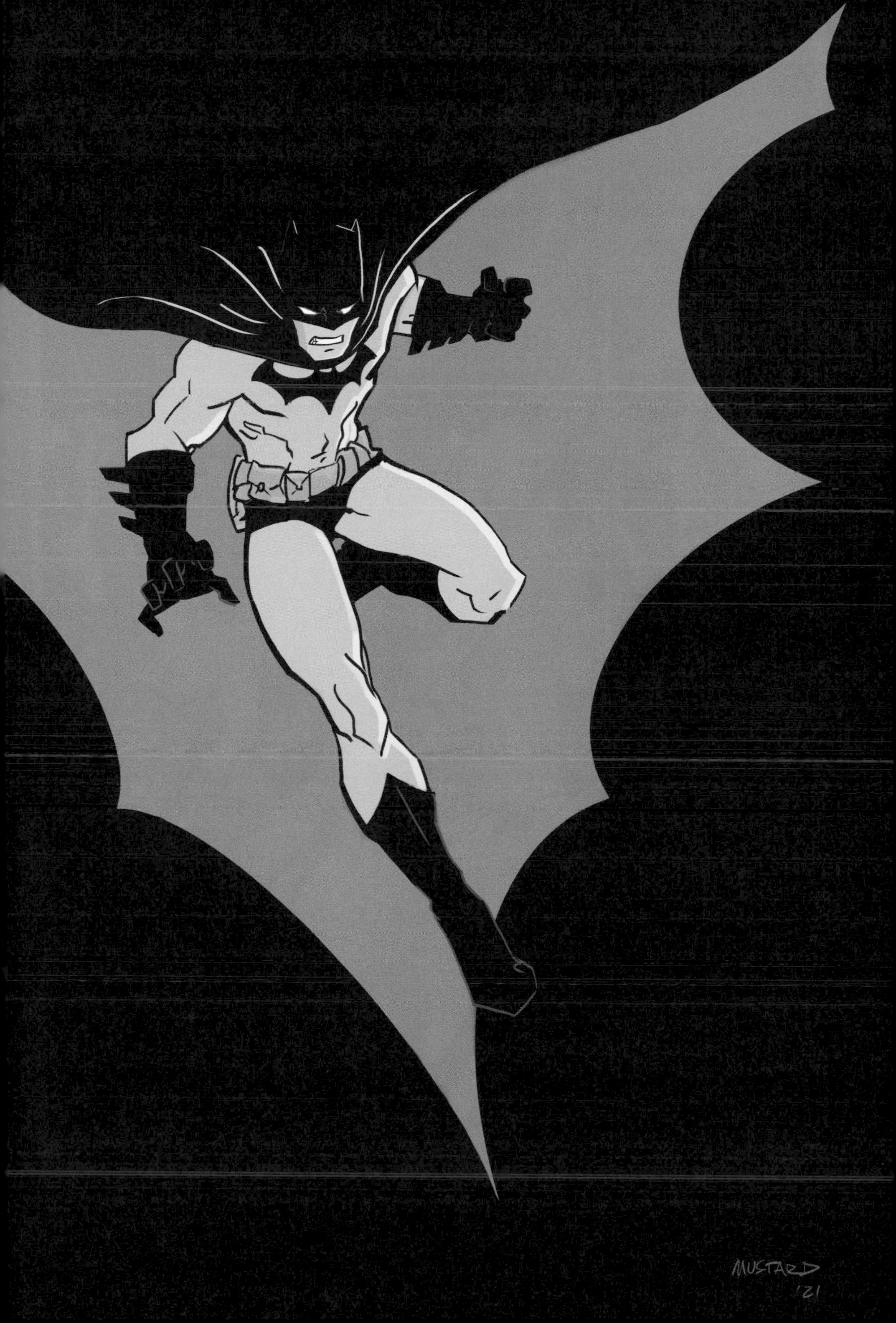
MUSTARD
'21

Batman/Fortnite: Zero Point #2
variant cover by ARTHUR ADAMS and SABINE RICH

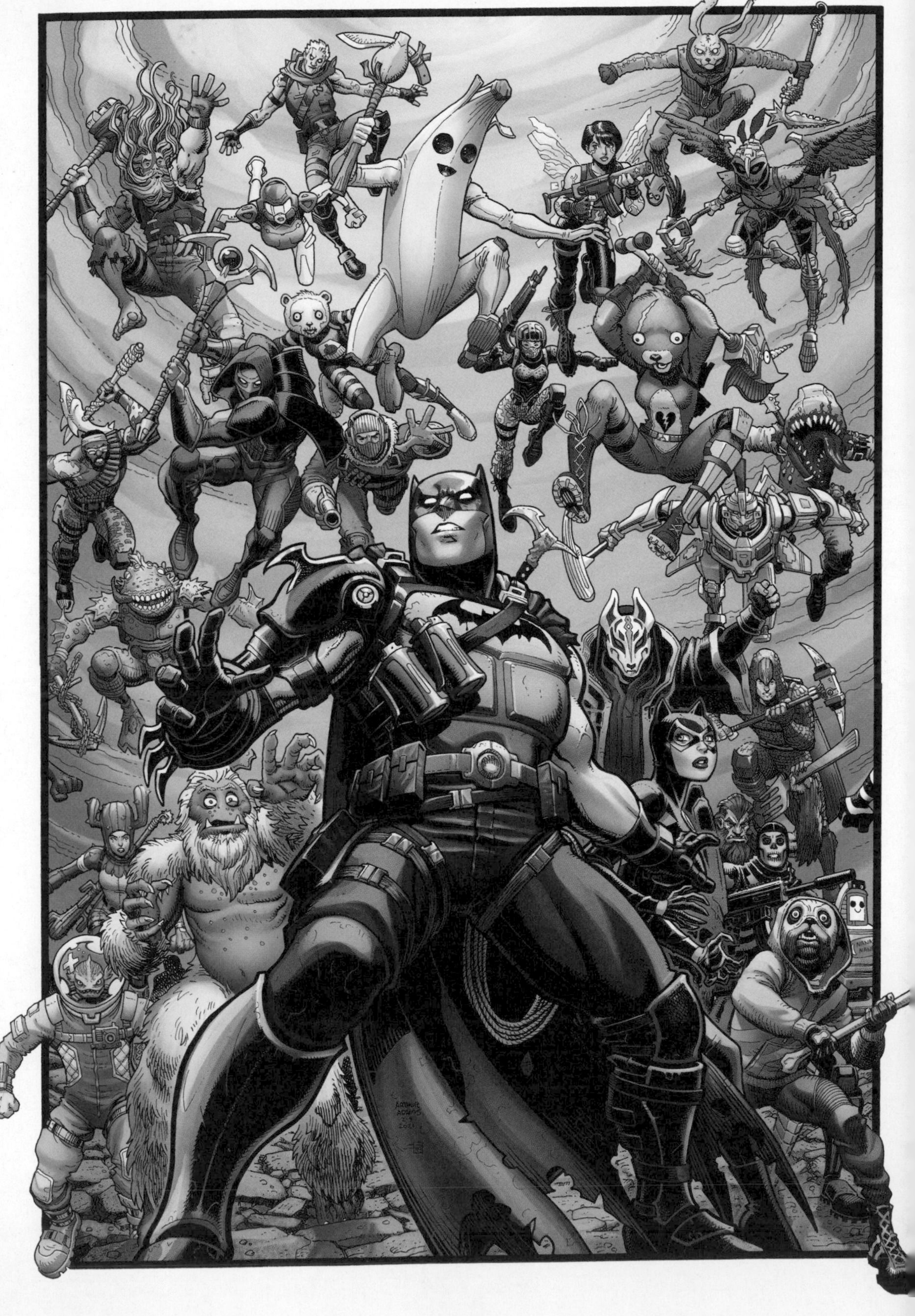

Batman/Fortnite: Zero Point #2
premium variant cover by DONALD MUSTARD

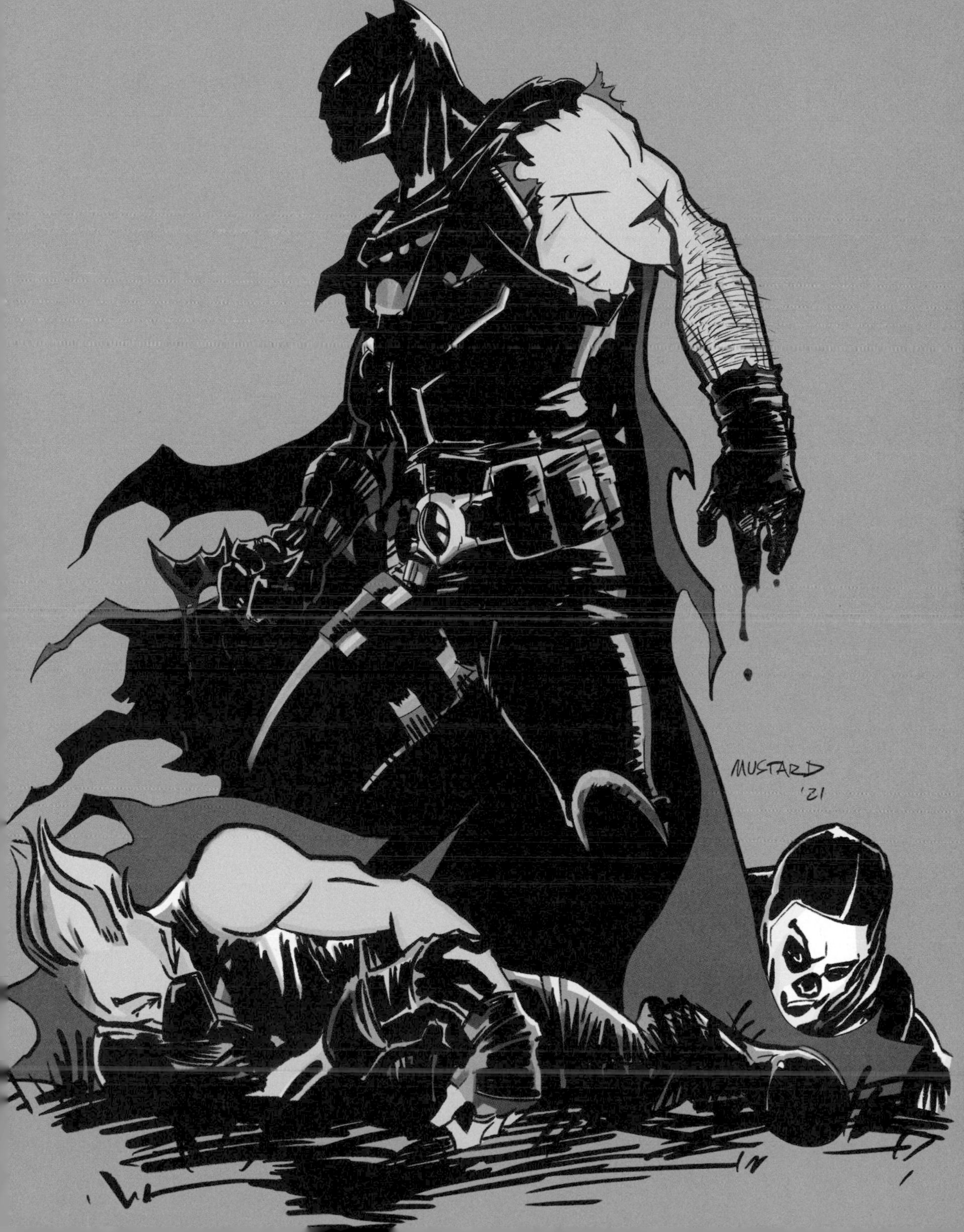
MUSTARD
'21

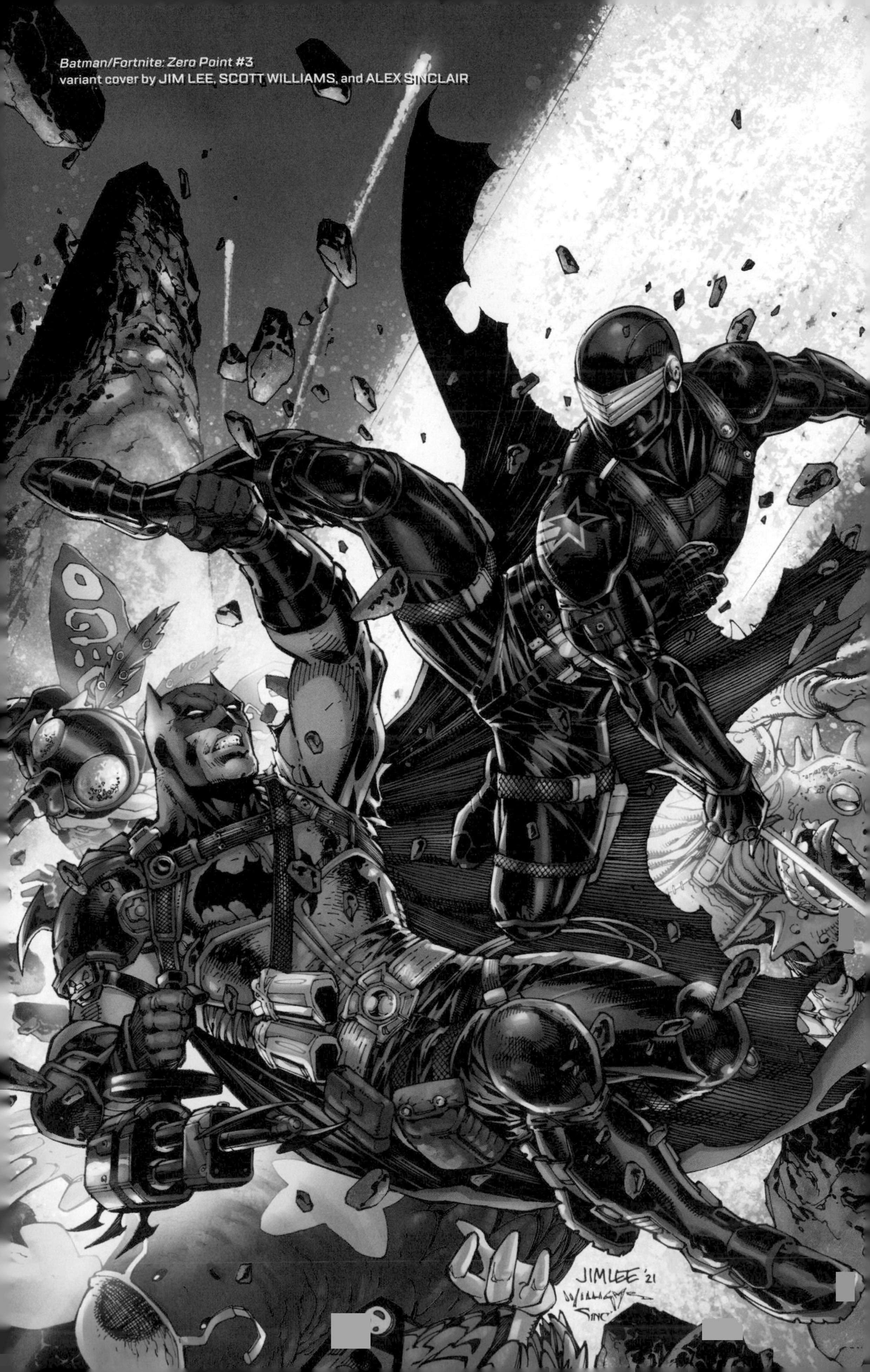
JIMLEE '21

Batman/Fortnite: Zero Point #3
variant cover by JIM LEE, SCOTT WILLIAMS, and ALEX SINCLAIR

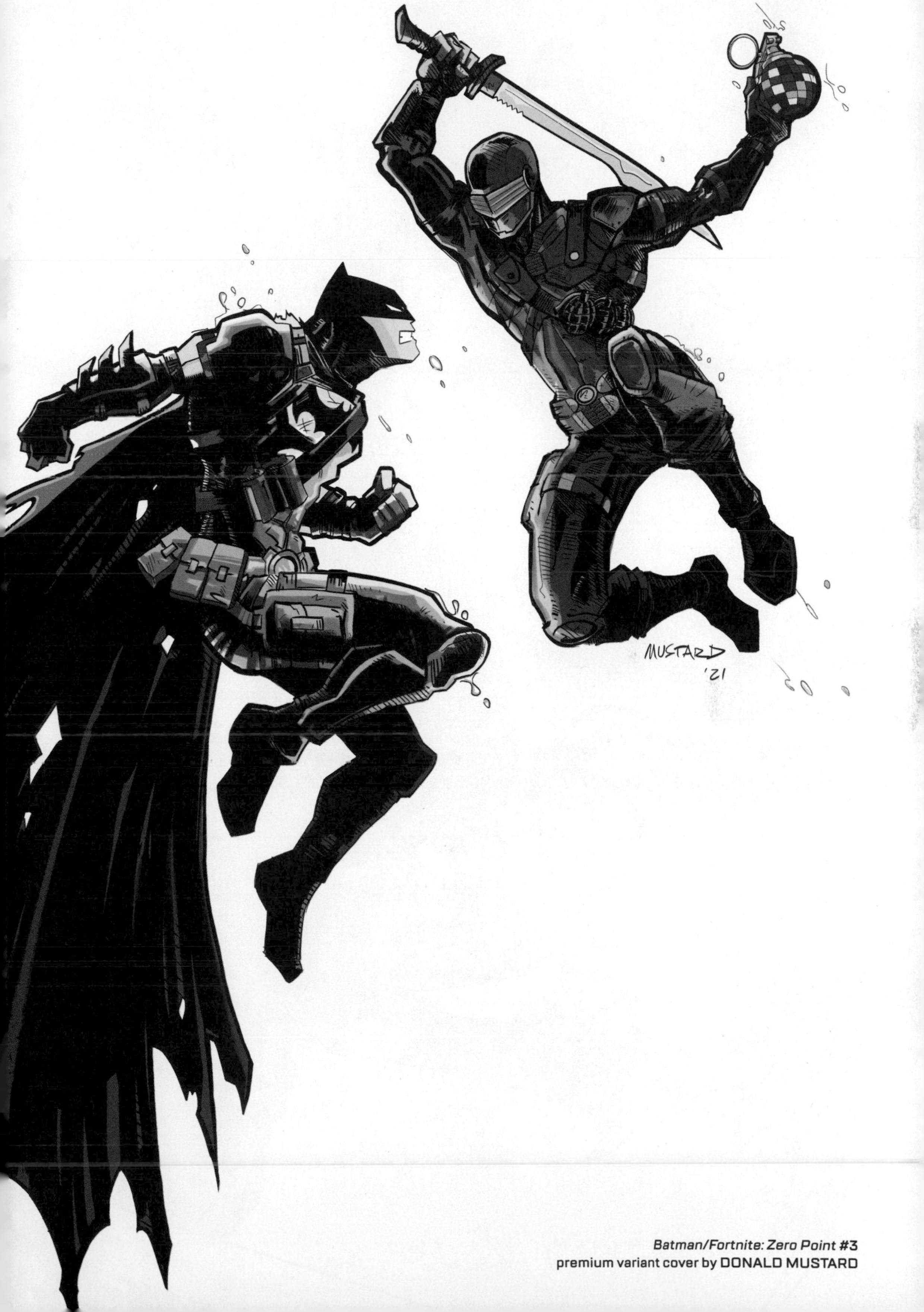
MUSTARD
'21

Batman/Fortnite: Zero Point #3
premium variant cover by DONALD MUSTARD

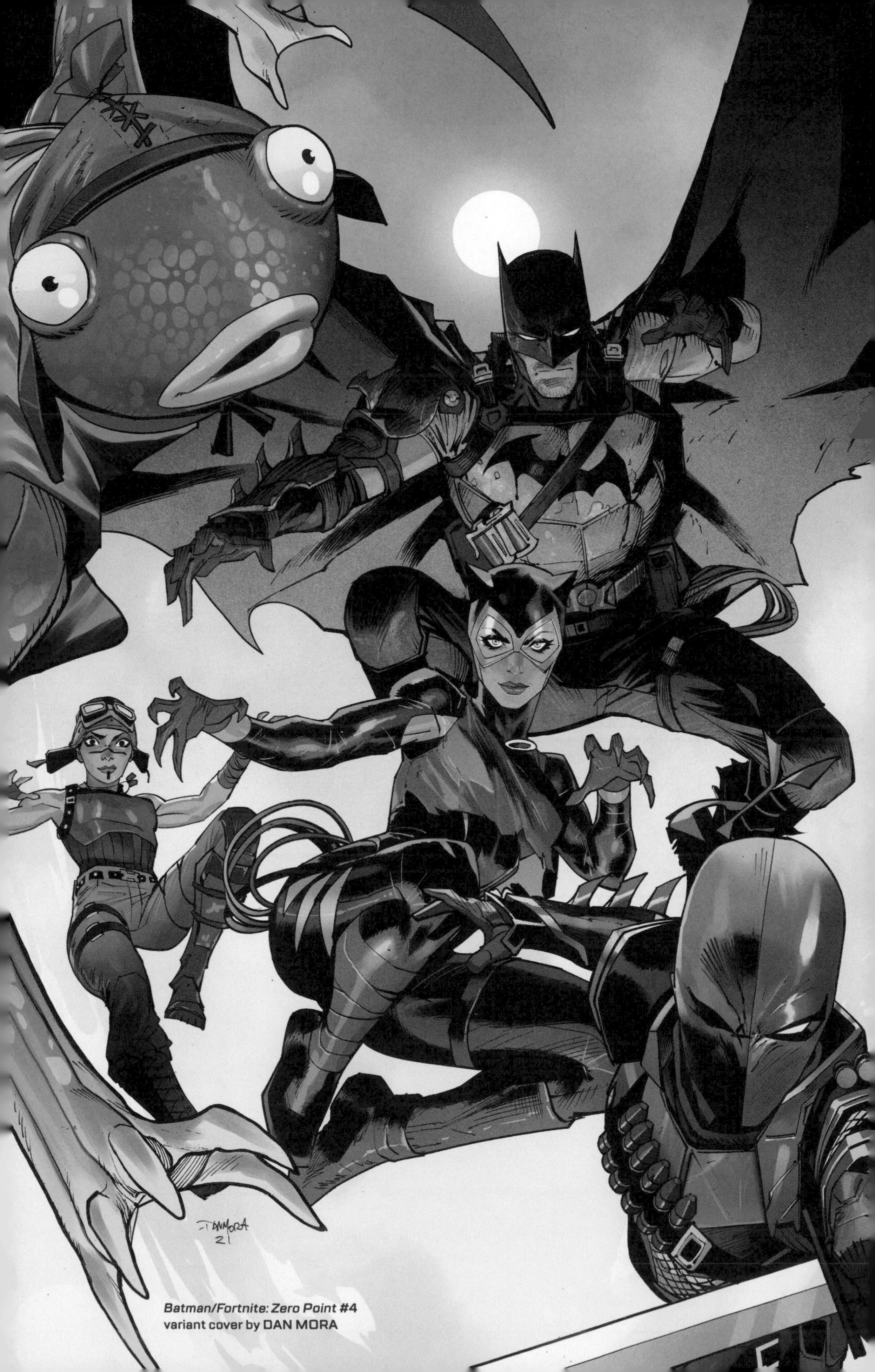
DANMORA
21

Batman/Fortnite: Zero Point **#4**
variant cover by **DAN MORA**

Batman/Fortnite: Zero Point #4
premium variant cover by DONALD MUSTARD

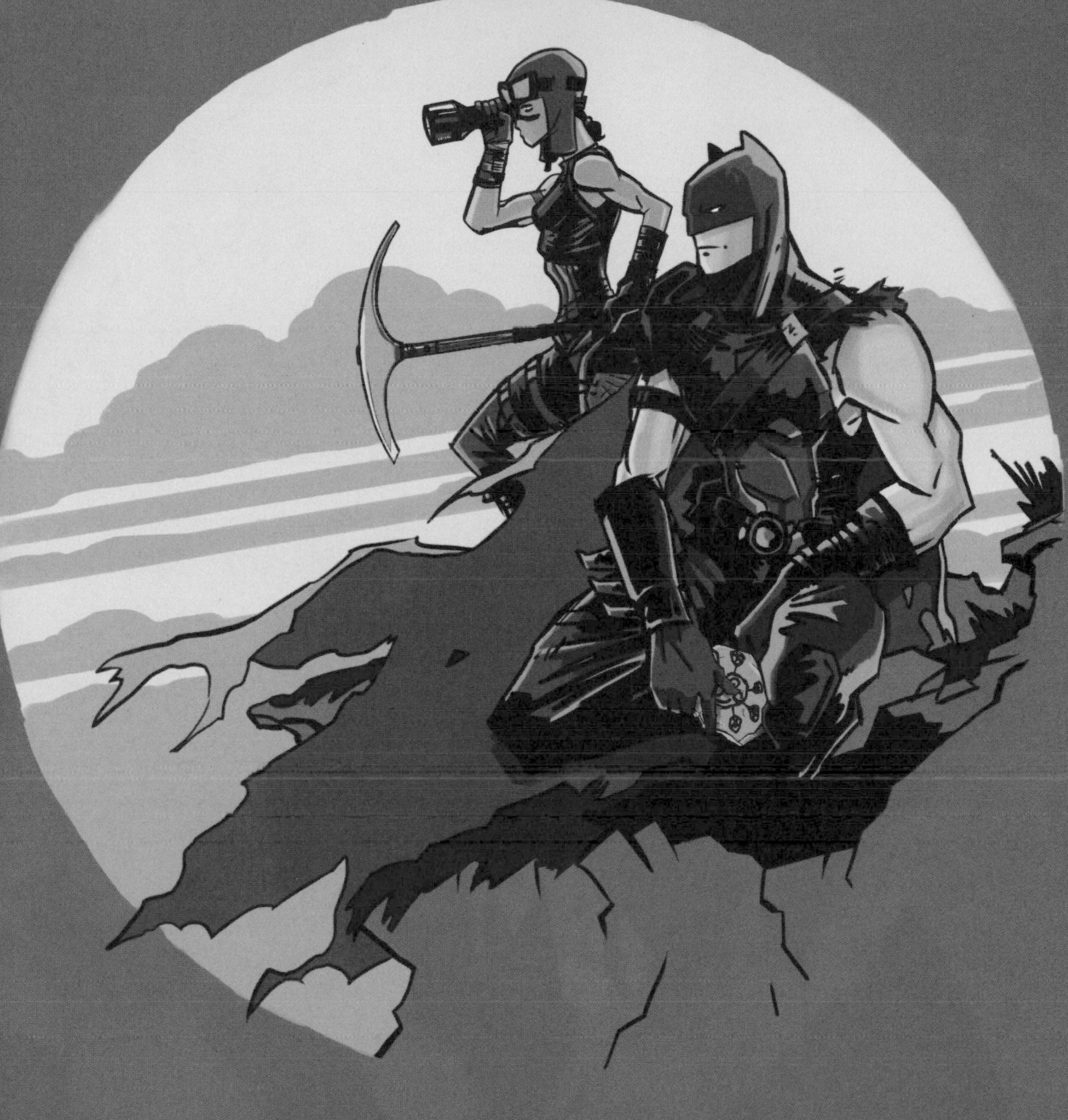

Batman/Fortnite: Zero Point #5
variant cover by AMANDA CONNER and ALEX SINCLAIR

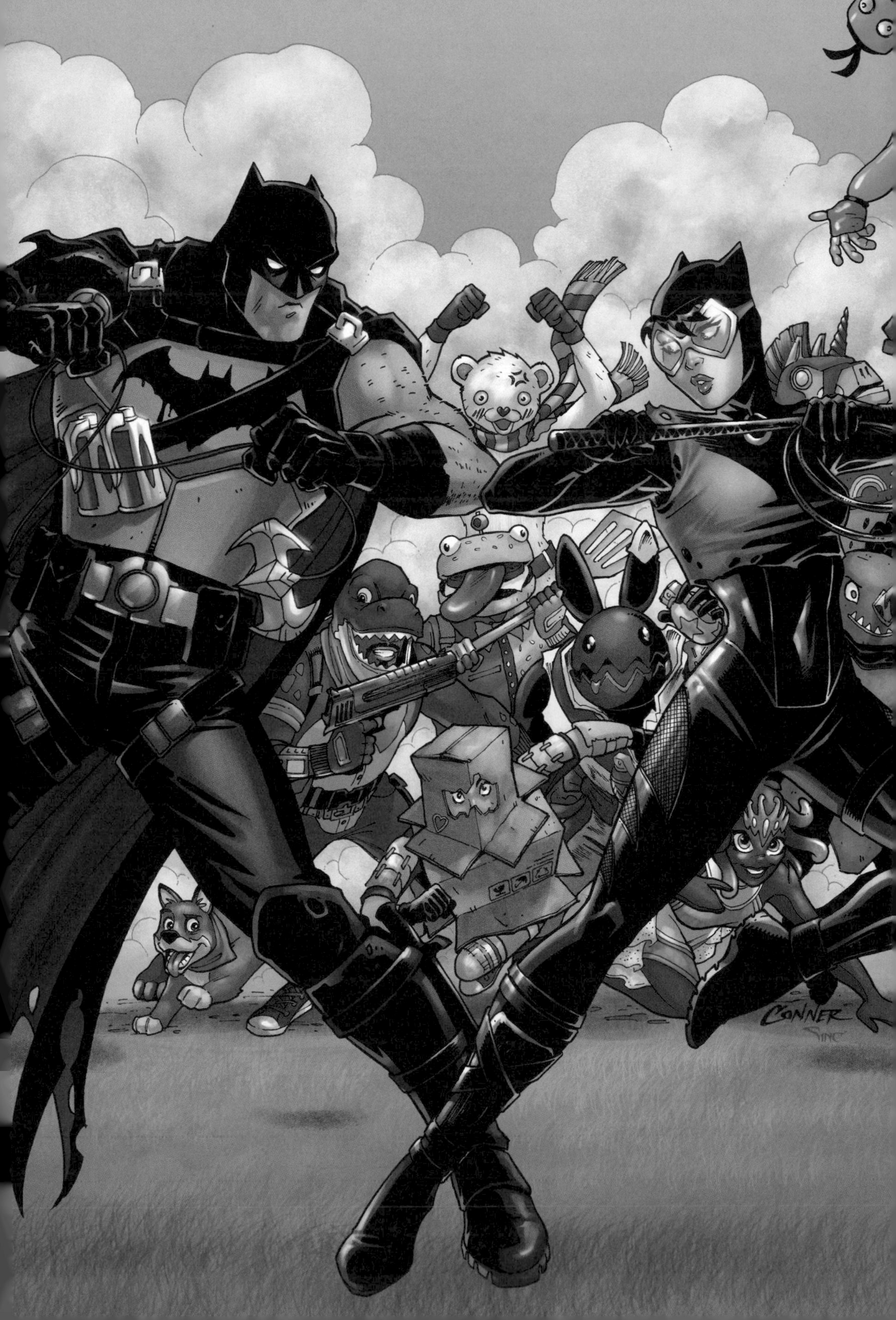
CONNER

Batman/Fortnite: Zero Point #5
premium variant cover by DONALD MUSTARD

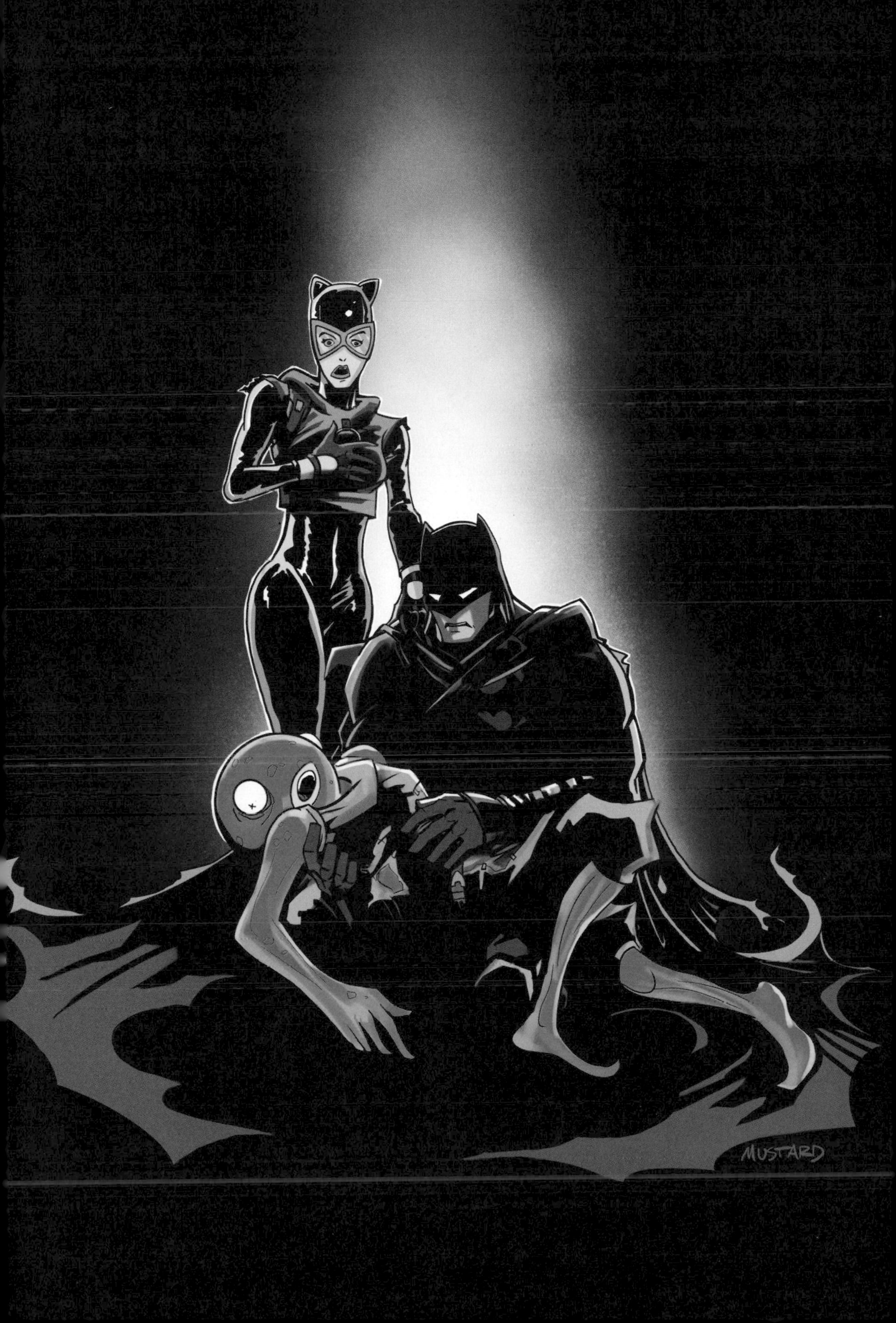
MUSTARD

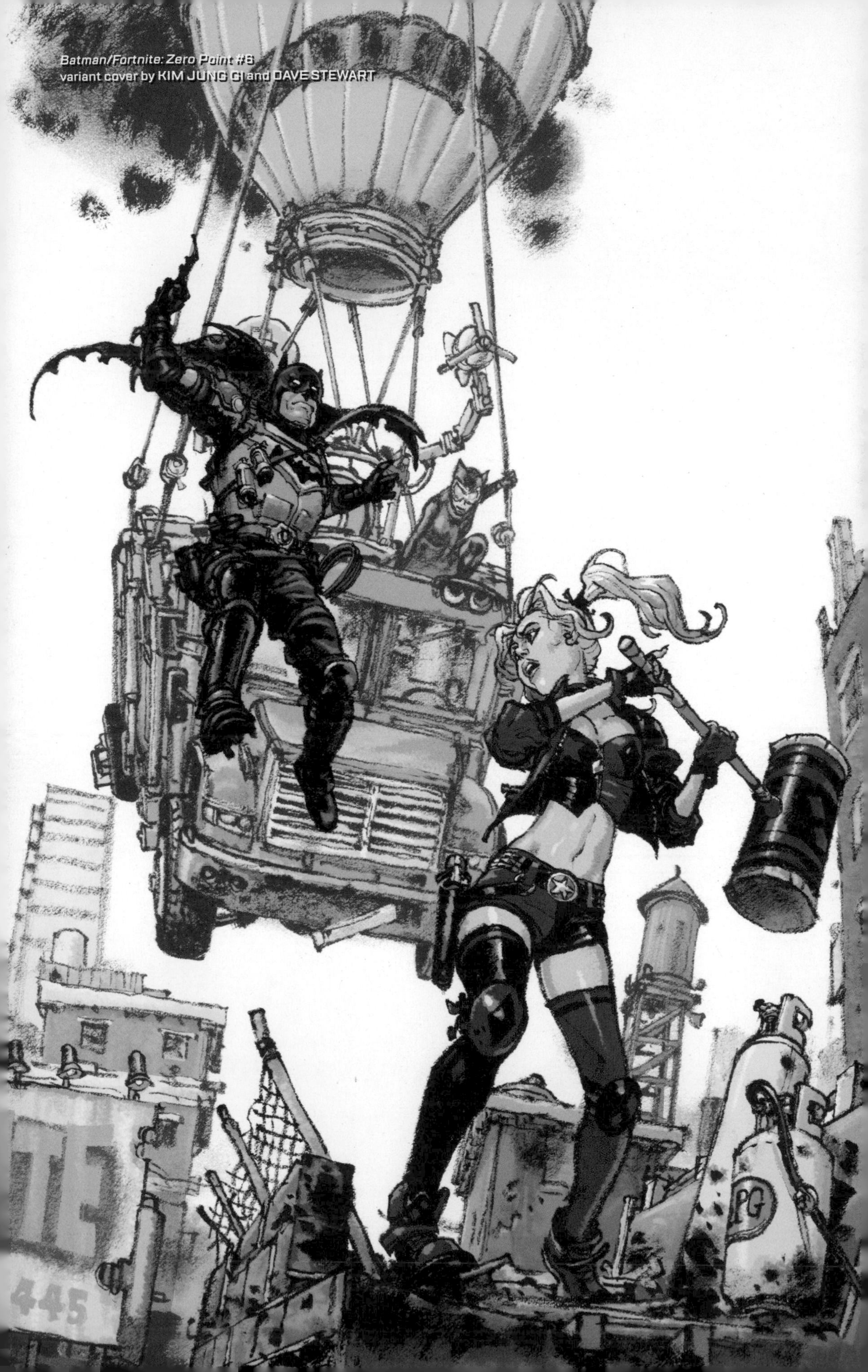
445
PG

Batman/Fortnite: Zero Point #6
variant cover by KIM JUNG GI and DAVE STEWART

Batman/Fortnite: Zero Point #6
premium variant cover by DONALD MUSTARD

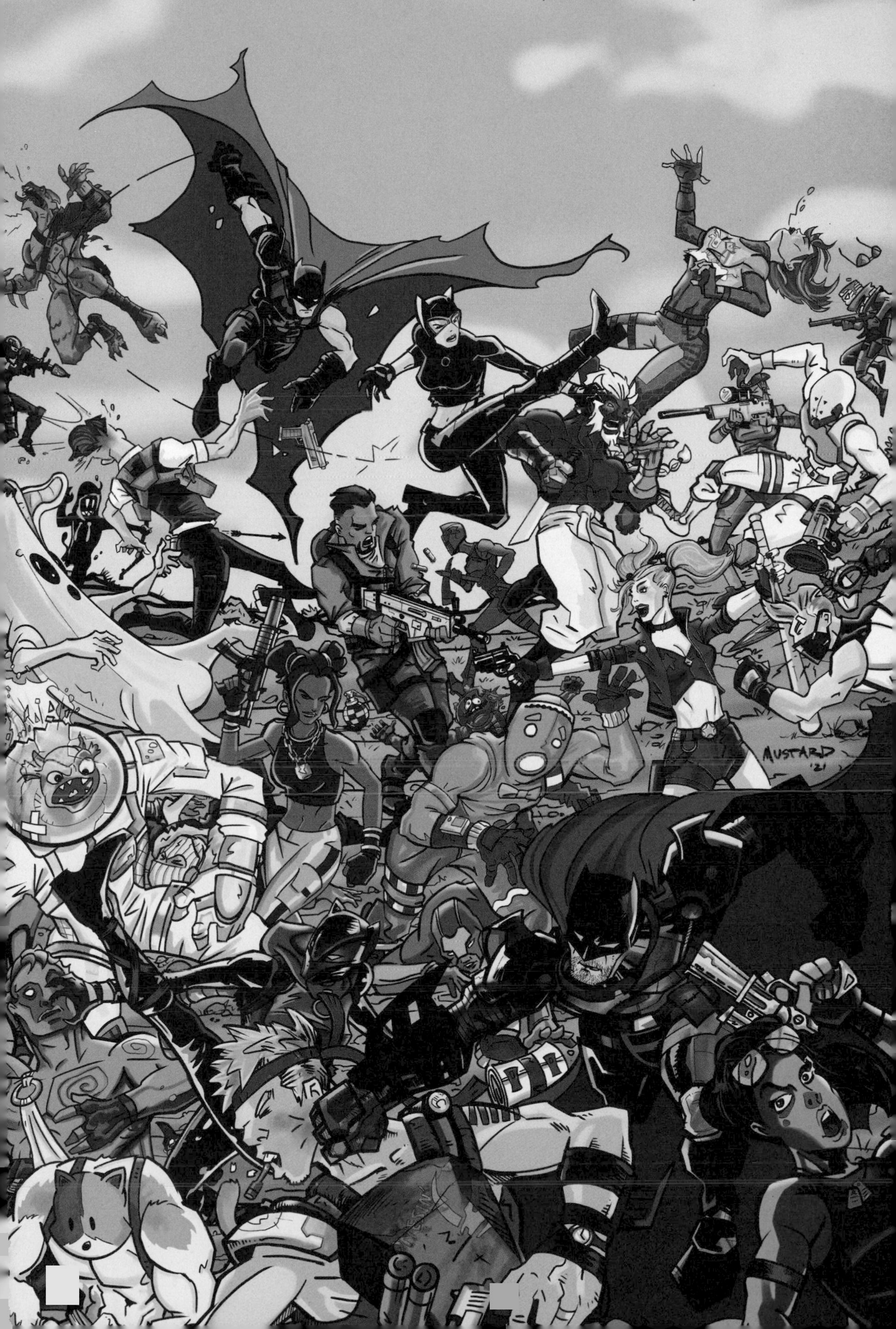
MUSTARD
'21

Batman Outfit concept designs by EPIC GAMES

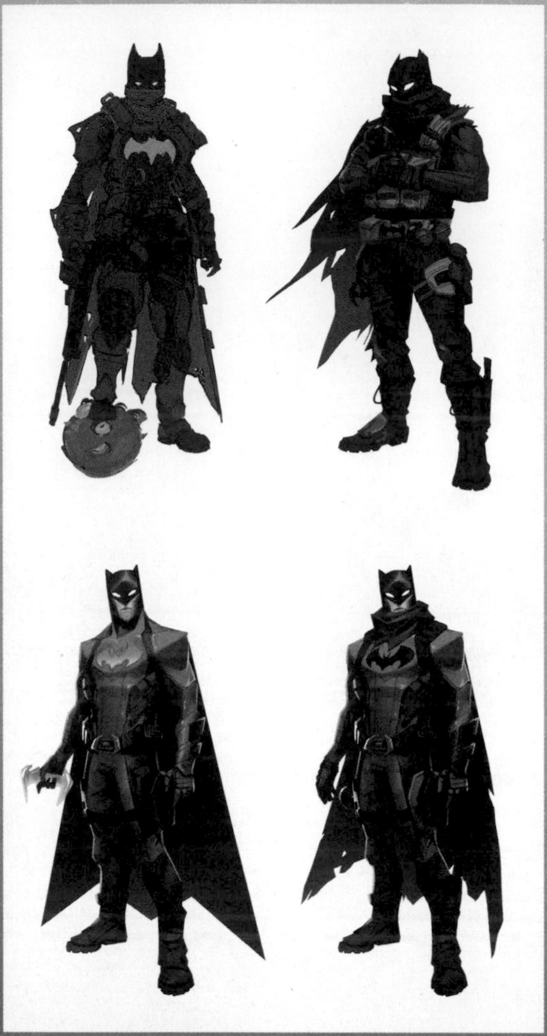

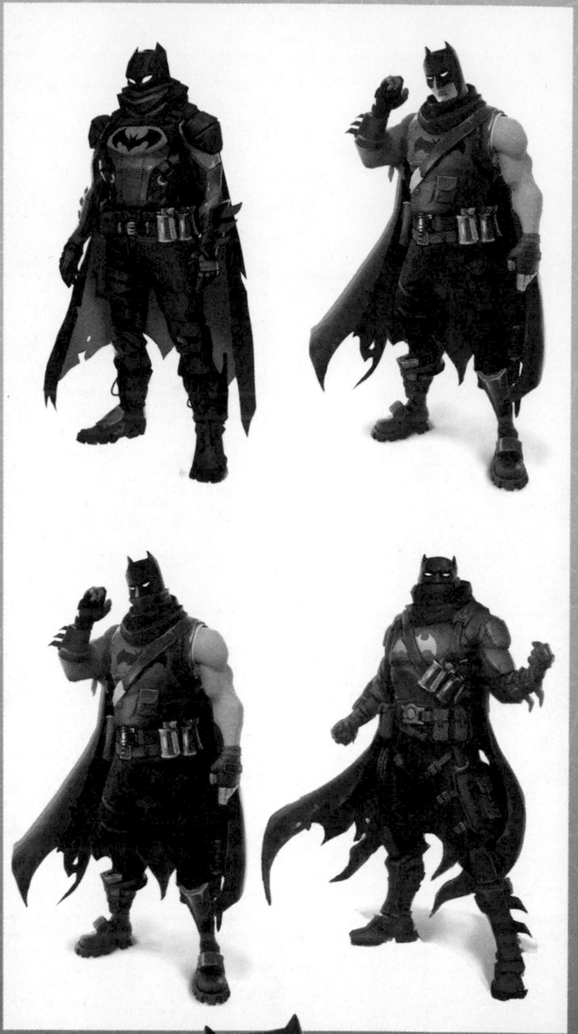

Batman Outfit design by EPIC GAMES

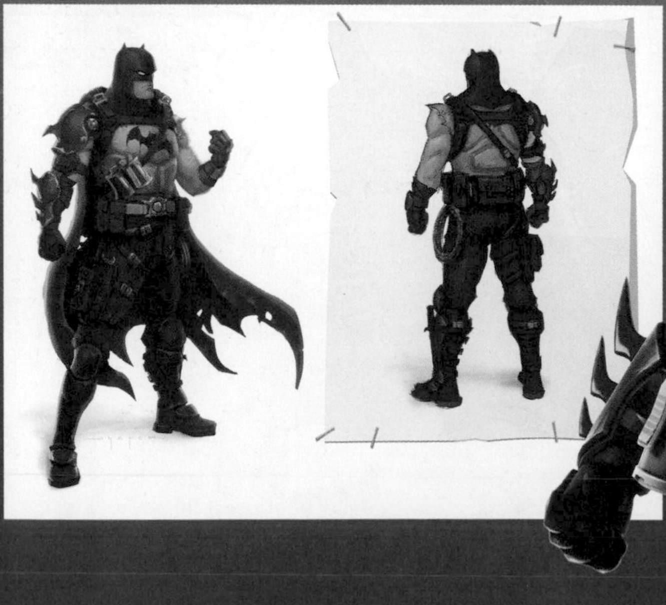

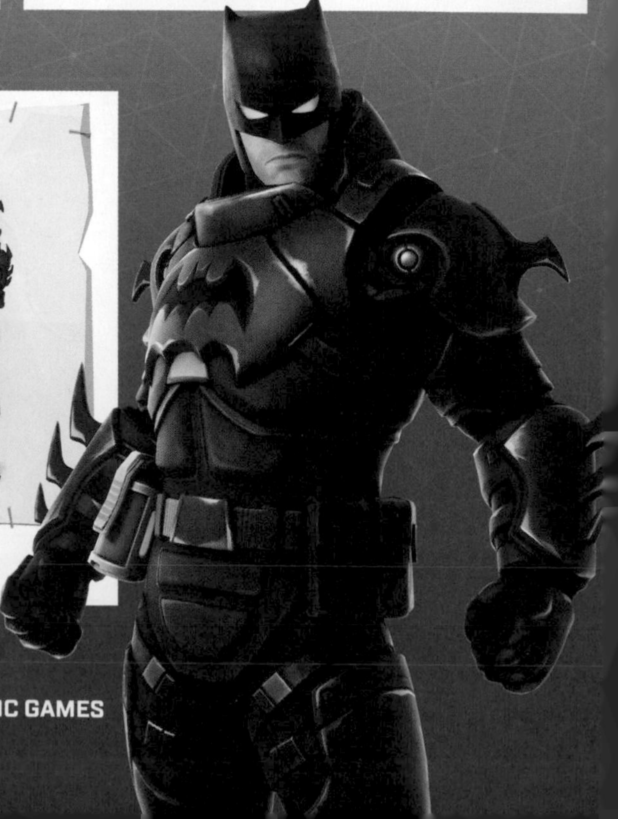

Armored Batman Zero Outfit design by EPIC GAMES

Catwoman Outfit concept designs by EPIC GAMES

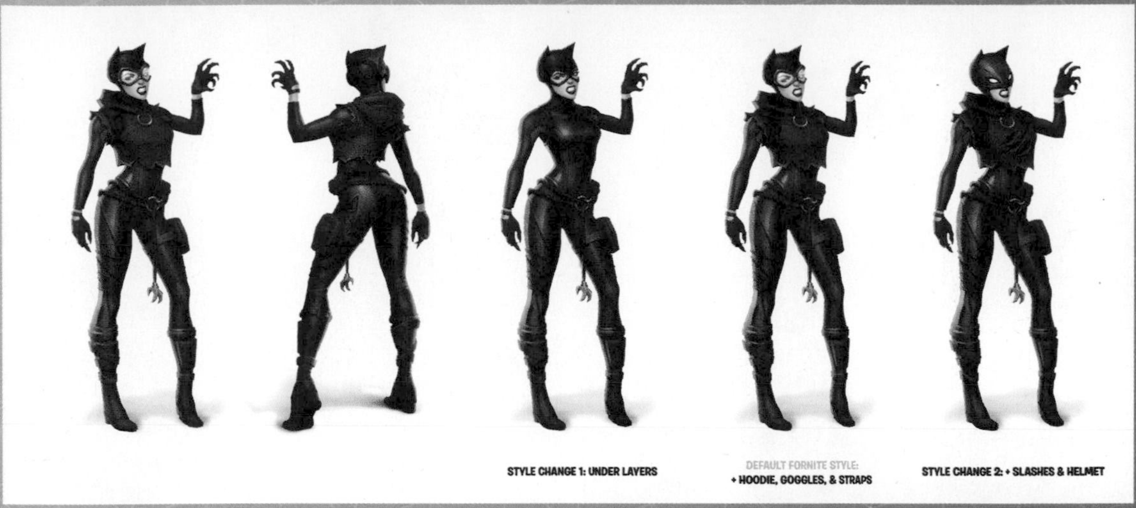

STYLE CHANGE 1: UNDER LAYERS
DEFAULT FORNITE STYLE:
+ HOODIE, GOGGLES, & STRAPS
STYLE CHANGE 2: + SLASHES & HELMET

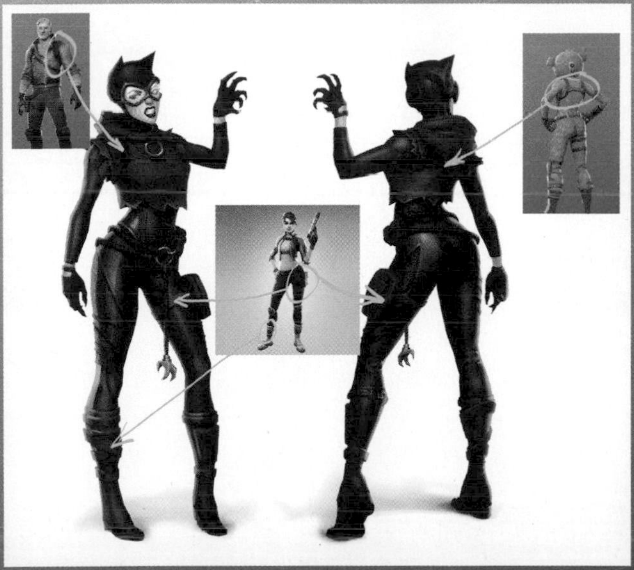

Catwoman Outfit final designs by EPIC GAMES

Deathstroke Outfit final designs by EPIC GAMES

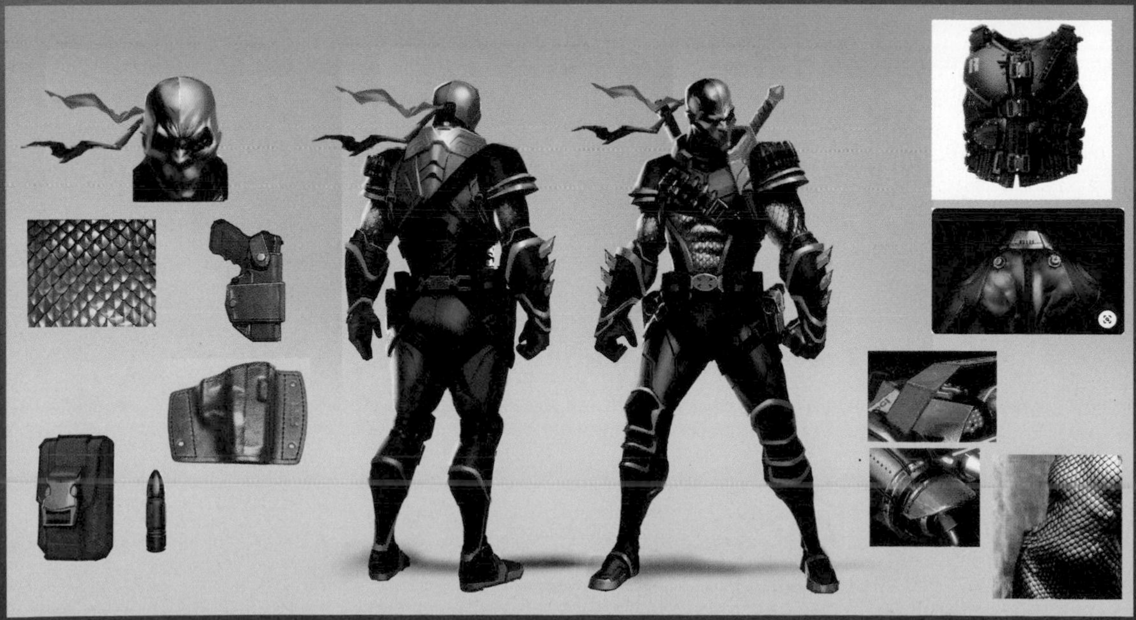

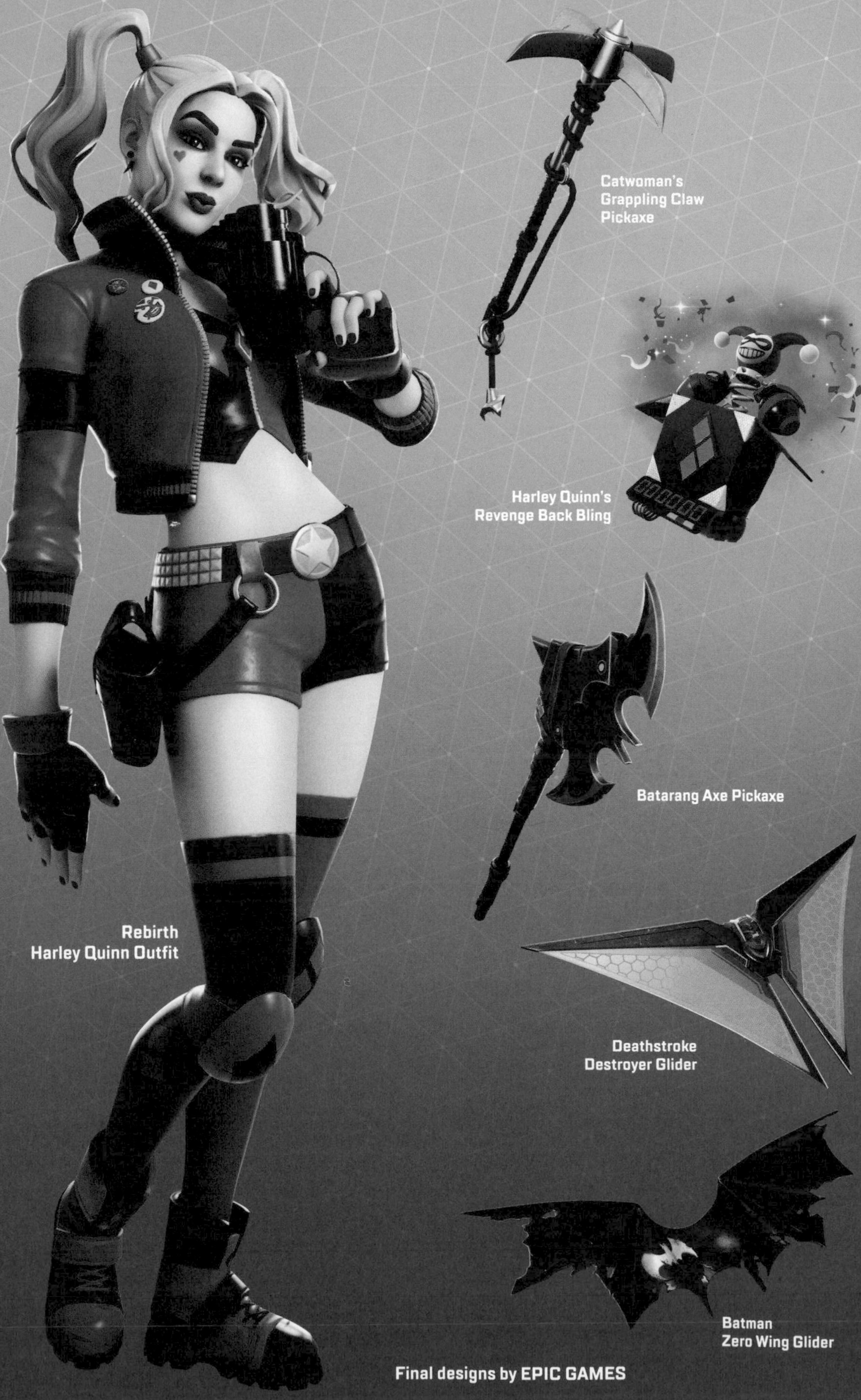
Catwoman's
Grappling Claw
Pickaxe
Harley Quinn's
Revenge Back Bling
Batarang Axe Pickaxe
Rebirth
Harley Quinn Outfit
Deathstroke
Destroyer Glider
Batman
Zero Wing Glider

Final designs by EPIC GAMES

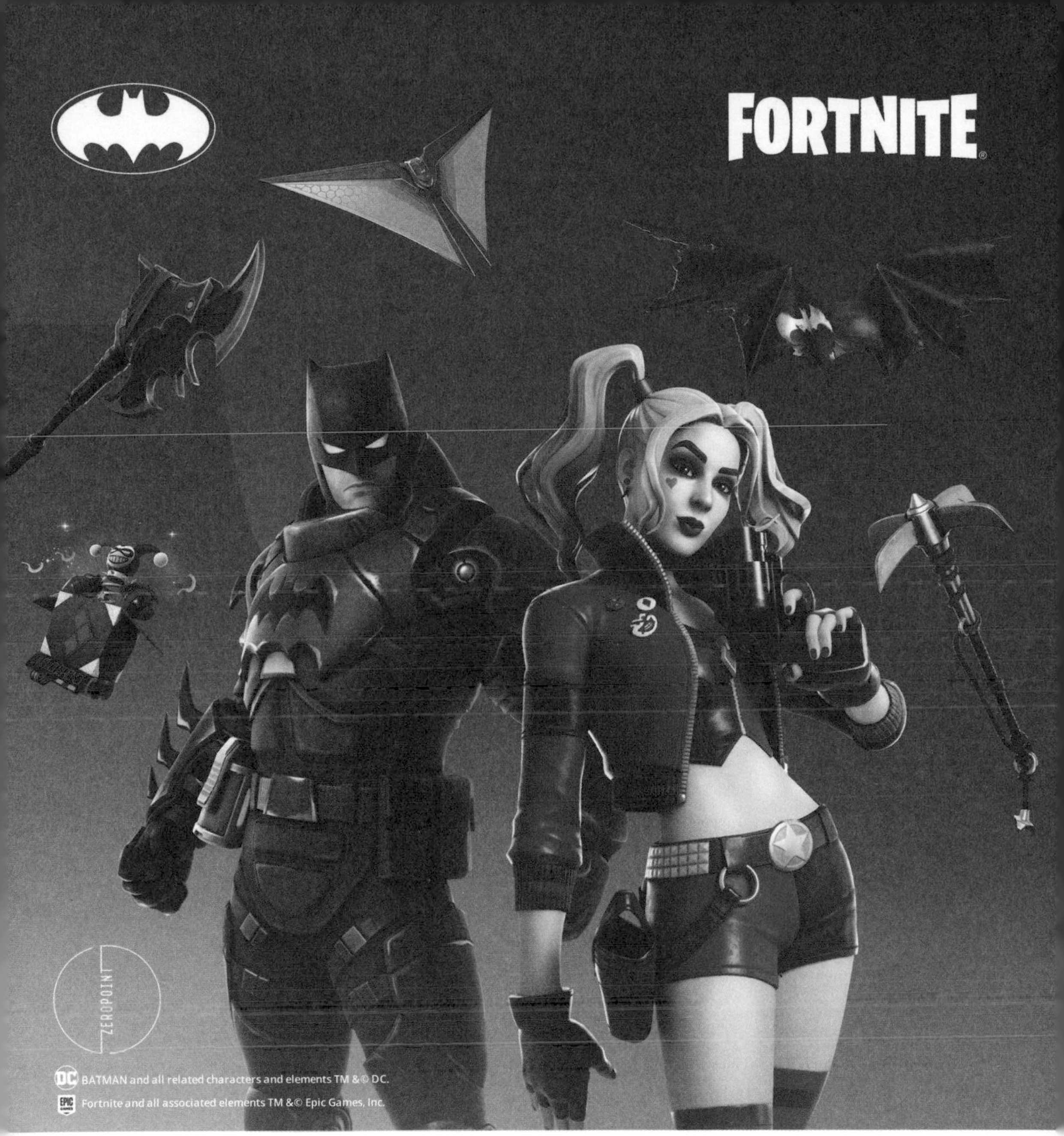
FORTNITE
ZEROPOINT
BATMAN and all related characters and elements TM & © DC.
Fortnite and all associated elements TM & © Epic Games, Inc.

ZPJZ6-6NQDT-
KPMG4-8ERD2

TO REDEEM YOUR BONUS FORTNITE COSMETIC ITEMS, VISIT FORTNITE.COM/REDEEM

- Codes can only be used once
- Only one code can be redeemed per account
- Codes expire on May 1, 2025